BUDMOUTH ESSAYS ON THOMAS HARDY

The Thomas Hardy Society was founded in 1967, and exists to honour the memory of a great writer, and encourage the study and appreciation of all aspects of his work. Its membership is world-wide.

The Society is a limited company and a registered charity. It publishes short guides to areas associated with Hardy's novels, and organizes annual programmes of lectures, film shows, and other activities. Members receive a quarterly newsletter, giving details of these, with book reviews and other information, as well as the annual *Review*.

Intending members are invited to write to the Hon. Secretary:

The Revd J. M. C. Yates
The Vicarage
Haselbury Plucknett
Crewkerne
Somerset
TA18 7PB.

The first major venture of the Society was the Thomas Hardy Festival of 1968; another is intended in 1978. A Summer School in 1973 resulted in the publication of *Thomas Hardy and the Modern World*, just as the present volume is the outcome of the second Summer School in 1975.

Please note that the only distributor of these books is the Secretary (at the above address). Retail prices are as follows, *with postage extra:*

THOMAS HARDY AND THE MODERN WORLD
Members £2.10 or $5.85 — Non-members £2.50 or $6.95

BUDMOUTH ESSAYS ON THOMAS HARDY
£3.60 or $9.00

Budmouth Essays on THOMAS HARDY

Papers presented at the 1975 Summer School

Edited by F. B. Pinion

The Thomas Hardy Society Ltd.

First published 1976 by
The Thomas Hardy Society Ltd.
Dorchester, Dorset.

ISBN 0 904398 15 3

Printed in Great Britain by
C. J. Creed, Printer, Broadoak, Bridport

CONTENTS

	Preface		7
1	*Desmond Hawkins*	The Strategy of the Novelist	9
2	*Robert C. Schweik*	The Narrative Structure of *Far from the Madding Crowd*	21
3	*H. A. T. Johnson*	In Defence of *The Trumpet-Major*	39
4	*Roy Morrell*	Some Aspects of Hardy's Minor Novels	60
5	*Maire A. Quinn*	Thomas Hardy and the Short Story	74
6	*Lennart A. Björk*	Psychological Vision and Social Criticism in *Desperate Remedies* and *Jude the Obscure*	86
7	*Melvyn Bragg*	Thomas Hardy and *Jude the Obscure*	106
8	*F. B. Pinion*	Hardy and Myth	125
9	*John Paterson*	The Continuing Miracle: Nature and Character in Thomas Hardy	140
10	*Walter F. Wright*	A Novel is an Impression, not an Argument	154
11	*Frank R. Giordano*	Hardy's Moments of Revision	168
12	*Harold Orel*	After *The Dynasts*: Hardy's Relationship to Christianity	180
13	*Tom Paulin*	Time and Sense Experience: Hardy and T. S. Eliot	192
14	*Keith Wilson*	The Personal Voice in the Poetry of Thomas Hardy	205
	Notes		218
	Notes on Contributors		224
	Index		226

PREFACE

The fourteen essays in this volume (with one exception, which had to be kept in reserve) were presented as papers at the second Summer School held by the Thomas Hardy Society at the College of Education, Weymouth, under the general chairmanship of Mr T. R. Wightman. Like the previous one, it was very successful, its smooth running affording the most expressive tribute to the work of its organizer, the Revd J. M. C. Yates. It is regretted that four talks or lectures are not available for publication: an illustrated opening one on Hardy's life and work by Norman Atkins, H. W. Bawden on the House of Macmillan and Hardy, Lord David Cecil on 'Hardy as Historian', and Dr Emma Clifford's unfinished study of *The Woodlanders*.

As in *Thomas Hardy and the Modern World,* contributions are arranged as far as possible with reference to the chronological order of Hardy's works, prose fiction taking precedence of poetry solely for this reason.

There have been some authorial revisions, and a few slight editorial economies. In substance, however, the papers remain unchanged. There may be doubt about biographical accuracy here and there, but any misrepresention of this kind is slight and has to be retained for the sake of the argument. The essays provide much to reflect on, and occasional conflicts of view among the critics add to their general interest.

The Society is grateful to the Macmillan Press Ltd for permission to quote from Hardy's prose and verse, and particularly from poems 85, 86, 109, 302, 439, 563, 580 in *The Complete Poems of Thomas Hardy* (ed. James Gibson), 1976. My thanks are due to the Revd J. M. C. Yates for his most valuable assistance in proof-checking.

F.B.P.

I

Desmond Hawkins:

THE STRATEGY OF THE NOVELIST

The contributions to this symposium will show a great variety of approaches to Hardy's work, but—if I may attempt a generalisation—I think we can recognise three main areas of preoccupation. There is firstly the area of Hardy's ideas, his philosophy, his intellectual concepts and beliefs. There is next the biographical and psychological element in his writings, the extent to which the real world of his personal history interacted with the imaginative world of his poetry. And there is finally the literary quality of his writings considered as a self-contained work of art, a thing in itself—a *Ding an sich*—an object having intrinsic value.

Each of these can help to enlarge and intensify our appreciation of Hardy. Whatever may be your final assessment of Hardy's ideas, you cannot ignore them and brush them aside. Hardy considered himself to be a thinker, presented himself to the public as a thinker—in the sense of the word that Rodin portrayed and the Victorians understood. *The Dynasts,* for example, could not have been written without the explicit formulation of a body of ideas about the Christian God and the process of Evolution, about Free Will and Determinism, and so on.

Similarly it is scarcely possible to read Hardy's poems without responding to his repeated hints to look for a further illumination in biographical contexts. He is a very personal writer, one who found an inexhaustible stimulation in his own inner drama. We need not beat our breasts too penitently about invasions of a privacy where the door was left so invitingly ajar. A properly conducted biographical scrutiny can hardly fail to enrich our insight into much that would otherwise be obscure and even impenetrable in Hardy. Let me instance a book published a few months ago, Robert Gittings' *Young Thomas Hardy,* as a case in point.

However, I want to address myself to the remaining category—to what might be considered Hardy's *professionalism* as a writer. I am not myself a philosopher or a psychoanalyst or a theologian. By trade and by instinct I am a literary critic, and this will account for my eagerness to redress the balance a bit, to swing the pendulum towards a Hardy whose most notable attribute is the pen in his hand. Many of his contemporaries held bold and controversial ideas; many of them had vivid and exciting lives. Where they differ from Hardy—and this is why we have forgotten them—is that they all omitted to write *Tess of the d'Urbervilles* and

'The Dance at the Phoenix' and 'The Phantom Horsewoman'. It was left to Hardy to do that. Therein lies his intrinsic quality and his unique importance.

I want therefore to concentrate on Hardy's technique as a novelist—and particularly on the way it developed in his early novels. Some of the views I am going to put before you were suggested to me by the experience of dramatising *Far from the Madding Crowd* for a centenary radio production by the B.B.C. last year. When you work over a book in this way—particularly if you already know it pretty well—some of its features show up in a very clear and interesting light.

Far from the Madding Crowd was the fourth of Hardy's novels. It followed *Desperate Remedies, Under the Greenwood Tree,* and *A Pair of Blue Eyes*; and it was his first really solid success. It led *The Spectator* to hail him as 'a new light among novelists', and we now recognise it as the first of the 'Great Six' novels (the others being *The Return of the Native, The Mayor of Casterbridge, The Woodlanders, Tess,* and *Jude*). In it we can discern the strategy of Hardy the novelist, imperfect as yet, incomplete in some respects, but revealing plainly enough the grand design that was to emerge, and be developed and refined, over the next twenty years. And what I aim to do now is to examine that strategy—the strategy of the novelist.

Let me begin by suggesting that the kind of novelist Hardy set out to be was very different from the kind of novelist he became. I believe his first conception of himself was as a satirist—a gentle and kindly satirist of the rural village life in which he grew up, and a more caustic and sophisticated satirist of the larger world of fashionable society. The first novel he *wrote, The Poor Man and the Lady,* was never published and the MS was destroyed, but we know—from the comments of those who read it—that it was rather 'socialistic' in tone and satirical in manner. His first *published* novel, *Desperate Remedies,* is a crudely melodramatic whodunnit of little merit, but it has some remarkable moments which reveal a good deal about the author. There is the passionate scene of extraordinary intensity between the heroine, Cytherea, and the wealthy woman who employs her, Miss Aldclyffe—to which I shall return later. And there is this striking comment on the attitude of the young hero, Edward Springrove, to Miss Aldclyffe in her role as his father's landlord:

> Miss Aldclyffe, like a good many others in her position, had plainly not realized that a son of her tenant and inferior could have become an educated man, who had learnt to feel his individuality, to view society from a Bohemian standpoint, far outside the farming grade in Carriford parish, and that hence he had all a developed man's unorthodox opinion about the subordination of classes.

There could be no clearer statement of the position that Hardy intended to adopt. His education emancipated him from the class structure and allowed him 'to view society from a Bohemian standpoint'. And the technical means for projecting that 'Bohemian standpoint' were satire and irony. It is no accident that Hardy called one of his books 'Satires of Circumstance' and another 'Life's Little Ironies'. They indicate the kind of 'ringing tone' that he was trying to get into his work. In his early novels he liked to spice his prose with the sort of tart aphorism that later became the stock-in-trade of Oscar Wilde. There is a sting of malice in his satirical portrait of the Revd Mr Swancourt in *A Pair of Blue Eyes* recalling his suspicions of the low birth of the young architect who dared to woo his daughter: 'I was inclined to suspect him, because he didn't care about sauces of any kind. I always did doubt a man's being a gentleman if his palate had no acquired tastes.'

The weapon of satire was one that Hardy always kept keen and bright in his armoury. At the very end of his career as a novelist, the scenes in *The Well-Beloved* that involve the Hon. Nicola Pine-Avon show all the old zest for lampooning the London fashionables.

With his rustic characters the touch is kindlier, the humour more genial, but there is no mistaking the satirical intention. Right at the beginning, in *Desperate Remedies,* there is that wonderful little sketch of Clerk Crickett—something incidental to the main fabric like a gargoyle or a misericord—whom Hardy immortalized with his description of the man as 'a kind of bowdlerized rake'. The words linger and echo on.

There are two other elements in Hardy's early writing that I want just to touch on briefly here, and to develop later. One is the tendency for Hardy's 'Bohemian standpoint' to foster a detachment, a disengagement—almost an alienation from society—which encouraged him to stand well back from his subject and see it in perspectives that extend far beyond the immediate time and place of the action. It is this which gives a majestic rhythm to the way Hardy sets the scene at the opening of *Far from the Madding Crowd.*

The other element which much preoccupied him was what I can best describe as the laodicean temperament, a dispassionate sceptical lukewarm view of matters that might inspire others to fanatical and impassioned devotion. Hardy called one of his novels 'A Laodicean' and he also used the word in *Desperate Remedies,* in *Under the Greenwood Tree,* and in *Far from the Madding Crowd.* This idea of a lukewarm nature, of an imperturbable disposition, was one that he was drawn to explore and inclined to admire.

I hope I have now done enough to identify some of the most important features in the way Hardy started to write *Far from the Madding Crowd.* In a dramatisation it is always tempting to put any narrative linking passages into the mouth of one of the characters, in order to maintain dramatic continuity; but in *Far from the Madding Crowd* Hardy's own narrative description of Norcombe Hill, which virtually opens the story, is so vital—so relevant to what follows—that it was imperative to use an impersonal narrator, as it might be Hardy himself, holding close to the descriptive passages in what surprisingly is not the first chapter in the book but the second. The first is really a little prologue—the initial encounter between Gabriel Oak and Bathsheba, something that a more mature Hardy might have found superfluous. The kind of opening to a novel that he gradually perfected was the broad landscape-with-figures, for which Norcombe Hill provided the prototype. Think of *The Woodlanders,* for example—the lonely roadside scene as the carrier's wagon approaches; or the tremendous evocation of Egdon Heath that opens *The Return of the Native.* Nowhere is Hardy's personal touch more evident than in these massive panoramic theatres of his imagination where the scene unfolds with a muted deliberation, and then—like the zooming of a camera—we are made to focus down on one small particular. In this case the wavering sound of Gabriel's flute.

But it is not just a theatrical device, a technical trick. At the same time he is charging the scene with the mood, the atmosphere, that he wants to create. What you will find in prose of this quality is that the author is pursuing several ends at the same time; that is what gives it its complexity of texture and also its impact. Instead of following a simple melodic line it is symphonic in character.

What Hardy has to say about Norcombe Hill is that it is ordinary and smoothly outlined and featureless but, for all that, it may survive 'on some great day of confusion, when far grander heights and dizzy granite precipices topple down'. Now if you consider the three men in Bathsheba's life, who constitute the whole drama of the book, you will recognise that Gabriel Oak is symbolised in Norcombe Hill, and that the more spectacular heights and depths that will eventually topple down are reflected in Sergeant Troy and Farmer Boldwood. To reinforce that, Hardy describes Oak as occupying 'morally the vast middle space of Laodicean neutrality'—as 'a man whose moral colour was a kind of pepper-and-salt mixture'. In short he was phlegmatic Norcombe Hill among the Alps of treachery and the Himalayas of passion.

Having thus stated the central theme of the book, Hardy next looks more closely at Gabriel Oak. And this he does with all the satirical virtuosity that now comes readily to his pen. Gabriel decides to go courting Bathsheba, who is staying with her aunt, Mrs Hurst, and Gabriel's preparations for this momentous interview provide Hardy with one of those classic occasions on which the tradition of English comic writing thrives. In *Much Ado* Shakespeare wrote 'If he be not in love with some woman, there is no believing old signs: a' brushes his hat o' mornings; what should that bode?' Gabriel does more than brush his hat—and Hardy describes the shepherd's preparations with great relish in Chapter IV.

In these early scenes Hardy is establishing an attractive young couple in a romantic situation—something that he regarded as almost obligatory in the kind of serial that magazine editors would buy. And he was very conscious of the financial necessity of showing himself to be a good hand at a serial. Consequently he seldom allows middle-aged or elderly characters to hold the centre of the stage for long. They have supporting roles. The Mayor of Casterbridge is about the only exception to the rule that Hardy's novels concern themselves *ostensibly*—I stress that, *ostensibly*—with the romantic fortunes, the love-life, of young people for whom the prospect of marriage is a dominating concern. At times, indeed, the heroines scarcely develop beyond the insipid dolls of routine love-stories. Even the most ardent of Hardy's admirers would find little delight, I am sure, in the prospect of an evening spent in the company of Fancy Day or Ann Garland—always assuming that one could even tell which was which.

But Bathsheba is a different matter. Hers is a lively and individual portrait. And more than that—she is to gain in stature from the new strategy that Hardy first perfects in this book. Unlike her less fortunate sisters she is swept by her creator far past that first joyous pealing of wedding bells which traditionally ends the tale. She has much more to taste, of the sweet and the bitter of life, before we finally leave her.

I hope I have now said enough on two counts to demonstrate what I believe was the dilemma that troubled Hardy when he started to write *Far from the Madding Crowd*. He was committed to some kind of romance between young lovers, which he was bound to find an increasingly limited and constricting framework. And he had this impulse towards satire, to lampoon the follies and frailties of the world, to express his sense of the ironies in human conduct.

What had he done so far to bring these conflicting elements into some sort of working relationship? Let us look first of all at *Under the Greenwood Tree*—and particularly at the final scene, which at first glance is the traditional happy ending. The young lovers, Fancy and Dick, are married:

> 'Fancy,' he said, 'why we are so happy is because there is such full confidence between us . . . We'll have no secrets from each other, darling, will we ever?—no secret at all.'
>
> 'None from today,' said Fancy. 'Hark! what's that? . . . O, 'tis the nightingale', murmurmed she, and thought of a secret she would never tell.

Those are the last words of the book and they contain a double irony. Dick is delighted with the apparent candour that had inspired Fancy to confess to a flirtation with a rival lover, Farmer Shiner, when in fact her confession was a sham, a make-believe device to provoke Dick to jealousy. On the other hand, the secret she will never tell him is that she had been on the verge of jilting him and marrying the better educated and more eligible Parson Maybold.

The story could of course have been rounded off as easily with the unalloyed sweetness of sentiment that is customary in romantic fiction. Hardy preferred to raise a doubt, to pose a question, to probe beyond the immediate bliss of the wedding-day. And in his next novel, *A Pair of Blue Eyes,* he made this matter of candour between lovers a main issue. This time the Poor Man loses the Lady. She does jilt him, and in her turn is hopelessly entangled in a web of deceit. As the story develops the action centres increasingly on such questions as 'Should a woman confess an earlier love? Can a man assume a right to find not only unfeigned devotion but unkissed lips?' And if these questions, put in such simple terms, suggest an ingenuousness in the author, let me emphasise that *A Pair of Blue Eyes* is very much the prototype of *Tess of the d'Urbervilles.*

If we now compare Gabriel and Bathsheba with their counterparts in the three earlier novels, there can be no doubt that in *Far from the Madding Crowd* Hardy was in command of a much sharper and more individualised characterisation. The dialogue is consistently lively and helps to animate the two of them. The satirical strokes that play about them give humour and humanity—attributes that romantic heroes and heroines often lack. Moreover they are dramatically poised; they have a reserve of strength, a readiness to move into more demanding situations as the plot develops.

I want to come on to the plot, but before I do so there is one other element to be considered—the rustic chorus. Hardy must have realised that, in his hands, the vernacular of Dorset was a weapon of great potential; but he did not find it easy to bring it into a well-proportioned relationship with the other ingredients of his early stories. In *Desperate Remedies* he gave it a very subordinate role—just one or two incidental scenes. In *Under the*

Greenwood Tree he went to the other extreme, showing an absolute mastery of the comic possibilities, but feeling perhaps that he had in some measure burlesqued the Mellstock musicians instead of giving them—in his own words—'a deeper, more essential, more transcendent handling'. In *A Pair of Blue Eyes* the dialect characters contribute little. They sound like Dorset folk uprooted and transplanted in Cornwall, where they wilt in an alien soil and climate.

In *Far from the Madding Crowd* Hardy discovered how to integrate this very rich material into the whole fabric of the novel. Joseph Poorgrass, Jan Coggan and the rest do not occupy such prominent positions as they would have done if the book had been another *Under the Greenwood Tree*; nor are they minor interludes with little bearing on the main action. They are part of the whole momentum of the story. Theirs is the testimony and theirs the commentary that give depth and resonance to the main events. And when the principal characters are caught up in the gathering tragedy of their destinies it is the curiosity, the sympathy, the tender philosophising, and the instinctive stoicism of the rustics which add a new and invaluable dimension to Hardy's writings. Thanks to them, what might have seemed high-flown at times and melodramatic is firmly secured in the credible realities that Hardy summoned up in his image of Wessex.

It was of course in *Far from the Madding Crowd* that he introduced this new concept, Wessex. The creation of a fictitious territory, in all seriousness and with an unremitting attention to detail, seems to us now so right, so necessary, that one is apt to forget that Hardy came to it only by degrees. His choice of names for people and places did not at first show the consistent gravity of demeanour that came later. In the satirical exuberance of his younger days he was inclined to send them up—Miss Vashti Sniff and Farmer Kex, for example, will hardly be found in any Dorset directory, and I don't suppose a conducted tour of the Hardy country has yet visited the villages of Tantrum Clangley and Puddle-sub-Mixen. I leave you to decide in which of his novels they are to be found—but I promise you they are there!

Where Wessex offered Hardy a much subtler outlet for his satirical impulse was in the conversation of the villagers. The dialogue at Warren's Malthouse in Chapter VIII for example, needs no justification and no explanation. Its quality is absolute and unmistakable. But as you listen to the conversation about Bathsheba's family, the Everdenes—and, I hope, enjoy the humour of the company at the Old Maltster's—you will recognise the scope that Hardy finds in his rustic worthies for that sceptical, mocking, laodicean philosophy that embodies his kind of satire. I do not want to be over-portentous about something that is essentially and joyously funny, but I think there is enough evidence here that Hardy adapted his rustics to the traditional role of the jester, the Court Fool—claiming the special privilege of mentioning the unmentionable. Let me instance that picture of the first Mrs Coggan—poor Charlotte in her strict godliness, so implacably opposed to 'Nature' and 'the good old word of sin', perhaps after all not getting into Heaven because ' 'a was never much in luck's way'.

This jocular, casual, uncommitted view of Heaven is carried on later—in Poorgrass's admission in Chapter XLII that he has been 'troubled with weak moments lately' and is determined 'not to go too far for safety', because 'Your next world is your next world, and not to be squandered off hand'. And there's his wry tribute in the same chapter to chapel-folk 'who are more hand-in-glove with them above than we'—which prompts Coggan to concede that 'if anybody do go to heaven, they will. They've worked hard for it and they deserve to have it, such as 'tis'. How characteristic is that murmured afterthought 'such as tis'! Even Heaven inspires only a *moderate* and qualified enthusiasm.

To appreciate the interaction between these scenes and the principal characters, we must look in some detail at the plot, the chain of events. And here the best pointer to the way Hardy's technique was evolving is *A Pair of Blue Eyes*. In that novel he first employed a method that was to become a feature of his strategy in his finest work. This was to take a theme of great simplicity and breadth of reference, and to group his events about this theme as variations on it. By so doing he achieved a homogeneity, an inter-relatedness, that accumulated the force which lifts the story to its climax. Let me give two examples from later novels. *The Woodlanders* has as its theme 'Fidelity and Infidelity, the spirit of marriage and the letter of marriage'; and at every turn of the story Hardy is probing and testing some aspect of this theme. *The Mayor of Casterbridge* is about Retribution; the whole massive weight of the blows that bring down Henchard comes from the working out of the theme of retribution.

In *A Pair of Blue Eyes* Hardy took Deception as his theme. In trying to be kind to Felix Jethway, Elfride innocently deceives him into believing that she loves him. When she disabuses him he deceives his mother into believing that Elfride has jilted him. Stephen Smith deceives Elfride and her father about his parentage. Elfride deceives first her father and later Henry Knight about her abortive elopement with Smith. And so on. By degrees we are made to realise what a chain of little white lies can lead to.

In these groupings of events Hardy found the moral dramas that stimulated him, and found also the satires of circumstance that accorded with his interpretation of human actions. To activate the plot of *Far from the Madding Crowd* he took as his theme one that has found a homely expression in the old saw which goes something like this—

For want of a nail the shoe was lost
For want of a shoe the horse was lost
For want of a horse the rider was lost
For want of a rider the battle was lost
And all for the want of a nail.

In other words the most trifling mischance can lead, step by step, to an overwhelming disaster. Thus, Gabriel's courtship of Bathsheba is terminated abruptly when his flock of sheep is driven over a precipice by a young half-trained dog—a disaster that could not have happened if Gabriel had remembered to shut the dog indoors at night in the way he normally did.

Fanny Robin's tragedy stems remorselessly from her silly little mistake in going to the wrong church when Frank Troy was ready to marry her. And Bathsheba just as inadvertently sets in motion her own tragedy when she commits a practical joke that misfires—the sending of an anonymous valentine to her stiff and rather pompous neighbour, Farmer Boldwood.

I want to dwell for a moment on the character of Boldwood, who might be described as a Malvolio transposed from a comic figure to a tragic one. One of the things that interested me particularly in the response of listeners to the radio dramatisation was the strong impression that Boldwood had made. This was due in no small measure to the actor James Grout, but not entirely so, I believe. In his creation of Boldwood Hardy relied largely on an extensive and vehement dialogue of a kind that he had used only once before—in Miss Aldclyffe's impassioned scene with Cytherea in *Desperate Remedies*. It is a dramatic style of utterance—a melodramatic style, if you prefer to call it so. When it is transferred from print, silently read, to an acted performance it can strikingly increase its impact. With the page in front of us we may have critical reservations that are swept away in the torrent of a dramatic rendering. The border between deeply felt emotion and what Hamlet called 'tearing a passion to tatters . . . out-heroding Herod' is sometimes an uncertain one. Hardy was certainly conscious of the danger when he wrote in *The Woodlanders*, 'It often happens that in situations of unrestraint . . . real feeling glides into a mode of manifestation not easly distinguishable from rodomontade.'

As a young writer he preferred not to risk another melodramatic outburst like Miss Aldclyffe's. *Under the Greenwood Tree* and *A Pair of Blue Eyes* both treat sexual love romantically and in a cool style. The stance of the author is detached, quizzical, concerned to add little touches of satire and not to tolerate a grand passion among his characters. I want particularly to stress the coolness of the writing—even when Henry Knight is facing a violent death on the cliff-face—as a contrast to the volcanic manner of Boldwood. In the evolution of his strategy as a novelist Hardy's biggest problem, in my view, was to reconcile by mutual adjustment these two very different sides of his genius. The crucial importance of *Far from the Madding Crowd* is that it brought him to grips with that problem.

When I use the word 'volcanic' to describe Boldwood's emotions I am recalling a sentence of D. H. Lawrence's—'Love passion, pitching along with its beauty and strange hate and suffering, remains the one living volcano of our souls.' Boldwood and Miss Aldclyffe display eruptions of a spectacular kind, but the volcano is a constant and menacing presence, from which lesser outbursts occur. Boldwood's rage at the thought of Bathsheba's being kissed by another man arouses a number of echoes in other contexts. For Hardy the act of kissing became a powerful symbol involving jealousy and possessiveness and guilt. There is Miss Aldclyffe saying, 'I thought I had at last found an artless woman who had not been sullied by a man's lips.' In *A Pair of Blue Eyes* Henry Knight pinned his hopes on kissing 'untried lips'. When Troy kissed Bathsheba she 'felt like one who has sinned a great sin. It had been a glory to her to know that her lips had been touched by no man's on earth.' And in *The Return of the Native* when Clym kisses Eustacia 'the impress was so real that he hardly dared to enter the house, for it seemed as if his mother might say, "What red spot is that glowing upon your mouth so vividly?" '

This, then, is the volcano that is gathering in Boldwood when he meets Bathsheba immediately after she has rejected him as a suitor and in his place accepted Sergeant Troy. The violently passionate outburst in Chapter XXXI shows Hardy venturing into the deep jungle country of unbridled emotion for the first time since the Cytherea/Aldclyffe duet in *Desperate Remedies*. We can see now that this exploration of the dark coiled-up vehemence in Boldwood's nature was a cardinal discovery that led Hardy on to the later tragedies.

I have one final backward glance to make to *A Pair of Blue Eyes*, and it takes the form of a comparison between Hardy's different ways of treating the rivalry between two men in love with the same woman. The difference is indeed so great that you may need to be reminded of the resemblance between the Bathsheba-Boldwood-Troy triangle and the Elfride-Stephen Smith-Henry Knight one. I have already spoken of the cool style of *A Pair of Blue Eyes*. Technically Hardy seems to be aiming at a well-behaved comedy of manners in the Jane Austen tradition—keeping powerful emotions below the surface and studying their reflections in the surface ripples they cause. And no amount of disappointment or jealousy or deceit is to be permitted to precipitate scenes of tragic drama.

The clash between Smith and Knight could have been as bitter and violent as that between Troy and Boldwood, but it is not. The climax of *A Pair of Blue Eyes* could have been as horrifying as the climax of *Far from the Madding Crowd,* but it is not. Smith is too magnanimous—or too irresolute—to urge his prior claim to Elfride, although it is perhaps a stronger claim than Boldwood's to Bathsheba. So the element of rivalry in *A Pair of Blue Eyes* is defused before it can accumulate any emotional power. And for the climax Hardy turns away from both romance and tragedy and opts for the kind of black comedy that he was again drawn to in the finale of *The Hand of Ethelberta.* Smith and Knight travel separately, but by a coincidence on the same train, from London to Cornwall to renew their courtship of Elfride. Neither knows that the train is also conveying Elfride—the corpse of Elfride in her coffin. It is a dry, ironical, anti-romantic, anti-heroic conclusion—very much to the taste of the young satirist.

But with Boldwood and Troy we are in different country. These men are the 'dizzy granite precipices' that will topple down on some 'great day of confusion' to which their unstable and volcanic temperaments have contributed, while the laodicean, middling ordinariness of a Norcombe Hill—or a Gabriel Oak—is quietly persistent and undisturbed. With that commitment to so dynamic and explosive a situation, Hardy was prepared to make the leap into what he conceived to be the tragic concept of Greek drama, transposed into the idiom of the Victorian novel—just as Shakespeare and his contemporaries had adapted it to the idiom of the Elizabethan theatre. It is that decision, made in *Far from the Madding Crowd,* which led to *The Return of the Native* and *The Mayor of Casterbridge,* to *Tess* and to *Jude.* It is the most far-reaching step that Hardy took in his evolution of a strategy of novel-writing.

As *Far from the Madding Crowd* gathers momentum we see how Hardy can now blend and harmonise what might have remained separate and conflicting techniques. The large detachment of the cosmic vision gives a grandeur and dignity to the drama; the ability to accept and be possessed by the volcanic nature of his characters gives an impassioned force to the tragic events; and the satirical humour of the Wessex chorus holds the highest flights of tragedy to a touchstone of reality.

This last point is nowhere better illustrated than in the return of Fanny Robin's corpse to Weatherbury from the Casterbridge workhouse. In order to set up the scene where Bathsheba is alone with Fanny's coffin, Hardy has to invent some reasonably plausible delay which postpones the burial. For this the perfect method is immediately to hand—Joseph Poorgrass's notorious intemperance. In place of some transparent contrivance, to which another novelist might have been driven, we have the normal course of events, requiring Poorgrass to take the farm wagon on this melancholy errand, delaying fatally at the inn where Coggan and Mark Clark prevail on him to join them. The consequent drinking-scene at the Buck's Head in Chapter XLII is a richly textured piece which is quite splendid in its own right, which binds the rustic characters into the mainstream of the story—instead of being decorative interludes—and which gives depth and contrast to Bathsheba's supreme moment of tragedy that immediately follows it.

It well illustrates what I said earlier about symphonic writing. Hardy is now controlling an elaborate dialogue between the various sections of his orchestra, moving us at will from one mood to another, exciting in us a sense of foreboding as he makes the first statement of the terrible revenge that Fanny in her innocence will take on Bathsheba—and then, when everything is ready and poised, leading us into the climax, Chapter XLIII, when Troy returns and finds Bathsheba standing beside the opened coffin in which the corpse of Fanny Robin lies with her still-born baby—of which Troy is of course the father.

Beyond that point there is little that calls for specific comment. As the years passed Hardy made improvements, changes of emphasis, modifications—but his strategy as a novelist proceeded from what he had achieved in *Far from the Madding Crowd*. The unifying theme, the detached panoramic vision, the command of volcanic emotion and specifically sexual passion, the ability to take his action to the limits of tragedy, the contrasting value of rural scenes and country voices offsetting the violence of the drama, the quiet playing of ironical treatments and satirical humours over the total scene—these are the distinctive attributes of his novels, and it was in the writing of *Far from the Madding Crowd* that they first came together in full force.

II

Robert C. Schweik:

THE NARRATIVE STRUCTURE OF "FAR FROM THE MADDING CROWD"

In spite of the scholarship which has been published in the last twenty years on the composition and revision of Hardy's novels, it is fair to say that by far the bulk of critical analysis of his fiction still proceeds on a fundamentally untenable basis—on the assumption that Hardy's novels can safely be discussed as if they were unified narrative constructs. In fact, Hardy's novels are more often characterized by marked shifts in narrative intention that came about in the process of composition, and any attempt to comment accurately on Hardy's fiction must take such shifts into account. *Far from the Madding Crowd* is a particularly clear example of the kind of narrative structure that can result from changes in narrative manner that grew out of the process of composition itself. In fact, the structure of *Far from the Madding Crowd* is something like a record of the ways that Hardy grappled with the problems of its composition—a record of some fine artistic successes achieved in the midst of extraordinary artistic uncertainty; a record of changing purposes, or narrative strategies tried and abandoned with varying degrees of care and carelessness; and a record of indecisions, compromises, and expedients accepted in an effort to get the thing done. My purpose in this paper is to trace that record in detail, and to suggest, by way of conclusion, what bearing this may have on future critical comment on the novel.

I

When the first five chapters of *Far from the Madding Crowd* appeared in *The Cornhill Magazine,* they dazzled one reviewer into speculating that they could be from the hand of George Eliot. Hardy himself was puzzled and annoyed by the comparison; and some later critics were inclined to displays of knowledgeable amazement that anyone could confuse the two. Yet these opening chapters were something different; of course they were not in the manner of George Eliot, but it would have been difficult to assign them to any other of Hardy's contemporaries either, nor were they quite what a reader of Hardy's earlier fiction might have expected from the writer himself. They deserve closer scrutiny than they have usually received, not only because they have the obvious importance of creating first impressions, but because they reveal some authorial difficulties which Hardy faced at the beginning of the novel, and because they provide a convenient benchmark against which his subsequent performance may be considered.

The effect created by the opening chapters of *Far from the Madding Crowd* results largely from a delicate shifting and balancing of narrative attitudes which range between serious concern and detached amusement. Hardy's initial description of Gabriel Oak, for example, begins with a paragraph of one sentence devoted to an exaggerated metaphoric description of Oak's smile, and immediately continues with a series of broad and obviously light-hearted generalizations on Oak's moral character—we are told that Oak is a 'young man of sound judgment, easy motions, proper dress, and general good character', that on Sundays he was given to 'misty views' and 'went to church but yawned privately by the time the congregation reached the Nicene creed', and that his friends considered him sometimes a good man, sometimes a bad man, and sometimes a salt-and-pepper mixture. These tongue-in-cheek observations on the subject of Oak's moral character (the manner, and in fact, some of the particulars are reminiscent of Hardy's description of William Dewy in *Under the Greenwood Tree)* are followed by remarks on the quaintly amusing details of his ordinary dress, and they culminate in a comic, almost mock-epic, account of Oak's watch. But following this account, which has become progressively more comic, Hardy begins to shift the tone of his description by introducing a suggestion that Oak might appear otherwise to 'thoughtful persons'. The more neutral attitude suggested by the lines which immediately follow—where we are told that Oak still retains the 'hues and curves of youth' and even 'some relics of the boy' while possessing a potentially imposing height and breadth—marks a transition from the amused playfulness with which Hardy had begun to a more serious attitude implied in the following passage:

> But there is a way some men have, rural and urban alike, for which the mind is more responsible than flesh and sinew; it is a way of curtailing their dimensions by their manner of showing them. And from a quiet modesty that would have become a vestal, which seemed to continually impress upon him that he had no great claim on the world's room, Oak walked unassumingly, and with a faintly perceptible bend, yet distinct from a bowing of the shoulders. This may be said to be a defect in an individual if he depends for his valuation more upon his appearance than upon his capacity to wear well, which Oak did not.

By the concluding sentence of this passage, however, Oak's quiet modesty has already been reduced to a less prepossessing 'capacity to wear well'; in the next paragraph Hardy gradually reassumes a more detached and less serious tone, then abruptly concludes his description of Oak with a casually reductive comment: 'In short, he was twenty-eight, and a bachelor.' Thus, in a matter of six paragraphs, Hardy moves from the amused and casual attitude which he adopts at the opening to a manner which implies a more serious concern about Oak's character, and he returns, finally, to end again on a lighter note with an off-hand quip.

This frequent shifting and balancing of attitudes toward his subject is characteristic of Hardy's manner throughout the first five chapters of *Far from the Madding Crowd.* In the process we are made aware that the relationship of Oak and Bathsheba involves some fundamentally serious concerns—the problem Bathsheba faces of attracting an acceptable lover, and the sexual need which underlies Oak's response to her. Hardy's descriptions of Bathsheba have a way of conveying Oak's interest in her unseen body, and her sexuality is discreetly suggested in the scenes in which Oak observes her—as she surveys herself in a looking glass ('her thoughts seeming to glide into far-off though likely dramas in which men would play a part') or rides astride ('in the manner demanded by the saddle, though hardly expected of the woman'). Their courtship takes place against a rural setting of lambing and calving, where, appropriately, Oak's conversation finally turns to babies, and Bathsheba struggles between her desire for independence ('I *hate* to be thought man's property in that way') and her desire to be dominated ('I want somebody to tame me; I am too independent'). Furthermore, Hardy reminds his readers from time to time that Oak and Bathsheba have qualities of character which are not to be taken lightly: in Oak's remark on Bathsheba's vanity there is a suggestion that her character may be seriously flawed, and there are pointed authorial comments to the effect that Oak has a 'special' if 'static' power, 'morally, physically, and mentally', that he is 'even-tempered' and faithful in love, and that he is an 'intensely humane man' who pities even the untimely fate of his sheep. Moreover, the action sometimes bears out Oak's special worthiness and Bathsheba's sturdy independence. But if the reader is expected to take Oak and Bathsheba with some seriousness, it is with a seriousness qualified by the comic aspect in which they are so often presented: Bathsheba haggling over twopence and huffily resenting Oak's payment of it ('in gaining her a passage he had lost her her point, and we know how women take a favour of that kind'); Oak returning to his work with 'an air between Tragedy and Comedy'; Oak's face 'rising like the moon behind the hedge' as he appears to Bathsheba; Oak dressed in his waistcoat 'patterned all over with the sprigs of an elegant flower uniting the beauties of both rose and lily without the defects of either', his hair slicked down to 'a splendidly novel colour between that of guano and Roman cement'; Bathsheba breathlessly pursuing Oak and explaining that she has difficulty thinking outdoors because her 'mind spreads away so';

Oak pursuing Bathsheba round a holly bush and responding to his rejected suit 'with the bearing of one who is going to give his days and nights to Ecclesiastes forever'.

There are similar variations of tone in Hardy's treatment of the rural setting in the first five chapters of the novel. His first description of the heavens in Chapter II is now a quite straightforward evocation of the solemnity and grandeur of the sky above Norcombe Hill, although in editions before 1912 the passage ended with a slightly mocking turn of phrase: 'After such a nocturnal reconnoitre among these astral clusters, aloft from the customary haunts of thought and vision, some men may feel raised to a capability for eternity at once.' A second passage in the same chapter shows similar alterations in tone:

> Castor and Pollux with their quiet shine were almost on the meridian: the barren and gloomy Square of Pegasus was creeping round to the north-west; far away through the plantation Vega sparkled like a lamp suspended amid the leafless trees, and Cassiopeia's chair stood daintily poised on the uppermost boughs.
>
> 'One o'clock,' said Gabriel.
>
> Being a man not without a frequent consciousness that there was some charm in this life he led, he stood still after looking at the sky as a useful instrument, and regarded it in an appreciative spirit, as a work of art superlatively beautiful. For a moment he seemed impressed with the speaking loneliness of the scene, or rather with the complete abstraction from all its compass of the sights and sounds of man. Human shapes, interferences, troubles, and joys were all as if they were not, and there seemed to be on the shaded hemisphere of the globe no sentient being save himself; he could fancy them all gone round to the sunny side.

The sober weight evoked by Hardy's description of 'barren and gloomy' Pegasus 'creeping round' contrasts with his image of the dainty poising of Cassiopeia's chair; the general picturesqueness of the constellations is juxtaposed incongruously against the matter-of-factness of Oak's 'One o'clock'; and narrative attitude ranges from reverence to playful imaginativeness as Hardy proceeds from his reference to the modest 'charm' of Oak's life, to an evocation of the 'speaking loneliness' Oak feels in gazing at the 'superlatively beautiful' sky, and then back to the more light-hearted 'fancy' of the concluding phrase.

Broader variations in tone are notable in Hardy's treatment of the smaller details of rural environment in the first five chapters of the novel. A feeling for the grimness in natural surroundings suggested by a remark like 'Many a small bird went to bed supperless that night among the bare boughs' will be countered by the playfully fanciful perspective supplied in another:

> Nothing disturbed the stillness of the cottage save the chatter of a knot of sparrows on the eaves; one might fancy scandal and rumour to be no less the staple topic of these little coteries on roofs than of those under them.

And, again, the activities of lambing and calving—the animal 'facts of life' at Norcombe—will sometimes be presented in a manner which emphasizes the precariousness of newborn life, and at other times be treated in a detached and fancifully comic way:

> The cow standing erect was of the Devon breed, and was encased in a tight warm hide of rich Indian red, as absolutely uniform from eyes to tail as if the animal had been dipped in a dye of that colour, her long back being mathematically level. The other was spotted, gray and white. Beside her Oak now noticed a little calf about a day old, looking idiotically at the two women, which showed it had not long been accustomed to the phenomenon of eyesight, and often turning to the lantern, which it apparently mistook for the moon, inherited instinct having as yet had little time for correction by experience. Between the sheep and the cows Lucina had been busy on Norcombe Hill lately.

Finally, there are similar variations of tone in Hardy's treatment of the two major crises which occur in the opening chapter of *Far from the Madding Crowd.* The critical moment in which Gabriel Oak almost loses his life by suffocation is really over before the reader is made aware of any cause for concern, and the potential seriousness of the event is minimized by the dialogue which follows it—a dialogue which slips almost imperceptibly towards the teasing playfulness of the conclusion in which Gabriel is allowed momentarily to hold Bathsheba's hand. Another and even more obvious effort to maintain a somewhat precarious balance between a serious and a comic attitude toward the action is notable in Hardy's account of the 'pastoral tragedy' of Chapter V. The incident itself is prefaced by two paragraphs which provide a broadly comic account of Oak's dogs, after which the narrative become increasingly sober as Hardy develops the events in which Oak loses sheep and farm, and culminates in passages of a grimly serious tone:

> It was a second to remember another phase of the matter. The sheep were not insured. All the savings of a frugal life had been dispersed at a blow; his hopes of being an independent farmer were laid low—possibly forever. Gabriel's energies, patience, and industry had been so severely taxed during the years of his life between eighteen and eight-and-twenty, to reach his present stage of progress, that no more seemed left in him. He leant down upon a rail, and covered his face with his hands.

But, as the chapter continues, Hardy's narrative manner once again changes; he supplies a more detached and crisply factual account of what must have happened to Oak's sheep, and returns, finally, to wryly humorous description of the fate of the offending dog:

> George's son had done his work so thoroughly that he was considered too good a workman to live, and was, in fact, taken and tragically shot at twelve o'clock that same day—another instance of the untoward fate which so often attends dogs and other philosophers who follow out a train of reasoning to its logical conclusion and attempt perfectly consistent conduct in a world so largely made up of compromise.

The effect, in short, is to qualify the otherwise restrained and moving account of Oak's personal misfortune by placing it within a comic frame.

This close balancing and interweaving of contrasting narrative tones throughout the first five chapters of *Far from the Madding Crowd* was certainly not characteristic of Hardy, nor was it likely to have been entirely congenial to him. Probably it came about as a result of his initial effort to combine a number of not entirely compatible objectives—the more serious treatment of character he had been groping toward in *A Pair of Blue Eyes,* the comic tone and rustic humour of *Under the Greenwood Tree* (which Leslie Stephen had praised in requesting a new novel for *The Cornhill Magazine),* and the 'incident' necessary to satisfy Stephen's demand for 'some distinct and well arranged plot'.[1] In any case, Hardy seems to have found the manner he had adopted increasingly difficult to maintain, and by Chapter V it had become something like a see-saw between wry comicality and profound seriousness. Yet, although Hardy no doubt felt the strain of keeping a balance between such diverse objectives, the result was a remarkably controlled opening; and his handling of scene and action leaves the impression of a narrator of broad awareness and flexible sensibility.

II

But the relatively self-contained action of the opening of the novel and its very indeterminateness of tone posed difficulties: the problem was to find a suitable continuation, and evidence of major revision in Chapters VI-XVIII of the manuscript testifies to Hardy's initial uncertainty about the direction the novel would take.[2] Hardy at first developed a continuation which differed very greatly from any version which appeared in print. Neither Boldwood nor Fanny Robin appear to have had any significant part in it, and its manner was thoroughly comic. Some idea of this original continuation may be had by reading in sequence the present Chapters VI, VIII, X, and XV, ignoring, however, all matters related to Boldwood and Fanny Robin. It was probably in this form that Hardy submitted the first nine chapters of *Far from the Madding Crowd* to Leslie Stephen in the spring of 1873, and what won Stephen's approval, then, was very likely something much closer to the rustic comedy of *Under the Greenwood Tree* than to the novel which finally appeared in print.[3] Although Stephen was enthusiastic, Hardy was not satisfied with the almost entirely comic turn which the novel had taken, and during the summer of 1873 he made revisions which brought Boldwood into the story and dramatized the Fanny Robin-Troy sub-plot; thus most of the material contained in what are now Chapters VII, IX, XI-XIV, and XVI was added. But while supplying a dramatic account of the Fanny-Troy relationship and developing Boldwood as a major character, Hardy had also to provide a continuation of the story of Bathsheba's adaptation to her new role, and of Oak to his. At best, such diverse matters would have been difficult to integrate smoothly, and, of course, some scenes (much of the present Chapters VI, VIII, X, and XV) had already been independently written. Hardy chose to take advantage of the situation by emphasizing the contrastive features inherent in the different matters he was presenting. Thus, within Chapters VI-XVI, all of the major character groups appear, but for the most part the various strands of their stories are developed separately, and the characters, so far as they act upon one another, do so mostly at a distance, separated physically and psychologically. This separation is further emphasized by marked differences in narrative manner, so that Hardy's treatment of Oak and the rustics, of the Fanny-Troy episodes, of Boldwood, and of Bathsheba, each has its distinct tone.

Perhaps most striking is the effect this change had upon the function of those scenes of rustic comedy already composed. Full as they are of the humour of rustic manners and rural anecdote, Hardy had certainly intended Chapters VIII, X, and XV to have their own intrinsic interest and special charm for urban readers; but with the introduction of the Fanny-Troy Chapters VII, XI, and XVI, they took on an additional function, for both the rustics' dialogues in Warren's malthouse and their meeting in Bathsheba's hall also convey particularly a sense of lives lived and experienced as social community, and these scenes, finally placed in immediate juxtaposition to the scenes devoted to the Fanny-Troy story in Chapters VII, XI, and XVI, serve to heighten the starkly evoked social isolation and helplessness of Fanny. The effect results from the sharply pointed contrasts in detail and emphasis which Hardy worked into the Fanny-Troy chapters. The shared community of the rustics had been most simply conveyed, of course, by their presence and activity as a group; but beyond this a complex of details serves to endow the rustic scenes with an aura of shared human sympathy. In Chapter X it emerges in expressions of concern for Fanny Robin. In the clubhouse atmosphere of the malthouse scenes it is rendered more immediately by the activities of passing round the communal mug and the sharing of bread and bacon in an atmosphere suffused by the ruddy glow of the kiln; by the presence of roasting potatoes and boiling coffee 'for the benefit of whosoever would call'; by the ready accommodations of the group to the foibles of its members—whether the maltster's insistence on his agedness or Oak's touchiness about Bathsheba; and by the shared memories of the story-telling and mutual reminiscing. By adding transitional matter to these scenes which so richly convey an impression of the communal life of the rustics, Hardy was able to set beside them the portions of the Fanny-Troy story detailed in Chapters VII, XI, and XVI. Of these, the meeting of Oak and Fanny in Chapter VII was composed most perfunctorily and depends most heavily on the trappings of melodrama—the silent, shivering, lonely girl, standing in the churchyard, her pulse 'beating with a throb of tragic intensity'. But Chapters XI and XVI are more carefully drafted, and each scene is treated with particular care to dehumanize the participants and so heighten the contrast they make with the shared life, common sympathy, and warm tones associated with the rustics. In Chapter XI, for example, Hardy carefully evokes the barrenness of the dreary moorland scene in which there are 'forms without features' shrouded in darkness and muffling snow, and Fanny herself is reduced to the blank anonymity of a 'spot' talking to a 'wall'.[4] Again, through most of Chapter XVI Troy stands with the abnormal rigidity of a church column while time is marked by the grotesque twitchings of a mechanical mannikin, and this exaggerated rigidity is carried over into his treatment of Fanny at the end of the chapter. Equally striking is the way laughter is used to convey the lack of human sympathy in these chapters—the 'low peal of laughter' over Fanny's plight which concludes Chapter XI, the titters and giggling of the bystanders in the church, and Troy's hoarse laugh as he deserts Fanny at the end of Chapter XVI.

Although they have such markedly contrasting features, the scenes which present the ballad-like tragedy of Fanny Robin in Chapters VII, XI, and XVI involve methods similar to those used for the rustic comedy of Chapters VII, X, and XV. Both present characters sketched with very broad strokes acting in relatively simple and sharply defined situations; both are devoid of authorial comment; and both depend heavily for their effects upon a carefully managed 'atmosphere' in which the action occurs.

In the groups of chapters devoted to Bathsheba and Boldwood in this portion of *Far from the Madding Crowd,* Hardy attempted to exploit a similar kind of contrast and a similar parallelism of method, but here the matter involved greater complexities both in character and situation, and the result was a more mixed success. The chapters devoted primarily to Bathsheba (IX, X, XII, and XIII) are handled in a way which most nearly continues the serio-comic tone of the opening of the novel. Again, within these chapters Hardy reminds his readers occasionally that there are some fundamentally serious issues at stake: there are further authorial comments on Bathsheba's sexuality ('there was potentially enough in that lithe slip of humanity for alarming exploits of sex, and daring enough to carry them out'), and further suggestions of her consciousness of male eyes, her vanity as a woman, and her instinct to 'walk as a queen among these gods of the fallow, like a little sister of a little Jove'. But although Hardy does from time to time inject such reminders—sometimes with what strikes modern readers as the clumsily blunt directness of authorial forewarning ('Of love as a spectacle Bathsheba had a fair knowledge; but of love subjectively she knew nothing')—the sequence of vignettes supplied in Chapters IX, X, XII, and XIII is predominantly devoted to presenting the comedy of Bathsheba's deliberate efforts to act out the role of a poised and businesslike mistress of the farm while instinctively playing the role of coquette; and for the most part Hardy conveys the incongruity with detached amusement. The stage for her activities is supplied with the humour of local colour —the descriptions of the quaint oddities of her house and the rustic peculiarities of the market-place—and we are provided with glimpses of Bathsheba at home in comic confusion over Boldwood's unexpected call, scenes with Liddy in which Bathsheba feigns an air of superior detachment in an attempt to conceal her impulsive 'womanishness', and the comedy of Chapter X in which Bathsheba plays the role of grande dame, complete with appropriate exit:

> Then this small thesmothete stepped from the table, and surged out of the hall, her black silk dress licking up a few straws and dragging them along with a scratching noise upon the floor. Liddy, elevating her feelings to the occasion from a sense of grandeur, floated off behind Bathsheba with a milder dignity not entirely free from travesty, and the door was closed.

It is worth remarking, too, that the scenes devoted to Bathsheba convey a sense of lively ambience—the bustle of servant women, the crowd of workers in the hall, the throng of farmers in the market-place; and, even when she is relatively alone, there is the presence of Liddy and the comedy of the dialogues between them.

On the other hand, the chapters primarily devoted to Boldwood (XIV, XVII, and XVIII) are entirely devoid of precisely those features which most prominently characterize the scenes given to Bathsheba; and Hardy's effort, obvious enough to seem heavy-handed, was to emphasize the ponderously serious, withdrawn, and lonely life of Boldwood in a way which makes for a high degree of contrast with the scenes in which Bathsheba predominates. Boldwood is made to appear characteristically alone —a solitary caller, an exception among farmers, a 'lonely and reserved man', a 'celibate' whose barn is his almonry and cloister and whose parlour has the atmosphere of a 'Puritan Sunday lasting all the week'. Instead of the commonplaces of farm and market life in which Bathsheba moves, Hardy evokes about Boldwood an atmosphere that is distinctly queer, and (most notably in Chapter XIV) almost surrealistically distorted. Equally pointed is the contrast between the casually impulsive 'womanishness' which motivates Bathsheba in this portion of the novel and the ponderous and violent forces (rendered by mechanical, elemental, and military metaphors) which Hardy uses to characterize Boldwood.[5]

In effect, then, in Chapters VI-XVIII of *Far from the Madding Crowd* Hardy worked out a continuation for the opening of the novel which for the moment retained, and in fact increased, the kinds of variation in narrative manner with which he had begun: but now these variations occur between elements of chapter length or more—units which allowed greater room for development and did not require the kind of close control demanded by the manner Hardy had adopted in the opening chapters. Of course the revisions which brought Fanny Robin and Boldwood into the story also considerably expanded the scope, and altered the direction, of the novel; it was, in fact, something like beginning another novel with the sixth chapter—a novel whose effects largely depended upon a counterpointing of chapters and groups of chapters against one another, so that throughout Chapters VI-XVIII marked shifts in narrative manner from chapter to chapter serve to emphasize the contrasts between lives lived psychologically and physically apart, in greatly different social situations and equally different emotional atmospheres.

III

These effects had been achieved, however, by treating the four major character groups as relatively separate units. In the chapters immediately following (XIX-XXIII), Hardy brought Oak, the rustics, Boldwood, and Bathsheba together in scenes which prohibited the sharply defined contrasts and marked tonal differences he had exploited earlier; this posed a new problem of integrating matters previously developed separately, and resulted in still another pronounced change in narrative mode.

There was, first of all, the problem of what to do with Boldwood. In Chapters VI-XVIII, Hardy had brought Boldwood forward prominently as a character of major significance: he had devoted the whole of Chapter XIV and portions of Chapters XVII and XVIII to the elaboration of Boldwood's character; he had allowed Oak to assume a relatively subordinate role as a member of the rustic group; and he had been willing to heighten Boldwood's importance even at the expense of explicitly minimizing Oak's character by an authorial comment on Oak's 'mediocrity of inadequacy' which remained in the novel until the edition of 1877. But in spite of the pains he had taken to present Boldwood as an unusual personality, Hardy's conception of him had remained fundamentally simple. He had concentrated particularly on Boldwood's ponderous seriousness, his social isolation, and his psychology as an equilibrium of vast forces—features which had provided as sharp as possible a contrast to Bathsheba; but the wealth of circumstantial detail and the variety of analogy he employed to achieve this effect accomplished, in fact, very little else, for although they had momentarily created the illusion of character depth, Boldwood remained simply an all-or-nothing personality whose possibilities for further action had been defined almost entirely by his capacity for being either indifferent or extreme. Given this initial simplicity in Hardy's conception, there was really little that he could do immediately with Boldwood (short of reorienting the novel toward a more minute exploration of character psychology) except to have him mechanically persist in his lonely and obsessive pursuit of Bathsheba. And this, in fact, constitutes the central action of Chapters XIX-XXIII: there is an initial proposal scene in Chapter XIX; Boldwood's suit is the subject of Bathsheba's quarrel with Oak in Chapters XX and XXI; Boldwood reappears as suitor in Chapter XXII to ride with Bathsheba; and the sequence concludes with his second declaration at the end of Chapter XXIII. But although Boldwood's suit obviously constitutes the central action of this sequence of chapters, Hardy devoted relatively little space directly to it: at the most, Chapter XIX, somewhat more than a page or so of Chapter XXII, and perhaps a third of Chapter XXIII. The reason for this is not difficult to see: clearly, on the level at which Hardy was dealing with Boldwood's character, it had required little practically to exhaust the limited dramatic possibilities inherent in Boldwood's obsessive pursuit and Bathsheba's guilty reluctance.

Yet it is also clear from the manuscript evidence that Hardy had intended to extend this action over at least six chapters, and what was not directly related to the necessarily limited treatment of Boldwood's suit had, of course, to be given over to other matters. It is not surprising, then, that throughout Chapters XIX-XXIII Hardy concentrated more intensively upon the details of farming life. He provided, in fact, a whole catalogue of farming matters (sheep-washing, shears-grinding, troubles in the sheepfold, the shearing-barn, the shearing process, the shearing-supper) and at the same time he introduced a secondary and related action—the quarrel of Oak and Bathsheba and the veterinary problems which lead to their reconciliation. Farming matters had, of course, an obvious relevance for this secondary action; but Hardy's effort to flesh out the scenes of Boldwood's strange courtship with carefully wrought and highly particularized accounts of the sheep-shearing process resulted (in spite of the excellence of Hardy's treatment of the matters themselves) in a curious sort of excrescence: for the farming background, at best only peripherally relevant to the Bathsheba-Boldwood affair, had to be brought to the foreground and allowed to assume proportions which nearly obscure the main action without providing any centre of its own.

Rather, Hardy gave to each of the farming scenes a different emphasis: there is the description of the sheep-washing with its concentration on the moist fertility of the scene, as Bathsheba in her elegant riding-habit watches her men dripping wet at their work; there is the sheep-shearing itself, with its memorable evocation of the timeless functionalism of the great barn;[6] and the shearing-supper with the comedy of rustic dialogue and the antics of Joseph Poorgrass and Bob Coggan—and, of course, none of this in any distinct way relevant to the Boldwood-Bathsheba courtship. To compare the way in which the activities of lambing and calving in the first five chapters of the novel are used to create a distinctly subordinate yet integral and relevant environment for Oak's courtship of Bathsheba is to see that Hardy had found no similar way to integrate his materials in Chapters XIX-XXIII. This fact did not go unnoticed by Leslie Stephen, who (always conscious of the importance of 'incident') gently suggested that Hardy was slowing the action too much:

> As you ask me for my opinion I will say frankly that I think the sheep-shearing rather long for the present purpose . . . For periodical purposes, I think it rather delays the action unnecessarily. What I should be inclined to do would be simply to omit the chapter headed the 'shearing supper' and to add a few paragraphs to the succeeding or preceding, just explaining that there had been a supper.

Hardy obliged by the deletion of an entire chapter, as Stephen suggested, but this, of course, simply rendered less obvious the real difficulty—the want of an integrated treatment of action and background.

IV

By the time he had reached Chapter XXIV of *Far from the Madding Crowd*, Hardy had already adopted three quite different approaches to his subject, and each successive change in narrative manner appears to have been dictated by the particular problem of composition he faced at the moment. In one respect, however, Hardy's method had remained remarkably consistent: throughout the first twenty-five chapters of *Far from the Madding Crowd* he frequently made use of direct authorial comments which relate the particulars of his narrative to some more general observation. The subjects of these authorial generalizations vary considerably and follow no particular pattern; the following examples are typically diverse:

> *On Oak's decision to make Bathsheba his wife*: Love is a possible strength in an actual weakness. Marriage transforms a distraction into a support, the power of which should be, and happily often is, in direct proportion to the degree of imbecility it supplants. Oak began now to see light in this direction . . . (IV).

On Bathsheba's farm workers: The assemblage—belonging to that class of society which casts its thoughts into the form of feeling, and its feelings into the form of commotion—set to work with a remarkable confusion of purpose (VI).

On Boldwood's address to Bathsheba: Silence has sometimes a remarkable power of showing itself as the disembodied soul of feeling wandering without its carcass, and it is then more impressive than speech. In the same way, to say a little is often to tell more than to say a great deal. Boldwood told everything in that word (XIX).

On preparations for sheep-shearing: Peace and war kiss each other at their hours of preparation—sickles, scythes, shears, and pruning-hooks ranking with swords, bayonets, and lances, in their common necessity for point and edge (XX).

Such authorial generalizations are, of course, part of the omniscient narrator's stock-in-trade. When used persistently, they have the effect of repeatedly inviting the reader to take (for the moment at least) a relatively more distant and detached view of the action—to see the immediate narrative particular within the larger perspective of a general observation on 'love' or 'woman' and so forth. What is striking about Hardy's use of such authorial generalizations in *Far from the Madding Crowd* is their unusual distribution: some sixty occur in the first twenty-five chapters of the novel, while in the remaining thirty-two chapters there are only twelve. This marked reduction in Hardy's use of authorial generalization after Chapter XXV was probably partly a result of the increased time pressure under which he worked;[7] in any case, it marks still another distinct shift in narrative method—and the beginning of a gradual decline into increasing dependence upon 'strong' effects, shock, surprise, and external melodrama.

This shift is not immediately noticeable, however, for after the introduction of Troy in Chapter XXIV Hardy began a sequence of seven chapters primarily devoted to the Troy-Bathsheba courtship, and particularly to the development of Troy's character; and here, once again, the new subject prompted still another adjustment in narrative method, and for a time carried the novel sufficiently to postpone until Chapter XXXI the obvious dependence upon the kinds of effects which mark the concluding portions of the novel. As a character, Troy leant himself more to the sorts of plot devices which Hardy could depend on to generate the 'incident' which Stephen had demanded—romantic entanglements, surprise discoveries, colourful and striking situations fraught with suspense. As a consequence, Hardy could now forego the detailed accounts of farming activities which had previously served to compensate for the cramping liabilities of Boldwood's character. Thus, throughout Chapters XXIV-XXX, Hardy provides only the briefest descriptions of hay-making and hiving, and both are made relatively integral parts of the main action. And, although once again in Chapter XXIX Hardy found occasion to bring Oak forward to act out his role as the mature, independent, critical, yet selflessly devoted lover of Bathsheba, certainly his central concern throughout Chapters XXIV-XXX was twofold: to establish Troy's untrustworthy character, and, at the time time, to render persuasively his attractiveness for Bathsheba. That Hardy conceived these as two relatively separate objectives is suggested by the strikingly different means he employed to achieve each. To establish Troy's character as unstable, untrustworthy, and unworthy of Bathsheba, Hardy relied largely on direct authorial comment. He approached Chapter XXV, 'The New Acquaintance Described', as a set piece—a strategy for character introduction which he would never entirely forego, even in his most mature work—but in this case he composed it with the ponderously inflated diction and laboriously balanced syntax notable in passages like the following:

> Troy was full of activity, but his activities were less of a locomotive than a vegetative nature; and, never being based upon any original choice of foundation or direction, they were exercised on whatever object chance might place in their way. Hence, whilst he sometimes reached the brilliant in speech because that was spontaneous, he fell below the commonplace in action, from inability to guide incipient effort. He had a quick comprehension and considerable force of character; but, being without the power to combine them, the comprehension became engaged with trivialities whilst waiting for the will to direct it, and the force wasted itself in useless grooves through unheeding the comprehension.

Similar efforts at elaborate balance and point (and with even more clumsy explicitness) appear elsewhere in Hardy's scattered authorial comments on Troy's character, as the following, from Chapter XXIX:

> And Troy's deformities lay deep down from a woman's vision, whilst his embellishments were upon the very surface; thus contrasting with the homely Oak, whose defects were patent to the blindest, and whose virtues were as metals in a mine.

Of course Troy's 'deformities' are occasionally dramatized (as by Oak's discovery in Chapter XXIX that Troy was not the churchgoer he claimed to be). It is in rendering Troy's attractiveness to Bathsheba, however, that Hardy relied primarily on a more oblique and evocative dramatizing of situations—and with considerably more persuasive art. This more dense and suggestive mode, involving a close interaction of setting, incident, and dialogue, first appears in Chapter XXIV, where the meeting of Troy and Bathsheba in the fir plantation is developed in a way which emphasizes the meeting as a sexual encounter. There is the dramatic effect of Troy as the lantern reveals him ('His sudden appearance was to darkness what the sound of a trumpet is to silence'), and the dialogue which underlines the simple difference of sex:

> 'We have got hitched together somehow, I think.'
> 'Yes.'
> 'Are you a woman?'
> 'Yes.'
> 'A lady, I should have said.'
> 'It doesn't matter.'
> 'I am a man.'
> 'Oh!'

And in other ways the setting is made to reinforce the same impression:

> He too stooped, and the lantern standing on the ground between them threw the gleam from its open side among the fir-tree needles and the blades of long damp grass with the effect of a large glow-worm. It radiated upwards into their faces, and sent over half the plantation gigantic shadows of both man and woman, each dusky shape becoming distorted and mangled upon the tree-trunks till it wasted away to nothing.

This same mode is exploited, largely by dialogue, in Chapter XXVI, 'On the Verge of the Hay Mead'; less fully in Chapter XXVII, 'Hiving the Bees'; and very fully indeed in Chapter XXVIII, 'The Hollow Amid the Ferns', where Troy's persuasive attractiveness is dramatized in a lush setting with its own phallic suggestiveness, and where action and dialogue combine conventional romantic gallantries with a description of a sword display whose erotic undertones can be felt even by readers quite innocent of any overt psychologizing over details. And much the same technique is employed in Chapter XXX, where the title, 'Hot Cheeks and Tearful Eyes' accurately describes what the chapter dramatizes.

V

But on the level at which Hardy was dealing with character, seven chapters were quite enough to exhaust even Troy's possibilities; thus by Chapter XXX Hardy had begun to reach the limits of what he could do in the mode he had adopted. No new characters remained to be introduced, and from Chapter XXXI on, then, through Chapter XLVII, Hardy slipped steadily toward a dependence on the kind of effects he could achieve by filling his narrative with mystery, physical threat, contrived surprise, and startling revelation. At this point, what had been a source of difficulty in earlier portions of the novel—Boldwood's simple characteristic tendency toward extremes—could now be exploited for its potential for active physical violence and otherwise kept as a threatening presence in the background. It is not surprising, then, that in Chapter XXXI Boldwood is brought forward to threaten violence on Troy, that he reappears in an even more threatening and violent posture in Chapter XXXIV, and that he is presented as driven nearly mad with despair by Chapter XXXVIII.

Nor is it surprising that the bulk of the action covered by Chapters XXXI-XLVII involves an elaborate and suspenseful series of mysteries, surprises, and revelations. There is the aura of doubt and mystery surrounding Bathsheba's trip, padded out with the details of the tracking skills of Coggan as he and Oak pursue a supposed thief,[8] and culminating in the surprise revelation of Bathsheba's marriage to Troy which occupies Chapters XXXII-XXXV; there is the dramatic race to save Bathsheba's grain against the advancing storm, and, of course, the violence of the storm scene itself in Chapters XXXVI-XXXVII; then the series of elaborately suspenseful scenes and dramatic revelations involving the death of Fanny Robin, which begins with Chapter XXXIX, 'Coming Home—A Cry', and culminates in Chapter XLIII, 'Fanny's Revenge', with its dramatic confrontation of Bathsheba and Troy over the open coffin of Fanny Robin and her child; and finally, there is the account of Troy's extraordinary reaction to Fanny's death, and the mystery of his disappearance after Chapter XLVII. An index of the extent to which Hardy was pressed to rely upon effects obtained by mystification and heightened suspense throughout Chapters XXXI-XLVII may be obtained from a consideration of an extensive revision which he made at the end of Chapter XLVII. As the manuscript shows, Hardy had originally intended to have Troy's fate not at all in doubt after he was nearly drowned while swimming; readers were originally informed at once that Troy signed on as a crewman of the ship that rescued him and undertook a voyage that would last at least six months. But Hardy took that information out of the conclusion of Chapter XLVII, so that we are now left only with the expectation that Troy was to be returned to land on the day following his rescue—and then told no more of him except that Bathsheba learns that his clothes have been discovered on shore in Chapter XLVIII. The arrangement Hardy finally chose, then, postponed an explanation of Troy's disappearance until Chapter L, and created for the space of two chapters a mystery where there formerly had not been one. It is this kind of mystification and dependence on 'surprise' revelations which particularly characterizes Hardy's narrative method in Chapters XXXI-XLVII.

But to say only this is, of course, to ignore an important qualification, for although in Chapters XXXI-XLVII Hardy slipped more and more into melodrama, he nevertheless often managed to achieve within this mode some of the most carefully wrought and memorable scenes in *Far from the Madding Crowd*: Joseph returning with Fanny Robin's body; Bathsheba and Troy before

Fanny's coffin; and Troy's moment of despairing self-awareness after the accidental destruction of his plantings over Fanny's grave. Certainly nowhere in the novel are there so many places where the fragility of human life, the bitterness of human anguish, the dignity of death, and the mysterious operation of natural forces are rendered so plangently.

Nevertheless, the increasing time pressures under which Hardy worked resulted, certainly, in a distinctly recognizable lowering of aims. It was only when he was in the later stages of composing *Far from the Madding Crowd* that Hardy wrote to Leslie Stephen that he wished 'merely to be considered a good hand at a serial'.[9] And of course the concluding chapters of *Far from the Madding Crowd* are notoriously weak. There is, for example, a passage in Chapter LV in which Oak and Smallbury have the following dialogue about Boldwood:

> 'Do ye think he really was out of his mind when he did it?' said Smallbury.
> 'I can't honestly say that I do,' Oak replied.

This passage constitutes an addition to the original text; it is not in the manuscript at all, and in its place is a passage in which Oak affirms that Boldwood's mind 'seems quite a wreck'. Significantly, such a radical alteration in Oak's view of Boldwood, which in other circumstances would have important implications, here makes no practical difference at all—a fact entirely characteristic of the looseness with which details in the final portion of the novel are related. And at worst the conclusion degenerates into such wildly extravagant matters as Troy's reappearance at the fair, acting the role of Dick Turpin, and reaching under the tent wall to snatch Pennyways' letter to Bathsheba out of her hand without being seen.

What in fact saves the conclusion of *Far from the Madding Crowd* is that with all the clumsy machinations of plot with which Hardy brings the novel to a close, he nevertheless manages in his treatment of Oak and Bathsheba to suggest a kind of relationship between them which plausibly yields a modest happiness achieved within the stringent limitations of ordinary human possibilities:

> They spoke very little of their mutual feelings: pretty phrases and warm expressions being probably unnecessary between such tried friends. Theirs was that substantial affection which arises (if any arises at all) when the two who are thrown together begin first by knowing the rougher sides of each other's character, and not the best till further on, the romance growing up in the interstices of a mass of hard prosaic reality.

It is a closing which is all the better for ending on such a finely restrained note, and even that is tempered and qualified by the comic wisdom of the concluding paragraphs. In ending, then, Hardy managed momentarily to recapture something of the finely balanced narrative mode with which he had begun, and the effect is perhaps enhanced because it comes almost as a surprise.

VI

What is clear from the foregoing examination, however, is that in *Far from the Madding Crowd* Hardy's method of composition was so thoroughly improvisatory that, taken as a whole, the resulting narrative structure is less a design than a record of changing narrative strategies and expedients involving alterations in matters so diverse as authorial distance, treatment of setting, narrative focus, use of imagery and symbol, and arrangement and subject of whole chapters. If Hardy may be said to have proceeded in *Far from the Madding Crowd* with 'immense assurance'[10] it was not that of a writer following a deliberate and well-defined plan but the assurance of an author confident of his powers to circumvent and overcome unforeseen narrative obstacles; and any critic who approaches *Far from the Madding Crowd* with the hope to discover in it some uniform and deliberate development of setting, imagery, symbol, or theme will be likely to succeed at the expense of creating the impression that the novel proceeds with more regularity and clarity of purpose than in fact is the case.

III

H. A. T. Johnson:

IN DEFENCE OF "THE TRUMPET-MAJOR"

It is, I suppose, unlikely that anyone would dispute the appropriateness of *The Trumpet-Major* to Hardy's Budmouth of all places. That Hardy knew the town well, that he had lived, worked, and been happy here, to this at least the book bears indisputable testimony:

> It was a clear day with little wind stirring, and the view from the downs, one of the most extensive in the country, was unclouded. The eye of any observer who cared for such things, swept over the wave-washed town, and the Bank beyond, and the Isle, with its pebble bank, lying on the sea to the left of these, like a great crouching animal tethered to the mainland. On the extreme east of the marine horizon, St Aldhelm's head closed the scene, the sea to the southward . . . gleaming like a mirror in the sun.

There architect, poet, painter, and topographer all meet. Happy the writer of a municipal guide who could rival that as an inducement to visit Weymouth!

But as to the book's eligibility for serious critical consideration on such an occasion as this, there are two opinions. Certainly a number of recent critics would contest the claim of *The Trumpet-Major* to anything more than a good-humoured pat on the spine, while some would consider even that over-indulgent. I must hope not too many of my audience will have taken up quite so damnatory a position just yet. For myself I will not pretend to neutrality—that last infirmity of ignoble minds; still, if I am to conduct a defence of *The Trumpet-Major,* I must obviously demonstrate that its detractors are not figments of my imagination.

Such a defence was not needed when *The Trumpet-Major* was published; indeed it received a remarkably unanimous chorus of critical acclaim on its first appearance during 1880 as a serial in *Good Words* (what Hardy, mistakenly, took to be Leslie Stephen's distaste for historical novels having denied it to *The Cornhill).* Possibly the fact that *Good Words* was, in today's jargon, a 'committed' magazine helped to muzzle those who had so strenuously objected to *The Return of the Native.* Hardy's new editor, the Revd Dr Norman Macleod, on being assailed by *The Society for the Diffusion of Pure Literature among the People*—and there is a whole chapter of Victorian social history in that sonorous title—replied to the grave charge that his periodical 'tempted . . . young persons . . . to read novels on Sundays' by this solemn affirmation: 'No infidel, no immoral man or woman, no one whom I could not receive into my family shall ever be permitted to write in *Good Words*.'[1] One wonders what he made of *Jude*, fourteen years later.

It does not appear that Hardy suffered much more than the expunging of a few military imprecations, however, together with the shifting of a lovers' assignation from Sunday to Saturday. It was not only novel-reading that was subject to the never-on-Sunday proscription.

It would accordingly be a mistake to suggest that the sunlit landscape of Overcombe, in pointed contrast to the Egdonian darkness of *The Return of the Native*, was somehow extorted from Hardy in opposition to his true bent for inspissated gloom. For, though it is by no means the 'idyll' some commentators have called it, this is a happy book, by and large; indeed its gaiety was stressed by most contemporary reviews.

Thus *The Spectator*, in a long, enthusiastic, and often discerning article, says that this is 'Hardy in his happiest vein . . . the story is replete with true comedy'. It adds that the plot 'is conceived with . . . capital ingenuity' and concludes, 'we are surprised, on a second reading, to find many verbal felicities we had forgotten'. *The Athenaeum*, recently so acidulated about *The Return of the Native*, makes amends, a trifle patronisingly, by commencing, 'Mr Hardy seems to be in the way to do for rural life what Dickens did for the town', and, although it cannot resist a dig about Cripplestraw's 'inappropriate idiom', it warmly commends such things as 'the Rabelaisian profusion of the wedding-feast', and concludes by placing the book in the category of 'those we keep on our shelves and look back into'. *The Times* also thought *The Trumpet-Major* a gay book, liking it better than *The Return of the Native*, and 'almost as well as *Far from the Madding Crowd*', while Havelock Ellis, in the most thorough and discriminating survey of Hardy's work to appear until then, and for some time after, wrote in *The Westminster Review* for April 1883 in the warmest terms of *The Trumpet-Major*'s 'verve [and] fresh and glowing vivacity'.

All this must have pleased the book's rather thin-skinned author a good deal, although initial sales were disappointing. But the determination of the reviews to stress the lighter side of *The Trumpet-Major* seems, less happily, to have set a pattern for critical response, where any at all was discernible, for the next seventy years or so. The common reader, 'slighted but enduring', has never had any doubts; *The Trumpet-Major* was reprinted every two or three years in the Pocket Edition between 1907 and 1970 (more often than *Jude the Obscure*, in fact) and, if you look on the shelves of any public library, you will more often find it out than in. Nevertheless, this initial genial reception, and continuing wide, if uncritical, popularity, must have dissuaded critics from considering the book at all; because of some twenty commentaries on Hardy's novels published between the wars, only two or three make more than glancing references to *The Trumpet-Major*.

Although H. C. Duffin, in whose nowadays unfairly neglected pages lurk a good few percipient comments, observed the occasional 'shadowing' of the book, he nevertheless discusses it mainly in terms of its 'sweetness' and 'idyllic quality', and while noting, acutely, the importance of the relationship between Bob and John, he sums up by saying that most of the book is 'conceived in the spirit of the highest comedy'. His is the one substantial notice; for W. R. Rutland, in 1933, this is a 'slight' if 'charming' book, 'lacking in characterisation'; Bob is 'unconvincing', and Anne 'hardly a character at all'. C. J. Weber, in 1940, thinks the conclusion 'lacks rightness and inevitability', while Edmund Blunden in 1942, surprisingly passes it by without a word, save to say that Hardy must have enjoyed writing it. And such comments are entirely typical of the period.

We may be forgiven if we begin to feel that, to some observers, *The Trumpet-Major*'s greatest defect is its apparent guilelessness, its innocence, in the original sense of the word. We all know that novels, like Adam and Eve, are more intriguing *after* the Fall; some indeed think criticism itself is a graft from the Tree that bore the Apple of Discord, though that perhaps is a point I had better not labour.

However, Lord David Cecil's Clark Lectures of 1942, though sparing only three pages or so to *The Trumpet-Major*, none the less offer a better basis for a serious consideration of the novel than any earlier assessment I know. I quote his conclusion: 'The trifling scene at the Mill becomes a window through which we are suddenly vouchsafed a glimpse of the sad, mysterious, fleetingness of human existence.' Like so much else in his book, that is both succinct and suggestive. It did not, however, prove fruitful.

Seven years later, in 1949, a much more captious and unaccommodating voice was raised on the other side of the Atlantic. It was, as might have been expected, the voice of a man with a thesis to expound, and a very good thesis too, as has been widely conceded. A. J. Guerard's case, as I understand it, amounts to an assertion that we, dwellers in an ever more implausible and bleakly ironical world, now see Hardy's work unblinkered, as it were, by the glib Victorian assumption that Progress must eventually lead us to a time when

> All men work in noble brotherhood,
> Breaking their mailed fleets and armed towers,
> And ruling by obeying Nature's powers,
> And gathering all the fruits of Earth and crowned with
> all her flowers.[2]

Passing by the question whether anyone, including Tennyson who wrote those lines, was ever quite so sanguine as Guerard implies, we may accept that what he says about Hardy's 'qualities as a popular entertainer and writer of comedy' being 'submerged under a great deal of sombre theorizing about his philosophy' has considerable weight. But whether we can swallow his next premiss that, because 'Victorian critics were nearly always polite and general in their literary studies', they therefore 'naturally preferred [Hardy's] worst books, *The Trumpet-Major* in particular', is at least disputable, particularly as it prompts him to dispose of those more recent critics, including Lord David Cecil, who have obstinately shared the Victorians' predilection for *The Trumpet-Major,* by lumping them together in a footnote which places them in 'an intellectual generation . . . earlier than that of Gide and Joyce'. Guerard's strictures on Victorian critics' generalising proclivities do not inhibit him from confining his own comments about *The Trumpet-Major* to such loose assertions as 'it refuses to get started' and 'it is lifeless until Bob Loveday and his dubious fiancée arrive and provoke complications to the plot'.

The trouble with theses is that what does not fit must be tailored into shape, as Procrustes' lodgers once painfully discovered. Accordingly if, like Guerard, you are determined to maintain that in Hardy's world as a rule 'everyday experience is both intolerable and improbable' you are likely to find in *The Trumpet-Major* an intractable obstacle. Least of all Hardy's novels will this one consent to fly Guerard's banner of 'a convincing foreshortening of the actual and absurd world'; more than any other perhaps, it does embrace precisely that 'finally unqualified faith in the goodness of a humanity more sinned against than sinning' which is just what, according to Guerard, we modern readers are 'repelled or left indifferent by'.

It must surely be evident that any attempt to account for *The Trumpet-Major* in terms of thorough-going despair or cynicism is doomed to failure. The fickle scape-grace Bob, the time-serving Matilda, the penny-pinching Uncle Benjy, all have salient redeeming features; Anne may be silly sometimes, but she is never calculating like Eustacia Vye, and never untrue to her heart's promptings. No one could fail to like Mrs Garland, or to admire the miller himself, while if we find John's simple rectitude too good to be true, so much the worse for us, surely? I lay stress on this point because it is, I believe, crucial, and I shall return to it later. In the meantime I submit that Guerard was unable to find what he was looking for in *The Trumpet-Major* because it isn't there and wasn't meant to be.

Perhaps I should pick one or two smaller bones with Guerard now, before proceeding to what I think are the roots of the dissension. First, the slow-paced start and Bob's delayed arrival are obviously strategies to establish the moving relationship between Anne and John, which is slow to develop because of their shared reticence. Indeed, Hardy's subtle and sensitive discrimination between love and liking is an important element in the book's success. Anne's reaction to the scalding incident, for example, has a quality of poignancy which is rare elsewhere in Hardy, though Marty's feeling for Giles in *The Woodlanders* echoes it. This has led many readers and some critics to say that she married the wrong man, but they miss the point; the sad truthfulness of Hardy's approach here is crystallised in a phrase from *Jude the Obscure*, 'The essence of love is its gratuitousness.'

Moreover, to use an epithet like 'lifeless' about *The Trumpet-Major*'s opening episodes argues an unreceptiveness to what is undeniably there in plenty—a humour more profuse and robust than anywhere else in Hardy, outside *A Few Crusted Characters* perhaps. Consider, for instance, the first appearance in the book of the ineffable Festus:

> the door opened, and in came a young man, about the size and weight of the Farnese Hercules, in the uniform of the yeomanry cavalry.
>
> 'Tis young Squire Derriman, old Mr. Derriman's nephew,' murmured voices in the background.
>
> Without waiting to address anybody or apparently seeing who were gathered there, the colossal man waved his cap above his head and went on in tones that shook the window-panes:—
>
> When husbands with their wives agree,
And maids won't wed from mod-es-ty,
Then Boney he'll come pouncing down
And march his men on London Town!
Chorus: Rollicum rorum, tolollorum, &c, &c.
>
> It was a verse which had been omitted by the gallant Stanner, out of respect to the ladies.
>
> The new-comer was red-haired and of florid complexion, and seemed full of a conviction that his whim of entering must be their pleasure, which for the moment it was.
>
> 'No ceremony, good men all,' he said; 'I was passing by, and my ear was caught by the singing. I like singing; 'tis warming and cheering, and shall not be put down. I should like to hear anyone say otherwise.'
>
> 'Welcome, Master Derriman,' said the miller, filling a glass and handing it to the yeoman. 'Come all the way from quarters, then? I hardly knowed 'ee in your soldier's clothes. You'd look more natural with a spud in your hand, sir. I shouldn't ha' known 'ee at all if I hadn't heard that you were called out.'
>
> 'More natural with a spud—have a care, miller,' said the young giant, the fire of his complexion increasing to scarlet. 'I don't mean anger, but—but—a soldier's honour, you know!'
>
> 'The military in the background laughed a little, and the yeoman then for the first time discovered that there were more regulars present than one. He looked momentarily disconcerted, but expanded again to full assurance.

It would be a jaundiced outlook that could call that lifeless, I feel, but it is all too easy to underrate such things. If we examine the quality of Hardy's writing here, I think it becomes apparent that he is taking just as many pains to perfect it as in, say, the first chapter of *The Return of the Native*. The initial sly allusion to the 'Farnese Hercules', quietly slipped in, and qualified with the mock-diffident 'about the size and weight' is perfectly congruent, unlike the Sudarium of St. Veronica to which Fitzpiers' bloody head is so obscurely compared in *The Woodlanders*. Again, how succinctly Hardy reveals Festus's character by his egregious speech and lofty unawareness; how drily effective the parenthetical phrase is in the sentence ending, 'his whim of entering must be their pleasure, which *for the moment* it was'. But the palm must go to the miller's superbly placed deflation, with its mock innocent admiration, 'Come all the way from quarters then? I hardly knowed 'ee in your soldier's clothes'. Notice the sly depreciation of *'soldier's clothes'*, suggesting dressing up, as opposed to uniform, to which lead-in the perfect humiliating coup de grâce is provided by the apparently guileless 'You'd look more natural with a spud in your hand, sir', the ambiguities of 'natural', the superb choice of 'spud' (as against 'sword'), and the pseudo-deferential 'sir' all salting the wound. This slow, sardonic quality typifies Hardy's country humorists, and that the miller spoke with calculated relish is made clear a little later. The temptation to go quoting the more hilarious incidents must be resisted; my point is that, despite his reference to Hardy's gifts as a writer of comedy, Guerard finds nothing to laugh at in Hardy's funniest book.

I cannot say that Dr Desmond Hawkins ignores *The Trumpet-Major* in his book on Hardy's novels, but he certainly did not like it much in 1950. He observes, rather tartly, that 'a Hardy without ideas would have written nothing better than *The Trumpet-Major*', a book he thinks was 'written to a box-office formula'; he concedes it has 'charm', and adds, 'but so has *Quality Street*'.

Irving Howe allows *The Trumpet-Major* 'small, steady pleasures', 'amiable domestic comedy, English ways and stuff' (whatever they may be), and 'a moderate toying with sentiment', but concludes by warning us solemnly that 'too much may be made of this novel, as indeed too much has been, both by the beef-and-ale critics of an earlier generation, and those of the present, like the *Scrutiny* group, who do not really like Hardy's major fiction'. I admire Howe's book, but these 'beef-and-ale critics' demonstrably belong to the good old school of Aunt Sally, set up only to be knocked down, while as for *Scrutiny*, the index hasn't a single mention of *The Trumpet-Major*.

It is possible Howe meant the late Douglas Brown and George Wing by his '*Scrutiny* group', but neither undervalues the major fiction, and though both are much more sympathetic and observant about *The Trumpet-Major* than is usual, their books are brief, and Brown's praise for Hardy's 'vivid feeling for the recollected past' and Wing's for his 'perceptive compassion' do not go far to disperse the cloud of disapprobation, and, what is worse, blank indifference, which gathers steadily round *The Trumpet-Major* as we draw near the present day. The nadir is reached when J. I. M. Stewart, in 1971, sternly relegates it to his chapter on 'Minor Fiction' because 'it has no serious designs on us' (a portentous accusation) and it is 'antiquarian rather than historical in temper'. Jean Brooks, in a judicious page or so, posits a 'mood of muted elegy', a dangerous if attractive half-truth. Michael Millgate, although his is easily the most substantial and informative of recent surveys, seems to me rather wide of the mark in his comparisons with Jane Austen (Cripplestraw? Festus?) and his remark that 'the novel exemplifies the power of simple sexuality just as surely as *The Return of the Native*, or *Tess*'. Several other recent books either ignore *The Trumpet-Major* or refer to it only dismissively and perfunctorily.

It is, I fear, a somewhat dispiriting decline from the glad, confident morning of 1880 when *The Times* hailed *The Trumpet-Major* as 'Mr Hardy's best novel so far'. The assailants are so vigorous, vehement, and aggressive, the defenders so few, so tentative, and inclined to retire hurt that my own extended diet of depreciation, preparatory to this lecture, has insidiously suggested to me that, while I may perhaps be allowed to like *The Trumpet-Major*, it would be in the last degree presumptuous actually to admire it. But this is a state of affairs, to borrow Dogberry's remark in *Much Ado About Nothing*, 'tolerable and not to be endured'. I do, in fact, greatly admire *The Trumpet-Major*, and, though I would place it short of the summits of Hardy's achievement, in *Far from the Madding Crowd*, *The Mayor of Casterbridge*, *Tess*, and *Jude*, it falls, in my considered opinion, only a little short of *The Woodlanders*, and stands level with *The Return of the Native*, and *Under the Greenwood Tree*, with the last of which it has a strong affinity. It is, incidentally, more than a little odd that Guerard should be so reluctant to let even a crumb of approbation fall on *The Trumpet-Major*, when he was happy to call *Under the Greenwood Tree* 'Hardy's most perfect work of art'.

Yet this apparent contradiction affords us a clue, I submit, to one reason why *The Trumpet-Major* has been so persistently under-rated or ignored. George Saintsbury, who himself considered that *The Trumpet-Major* displayed 'delicate composition and carefully elaborated grace',[3] once formulated what he called a 'cardinal neglected rule of criticism', namely: 'A is not bad because it is not B, no matter how good B is.'

It is my contention that nearly all the detractors of *The*

Trumpet-Major lay themselves open to that particular indictment, for one implicit premiss of much adverse comment is that Hardy, in deserting his usual method and manner, was somehow culpable, that he ought to have written something further in the vein of his preceding work. Yet the fact that *The Trumpet-Major* is incontestably not *like* Hardy's other novels is, after all, no sort of evidence for its inferiority to them (or its superiority for that matter). It is different; that is all.

Perhaps not so very different either, for though Hardy later labelled it a 'Romance' it is just as much a 'Novel of Character and Environment' as any of the others in that category, where it matters. The book is as rooted in Wessex, all the characters as indigenous, the dialogue as authentic, the incident as persuasive, as in any. True, there is none of the coincidental absurdity of *Desperate Remedies*, none of the stilted intellectualism that flaws *A Pair of Blue Eyes*. We are spared the flatfooted 'high society' dialogue of *Ethelberta*, and the heavy cultural mulch that is poured over some pages of *The Woodlanders*. The over-ambitious 'fine writing' of *The Return of the Native*, even the potted philosophising that mars some pages of *Tess*, triumphant novel as it is, are absent. It seems to me that we can do very well without them.

Again even if *The Trumpet-Major* is 'good box-office', is that really so damning? One of the most irritating of modern critical heresies is the assumption, usually unargued, that an automatic stigma attaches to popularity. If we take the trouble to examine the statistics of what the Victorians actually bought and presumably read, we have to concede that an astonishingly high proportion of what was popular was also of the highest distinction, and has lasted.

Hardy did not disdain, or over-value, success, but he would, I think, have been justly vexed by Irving Howe's dismissal of his meticulously researched detail of the social scene, the distant thunder of war, the sprightly comedy and occasional farce, as merely 'English ways and stuff', a slightly supercilious pronouncement which chimes with Hawkins' jibe about '*Quality Street*', and perhaps Millgate's Jane Austen analogue, too. These innovations, these supposed incongruities, were not the result of a wish to pad out a thin plot; the 'Trumpet-Major' Notebook shows how painstaking Hardy was in his pursuit of authenticity. The long sessions in the British Museum were integral to Hardy's purpose, which was not, indeed, obscure or recondite, not even to show that 'in real life the meaning is frequently secondary to the glory . . . of the moment' as one of the most recent critics has contended,[4] but something much simpler than that, and, I think, more worthwhile.

I am well aware of the dangers to which I now expose

myself. T. S. Eliot drily identified those who attempt 'to reveal for the first time the gospel of some dead sage . . . which owing to the backward and confused state of men's minds has lain unknown until this very moment'. Perhaps the best way to avoid this pitfall is to identify, as far as is feasible, what the author himself was trying to do; and here the title-page, with its elaboration, and especially the sub-title, 'A Tale', offer us a clue, in that they make explicit what Donald Davidson, in 'The Traditional Basis of Thomas Hardy's Fiction', says about most of Hardy's novels being 'composed as a told . . . or sung story'. The soldier, the sailor, faithful or unfaithful, the jolly miller, the braggart put down, the girl who can't make up her mind, the miserly squire—all come straight out of the ballad tradition. Futhermore the 1895 Preface is quite unequivocal about Hardy's purpose to include 'the unexaggerated reproduction of the recollections of old persons . . . who were eye-witnesses'. The authenticity of the detail, the basis in oral tradition, the emphasis on a tale to be told, are all vouched for, but this, I think, made Hardy aware of another requirement, that of an appropriate narrative tone, distinctive yet not compact of gadzookery. For this purpose I suggest he deliberately went back to an earlier period of the English novel's development.

Hardy's liking for, and long-standing acquaintance with, the Augustan novel is well attested. Defoe, Swift, Richardson, and Sterne, all figure in *The Life,* as does Henry Fielding who is also the pre-eminent examplar in Hardy's 'The Profitable Reading of Fiction'. Perhaps the most significant references occur in *The Life,* where he compares his own rustic humour to Fielding's, says that he has 'felt akin locally to Fielding', and observes in a letter that 'Fielding as a local novelist has never been clearly regarded.'[5] Surely then if Hardy wanted a stylistic model to suggest the ambience of an earlier period, he had a congenial and familiar one in Fielding, an edition of whose novels he was once invited to introduce, although, regrettably, he declined the offer.

The moment we open *The Trumpet-Major* there are clues; the sardonic chapter headings for example, although these are more redolent of Smollett, whose *Humphry Clinker* (notable for its gallery of eccentrics and its authentic social background) Hardy read while doing his *Trumpet-Major*—together with Smollett's other works. (The chapter headings of Smollett's *Sir Lancelot Greaves* incidentally bear a striking resemblance to those of *The Trumpet-Major.*)[6]

Fielding's benevolent influence is felt in the slight dryness that checks any incipient sentimentality in the portrayal of Anne, who has been unfairly treated by the commentators who see only her vacillation. She is reminiscent of Fielding's lively Sophia in *Tom Jones;* her spirited baiting of Festus in Chapter VII (where Hardy most effectively transcribes a page of the *Standing Orders of the 2nd Dragoon Guards,* relating to the pistol in horse-drill),[7] not to mention her precipitation of him into the stream, and her theft of his horse, make her something quite unlike Guerard's 'ingénue', and not at all Victorian.

As for style, there is a sentence at the opening of the novel which ends, 'they had the pleasure of knowing that there crept in through every crevice, door and window of their dwelling, however tightly closed, a subtle mist of superfine flour from the grinding-room, quite invisible, but making its presence known in the course of time by giving a pallid and ghostly look to the best furniture'. The poised sardonic phrasing in 'pleasure of knowing', 'subtle mist of superfine flour' and 'pallid and ghostly look to the best furniture' is surely very like Fielding's, while the frequent authorial interjections Hardy allows himself are a hall-mark of Fielding's style too, of course. Even more sharply reminiscent is the mordant wit of the opening of the description of Oxwell Hall (in Chapter VI), with its formal antitheses and iterations: 'The rambling and neglected dwelling had all the romantic excellencies and practical drawbacks which such mildewed places share in common with caves, mountains, wildernesses, glens, and other homes of poesy that people of taste wish to live and die in.' 'Homes of poesy . . . people of taste'—it exudes a robust and contemptuous commonsense, a whiff of the eighteenth century, which admirably offsets the much more characteristically Hardyan conclusion to the same passage. I could instance a good few other passages, and many small details—the names of the officers of the German Legion, the drill-scene, not to mention Bob, in some respects plainly descended from Tom Jones—but consider this passage from Chapter XVI:

> The afternoon sermons at this church being of a dry and metaphysical nature at that date, it was by special providence that the waggon-office was placed near the ancient fabric, so that whenever the Sunday waggon was late, which it always was in hot weather, in cold weather, in wet weather, and in weather of almost every other sort, the rattle, dismounting, and swearing outside completely drowned the parson's voice within, and sustained the flagging interest of the congregation at precisely the right moment.

The controlled movement of that whole, long, balanced sentence; the cumulation of 'weathers', the sly irony of 'special providence', the polished acerbity of 'sustained the flagging interest of the congregation', these are surely Fielding to the life.

Then again we have Festus, who has been called a 'mere *miles gloriosus*'. Well, Hardy knew his Latin, but both Plautus and Ralph Roister Doister, come to that, are unnecessarily distant ancestors. In Fielding's *Joseph Andrews,* Parson Adams, a character Hardy relished, meets a man who proclaims his courage in round terms as follows: 'Damn me, what's a man's life when his country demands it? . . . A man who won't sacrifice his life for his country deserves to be hanged, damn me!' Chancing on a highway robbery, Adams wants to give help, and attempt to borrow the 'valiant man's' gun. But he demurs: 'I hope you are not mad enough', says the gentleman, trembling. 'Do you consider this gun is only charged with shot, and that the robbers are most probably furnished with pistols loaded with bullets!' Compare that with some typical Festus, in hortatory mood, 'The man who quails . . . is unworthy of the name of yeoman . . . I'll take three frog-eating Frenchmen single-handed.' The similarity between two bits of bombast is striking, but Festus's shared capacity for brisk rationalisation suggests something more; 'No skill is required of a forlorn hope' and his superb 'Of course I would not hide in any mean sense . . . ' argue, I think, for a line of descent, while certainly Fielding's insistence on 'Affectation' as the true source of humour was very much in Hardy's mind when he created Festus. As for Cripplestraw, foil to Festus, he comes straight from the pages of eighteenth-century comedy (a whole crop of which Hardy read while preparing for *The Trumpet-Major),* as does Uncle Benjy, while finally Matilda, with her quick eye for the main chance, is a near relation of Fielding's Mrs Waters, slightly shop-soiled, but undaunted and not unlikeable, able to teach Anne at least one useful lesson.

This Augustan atmosphere, which I think is often discernible in *The Trumpet-Major,* has other merits besides those of stylistic appropriateness. It also offers Hardy a certain coolness of *tone* which, especially in the comic scenes, he uses to advantage, and it probably helps to account for the steady avoidance of that literary over-reaching which damages parts of *The Return of the Native.* However, if Hardy deliberately adopted a manner different from that of his earlier novels, it was not, I think, the product of a simple wish to suggest a historical period. He always disliked mere decoration, however appropriate, and I believe he also wished to define an authorial stance, a viewpoint, radically different from any he had taken up hitherto. He set out, I suggest, to achieve a calculated distancing effect, to instil in his readers a continuous undercurrent of awareness that all these events are long past, that all the actors have long left the stage, precisely because it was his intention to write a new kind of novel, one which would embody his own conviction that, as he put it in *The Life,* 'History is rather a stream than a tree . . . with nothing systematic in its development.'[8] The past, for all that he had an uncommonly powerful awareness of it, for all that it often 'seized upon him with a phantom hand', as it did Clym in *The Return of the Native,* was not for Hardy anything at all like what his contemporaries made it out to be. For them, historians and novelists alike, with few exceptions, History was an escalator, moving, even if by fits and starts, inexorably upwards to a higher station for mankind; for Hardy it was nothing of the sort.

At this point it is informative to consider Hardy's choice of his favourite prose passage for *The Fortnightly Review*. By Carlyle, from *The French Revolution*, it uses the metaphor of an oak's slow, almost imperceptible growth to suggest that 'foolish History . . . knows so little that were not as well unknown. Attila invasions . . . Sicilian Vespers, Thirty-Years Wars: mere sin and misery; not work, but hindrance of work! For the Earth, all this while, was yearly green and yellow with her kind harvests; the hand of the craftsman, the mind of the thinker rested not . . . ' And Carlyle concludes by citing the aphorism: 'Happy the people whose annals are vacant'.[9]

Now it is surely evident from almost every other page of *The Trumpet-Major* that Hardy concurred with Carlyle here in every particular; indeed the passage might well have served as an epigraph for the novel. For the people of Overcombe, as for Carlyle's oak, 'This hour seemed altogether as the last was, as the next would be.' Large general notions of progress are nothing to them, yet their experience of life has value, for us as well as for them, a value bound up with the way, as Hardy put it in *The Woodlanders*, 'to those long settled in a spot . . . there is a richness of memory and old association . . . with every object, animate or inanimate, within the observer's horizon'. So in *The Trumpet-Major* the horizon is deliberately limited, yet upon the whole book this informing sense of the past lies as densely, and as lightly, as moss on an old stone roof. It is a sense which another poet, Edward Thomas, an early admirer of Hardy, caught supremely well in his *Haymaking*, of which I quote the last few lines:

All was old,
This morning time, with a great age untold,
Older than Clare and Cobbett, Morland and Crome,
Than, at the field's far edge, the farmer's home,
A white house crouched at the foot of a great tree.
Under the heavens that know not what years be
The men, the beasts, the trees, the implements
Uttered even what they will in times far hence—
All of us gone out of the reach of change—
Immortal in a picture of an old grange.

I find a remarkably close correspondence between Thomas's 'old grange' and Hardy's 'ancient manor house' of Overcombe, and I suggest that it is also true to say that each asserts a sense of values shared by Hardy and Thomas, values sharply opposed to an interpretation of history in terms of 'great men' and 'great events', leaning rather towards the King of Brobdingnag's opinion, in *Gulliver's Travels,* 'that whoever could make two ears of corn or two blades of grass to grow upon a spot where only one had grown before, would deserve better of mankind, and do more essential service to his country than the whole race of politicians put together'.

Still, a Swiftian disenchantment with 'greatness' will hardly serve as a catalyst for *The Trumpet-Major,* though I think it goes some way to account for its mood; something more positive is required. What then, if any, are the moral imperatives which Hardy puts forward, as against those of, say, *Ben Hur,* the archetypal historical 'epic' published in the same year? For if the people of Overcombe mediate to us anything of universal relevance, they plainly don't do it very dramatically; the review and the alarm can't be set against the chariot race and the Colosseum scenes in *Ben Hur,* for example. In *The Dynasts* there are ordinary Wessex folk of the same stock as the Overcombers, to be sure; but there we are asked to view them not only in close-up amongst the horrors of war, but also against the back-cloth of a vast spiritual cosmos, *sub specie aeternitatis.* In *The Trumpet-Major* the minimum essential historical perspective is given by a few set-pieces, sometimes pointed up by mordant authorial comment, like the review on the downs with its grim threnody for the 'military and other dust, some at Talavera, Albuera, Salamanca, Vittoria, Toulouse and Waterloo; some in home churchyards; and a few small handfuls in royal vaults' (Chapter XII). Although these passages have been sniped at by R. J. White in *Hardy and History,* I feel that they merely serve to enhance, by contrast, the fact that our immersion in the little world of Overcombe is what matters to Hardy. The war, he implies, with all its paraphernalia, with Napoleon the bogey-man, is something for which the pike-shafts mouldering in the church tower, turned into 'rake-stems, benefit-club staves and pick-handles', constitute an effective paradigm. Seen close, the splendours of the court grow trivial, those of martial pageantry tarnished and insignificant. It is the day-to-day business of living and what we make of it, the ordinary, unremarkable, indeed often dull stuff of life that *The Trumpet-Major* is really about; and in one of his finest Boer War poems, 'The Souls of the Slain', Hardy has provided us with a key to what he is saying on the broader canvas of the novel. The spirits of the Boer War dead from Wessex are returning over 'The Isle by the Race'—exactly where Anne watched *The Victory's* departure. They hope to feast on their fame, but the spirit who meets them scorns that idea, telling them it is their 'Deeds of home that live yet/Fresh as new', and they realise

> that our glory
> Weighs less in their thought
> Than our old homely acts,
> And the long-ago commonplace facts
> Of our lives—held by us as scarce part of our story,
> And rated as nought!

That, to my mind, sums up, succinctly and precisely, the message of *The Trumpet-Major*. It needs to be stressed, however, that by this insistence on ordinariness, Hardy was making an unavoidable renunciation of much that had served him well in earlier novels, in particular the Websterian turbulence of *The Return of the Native*, and the volcanic passion of Boldwood in *Far from the Madding Crowd*. We have only to think of the humdrum routine of the mill, the easy-going miller, with his philosophy that 'It's as well to be neighbourly with folks . . . if they be not quite onbearable', of Anne's gentle if slightly indeterminate sweetness, John's sobriety and control, even Bob's fundamental goodheartedness, to see that there is no place here for a Eustacia Vye, still less for a Mephistophelean visitant! Too much rapture, too much despair, would irretrievably dissipate the aura of peace breathed out by so many pages of *The Trumpet-Major*, and Hardy's progressive reduction of Festus to impotent buffoonery shows his awareness that to make him a real threat to Anne (as he had once intended) would disturb the tone of *The Trumpet-Major*, on which so much depends.

Nevertheless this unemphatic quality, which corresponds to Hardy's conviction, stated in *The Life*, that history is anything but 'systematic', that 'It flows on like a thunder-storm rill by a road-side; now a straw turns it this way, now a tiny barrier of sand that', plainly does not allow for the kind of directly unifying impulse which a novel presenting George III, say, or Captain Hardy even, would claim; nor the immediacy of one where Bob or John was a participant, however insignificant personally, at Trafalgar or Waterloo. The methods of Scott or Thackeray, both of whom he admired, were not to Hardy's purpose.

Here, I believe, we arrive at the true, if tacit, crux of the quarrel that *The Trumpet-Major's* opponents have with it. They fail to detect in it the normal, the expected, the—one might almost say—Hardyan, unifying principle of, to put it in Hardy's own words, 'the worthy compassed by the inevitable'. And they are right of course; it isn't there! It is true that in all Hardy's other major novels this principle, even if at times it sags into an over-heavy purposiveness, makes for a recognisable leit-motif, especially useful for examinees. But it by no means follows that, because *The*

Trumpet-Major lacks this kind of unity, it therefore can have none, that it qualifies only as one of Henry James's 'loose, baggy monsters', and therefore, to return to J. I. M. Stewart's condemnation, representative of many others, it 'has no serious designs on us'.

It is my contention that in *The Trumpet-Major,* for that schematic and purposive view of human destiny which marks, and (if we are honest) also occasionally mars, his other great novels so strongly, Hardy here substitutes, in accord with his own expressed views on history, a poetic integrity. His concentration on the humble and prosaic doings at Overcombe displays exactly that 'certain provincialism of feeling' which he once asserted was 'invaluable to the writer', and the particular device which illuminates the book, subtly engages and holds the reader's interest, and often carries the latent burden of what the novel is *saying,* is Hardy's use, very much a poet's use, of two recurrent and interrelated images, which I shall entitle those of the Mill and the Camp, and which I consider embody and convey the leading theme of the book with unobtrusive yet persuasive force.

I am suggesting that Hardy here originated something later used to notable effect by E. M. Forster in *Howards End,* that the sense of place, which effects so significant a counterpoint in *The Return of the Native,* here becomes a vehicle for this novel's central harmony, for what it has to say to us as a whole. I need not remind you how recurrent and crucial a role this sense of place has to play in Hardy's poetry generally, or of how often it fulfils, in poems like 'Wessex Heights' or 'In Front of the Landscape' a function which the word 'topographical' is wholly inadequate to convey. What I want to argue here is that Hardy has extended into *The Trumpet-Major* a method by which in his poems he gives to certain locations, to features of the landscape or to the marks of man's passing upon it, a weight of connotative significance at times almost numinous.

The reconstruction of Hardy's original sketch, used for the blind-stamp cover of the first bound edition of *The Trumpet-Major,* makes it clear that these two images were both powerfully present and linked in Hardy's mind, and while it stresses the permanence and solidity of the mill, rooted at the hill's foot, the drawing also emphasises the scrappy transience of the camp on the bare down above. Plainly Hardy took great pains here to depict the mill as he conceived it in his mind's eye, while Denys Kay-Robinson's convincing demonstration that Overcombe Mill was, in fact, an amalgam of two actual mills strengthens the case for its symbolic status.

Significantly we first encounter the mill through its function. In a passage nicely poised between irony and accuracy, Hardy compares the notes made by the mill to 'the stopped diapason' of an organ, the full range of harmony that is, an interesting choice of simile, the organ being, according to Browning's 'Abt Vogler' (a poem Hardy quotes in *The Life)* 'all triumphant art, but art in obedience to laws'. Any whiff of sarcasm is dispelled by Mrs Garland's refusal to be put out by the omnipresent flour, however, because it is, she says, 'the blessed staff of life itself', a saying which sharply reminds me of my own mother's stubborn refusal ever to burn bread. Thus a picture of a kind of beauty intimately associated with function is established at the outset, and this is, I think, of such crucial importance that I shall return to it later.

We next see the exterior of the mill, through Anne's eyes. Part of this description runs:

> The water with its flowing leaves,
> And spots of froth was stealing away like Time
> Under the dark arch to tumble over
> The great slimy wheel within.

That is so remarkably near to regular verse that I have ventured to set it out as if it were; it also very beautifully introduces that recurrent stress on Time and Mutability which, throughout, balances what may be called the Elysian aspect of the mill, which is thus never allowed to become an idyll, where 'Neither sorrow comes nor tired old age', but always retains contact with normal human experience.

Chapter II offers a long visual description of the mill's exterior, stressing its age, and conveying on the one hand its simple functional properties—the double doors, the 'gaping arch vomiting the river'; on the other its charm—'snowy dimity curtains', its leafiness and quietude. At one level this simply verbalises the sketch; at another it endows the building with a kind of personality, for it is 'half-cloaked' and 'round-shouldered', and has 'hips instead of gables'. So, too, the worn-out millstones have a continuing usefulness, and only the weather-vane, signifying a rather futile changeableness, is purposeless here, where what Hardy calls 'the Elysian climate' 'makes spring into summer and allows myrtle to flourish out of doors'.

A further stage is reached in the next chapter with the beautiful vignette of the soldiers eating cherries at the mill:

> It was a cheerful, careless, unpremeditated half-hour, which returned like the scent of a flower to the memories of some of those who enjoyed it, even at a distance of many years after, when they lay wounded and weak in foreign lands.

Here the emblematic role of the mill becomes explicit. For the soldiers it is to constitute an enduring image of peace and happiness, opposed to the wanton destructiveness of war; and the chapter ends with a return to the mill as an image of both mutability and community:

> Thus they crossed the threshold of the mill-house and up the passage, the paving of which was worn into a gutter by the ebb and flow of feet that had been going on there ever since Tudor times.

That has a delicately admonitory quality, hinting at the insignificance of any particular individual, yet also suggesting continuity and harmony between past and present.

The interior of the mill is the scene of the party of Chapter IV, which with its 'hilarity' and 'bursts of gaiety' eventually moves Mrs Garland to compare 'the other side of the wall' with 'Paradise', and which also looks forward to that infectious relish for unsophisticated pleasure that marks the wedding preparations. The famous invocation of Casterbrige ale has been quoted often enough before:

> It was of the most beautiful colour that the eye of an artist in beer could desire, full in body, yet brisk as a volcano; piquant, yet without a twang; luminous as an autumn sunset; free from streakiness of taste; but, finally rather heady.

Yet this, with the rest of the harmless gaiety and high spirits that spills over everywhere in the book, is only another way of saying what Hardy expressed more directly in a poem:

> Let me enjoy the earth no less
> Because the all-enacting Might
> That fashioned forth its loveliness
> Had other aims than my delight.10

It finds an echo in the attitude of the Overcombers generally. Bob's real disappointment about Matilda is assuaged by seedy cake and fat eels, tangible if unromantic; Anne keeps her chin up despite some wounding disappointments; the miller's unassuming courage is notable; but even Uncle Benjy has admirable bounce; while John, who suffers most and most undeservedly, doesn't lapse into a green melancholy, like the hussar in Hardy's short story of the same date. In a word they are resilient; they enjoy that sub-stratum of tough commonsense which enables them to survive and enjoy life, unlike so many of Hardy's major characters who, as Roy Morrell has observed, are deficient in these qualities. For the mill and those who dwell in it, the famous aside in *The Revenger's Tragedy*, 'Joy's a subtle elf,/I think man's happiest when he forgets himself' is peculiarly appropriate.

Nevertheless the mill has a wide range of suggestion; we

see it very differently during John's midnight vigil when, as he watches, Anne shuts the casement with a candle in her hand, and

> The light shone out upon the broad and deep mill-head, illuminating to a distinct individuality every moth and gnat that entered the quivering chain of radiance stretching across the water towards him, and every bubble or atom of froth that floated into its width.

Here the mill, silent and at night, mirrors the romantic longing of John; the utilitarian mill-pond is transformed, endowed with a fragile beauty, which daylight will dispel.

At a critical point in the story the mill has a particularly important role to play in the book's development. It is where Hardy has contrived to isolate the returning Bob when he reaches the mill after a long absence:

> though Bob had been all over the world from Cape Horn to Pekin, and from India's coral strand to the White Sea, the most conspicuous of all the marks which he had brought back with him was an increased resemblance to his mother, who had lain all the time beneath Overcombe church wall.

How telling that is with its retrospective and premonitory undertones. Though neither he, nor the reader knows it yet, this is where Bob truly belongs, and Hardy continues after this subtle opening, to convey Bob's half-puzzled recognition, one by one, of the mill's familiar features, and their significance to him:

> the panes of the grinding-room, now as heretofore clouded with flour as with stale hoar-frost; the meal lodged in the corners of the window-sills, forming a soil in which lichens grew without getting any bigger, as they had done since his dimmest infancy . . . the penned mill-pond, now as ever on the point of overflowing into the garden. Everything was the same.

Here Hardy returns to that dual emphasis on the mill's function and its apparent impermeability to time, though that, as a comparison with nearby Oxwell Hall shows, is contingent on the continuing usefulness of the building. I am sure that, in bringing us here, at a turning-point in the narrative, to a renewed sense of the mill's purposefulness, durability, and unassuming beauty, and of the ways in which those qualities are bound up with the lives of those who dwell in it, Hardy is asserting, as often elsewhere, something he once expressed more explicitly in Chapter XXII of *Far from the Madding Crowd.* There, Hardy says of the Great Barn, after praising its architectural splendours:

> the eye regarded its present usage, the mind dwelt upon its past history, with a satisfied sense of functional continuity throughout—a feeling almost of gratitude and quite of pride, at the permanence of the idea that had heaped it up.

A good deal of that chapter is relevant to an understanding of the mill, its ancient walls, like those of the great barn, having 'grandeur in their very simplicity', its garden fat with centuries of cultivation, its machinery 'making music day and night', its lawns murmurous with streams, its waters full of fish and its granaries with corn, while its inhabitants, by their generosity and general unselfishness, make it a natural centre for gaiety and high spirits in the neighbourhood, the miller's unfailing warmth and openness making as good a touchstone as we have for what Hardy thought human decency could rise to. I suggest that the mill becomes in Hardy's hands, not just an artefact, however old or richly suggestive, nor even an emblem, like the Great Barn, of a particular idea at a particular moment, but something we might call a 'memorial presence', following Hardy in his essay on Church Restoration, where he says of an old building that 'though limestones and sandstones have passed into its form, yet it is an idea independent of them, a blend of the æsthetic and memorial or associative'.[11] For the mill assists both the miller's romance and Bob's; it helps to deliver John from a potentially tragic misconception, while its intimacy and warmth contributes insensibly to wearing down the incipient snobbery of first Mrs Garland and then Anne, into an acceptance of the unaffected life within it; indeed it acts, throughout, as a sort of lodestone for true feeling. Bob, especially, is really himself at the mill; it is only away from it that his rosebud-gathering tendencies flourish; at home he is a different man, while even Matilda is not unaffected by the mill's atmosphere. More directly, Bob's escape from the press-gang is furthered by the mill's curious architecture and machinery, too.

If the Mill asserts a positive, the Camp signifies a negative: the intrusive and ephemeral military life which the war has brought to Overcombe. It is glamorous on first appearance when 'The two troopers rode proudly on as if nothing less than crowns and empires ever concerned their magnificent minds', but there is at once apparent an undertone of tart irony, which continually recurs whenever Hardy reverts to the image of the camp. Thus the machine-like organisation, glittering and attractive to the eye, is stressed early on, yet sharply devalued as serving no useful end, once we contrast it with the mill. The gorgeous uniforms get full treatment, but Hardy sardonically notes that 'The historic pelisse . . . is a fascination to women and an encumbrance to the wearer.' Again, the soldiers' brassy splendour is tellingly opposed to the bedraggled finery of their wives, while the pictures of the camp breaking up and the pathetic sale of oddments, express the depressing reality of military life. A particularly effective moment occurs when Anne looks out at the moon-lit camp and beyond it hears 'the miles-long voice of the sea', the melancholy sound emphasising the restless and rootless condition of the soldiers.

Everywhere there occurs this deflation of the dubious rewards of uniform and glory; old Corporal Tullidge's arm-grinding party piece is partly comic perhaps, but it is a much blacker comedy than *The Trumpet-Major* deals in elsewhere. Even John, for all his uprightness and probity, cannot offer Anne any sort of permanence, bound as he is to the army while the war lasts. Hardy has a strong sense of what is valuable in patriotism, a keen awareness of the true nature of courage (notice how his regular soldiers are bored by war); but he has an even stronger sense that, an inch below the bright surface of battle, are death, maiming, and suffering, often futile, and he never allows us to forget it.

The most powerful of all Hardy's images of war is one which, paradoxically, has to do with the single intrusion of the true epic temper on the scene. It is the passing of *The Victory,* which, for all its authentically heroic associations, is as profoundly melancholy as anything in the book. The association of the blind old man and the helpless girl with the weird moon-landscape of Portland, brilliantly evokes the fate of ordinary folk caught up in war, able only to watch and to despair. The whole piece is a threnody for those about to die, for the futility of man's pursuit of an illusory glory; and Hardy's metaphors and similes for *The Victory,* seen throughout as a wraith, and described successively as 'a large white bat, sometimes . . . a grey one', 'the form of an egg on end', and finally as 'a dead fly's wing on a sheet of spider's web', impart poetically far more than they tell directly, the last especially subsuming the great ship into an apotheosis of frailty and decay.

At this point, Anne's despair and grief might be unsupportable, her encounter with the King merely demonstrating how equally powerless to influence events he is—but that she has somewhere to go, even someone to lean on. Life at the mill, with which she has now identified herself, goes on; she can draw strength from it because she belongs to it; John, unable to help as he would like, can still do something for her. It is certainly the benevolent ambience of the mill that helps reconcile her to Bob at last, for, we are told, 'There were so many nooks and corners she could never be sure he would not turn up within a foot of her', and while the darkness of the attic during the firework display enables him to 'imprison' first her hand, and then her waist, eventually, after she has—not quite convincingly—tried to elude him through several rooms, she goes into the bakehouse, 'where there were no means of exit whatsoever'. Though she grows angry with him and he storms out, 'left to herself in the large vacant old apartment, she grew calm'. Might we perhaps say, then, that the Mill has done it again?

It may be that the theme of *The Trumpet-Major* which I have postulated is, even if plausible, not of much apparent moment. Before we write off Overcombe as dull and undemanding, we might do well to listen to Dr Johnson, writing in the penultimate number of *The Adventurer.* He says:

> The business of life is carried on by a general co-operation, in which the part of any single man can no more be distinguished than the effect of a particular drop when the meadows are floated by a summer shower, yet every drop increases the inundation, and every hand adds to the happiness or the misery of mankind.

If that is disillusion, it is a noble disillusion, of which I think Thomas Hardy would have approved; indeed I think that he was saying something very close to that in *The Trumpet-Major.*

IV

Roy Morrell:

SOME ASPECTS OF HARDY'S MINOR NOVELS

It has long seemed to me that Hardy's minor novels deserve more attention than they get. Unfortunately this does not mean that they make a good subject for a lecture. Hardy published fourteen novels; six of them are often acclaimed masterpieces. To examine the remaining eight in a single lecture would be impossible, and I must content myself with making suggestions and asking a few questions.

First: is there a real dividing line between the 'major' and the 'minor' works? If we did not have the six best, would we be happy with the next four or five on the list, and still rank Hardy high among English novelists? Do we neglect the minor novels only because we have the better ones?

Or, if we accept that there is a real difference—a difference in kind—between the great novels and some at least of the remainder, in what does that difference consist? What are our criteria? What do we most value in Hardy's books?

Personally I should attempt to answer this last question in terms of human character and the human situation. Hardy's approach to the human condition is characteristically a serious one, as we should all agree. His best novels are concerned with men and women coping with greater or lesser success with the business of life. He is much concerned with love, with the relationship between a man and woman, and often deals with romantic love, but seldom uncritically; we seldom find him accepting purely romantic values. Kenneth Clark qualifies his admiration for Turner's romantic landscapes by remarking that far greater intensity of feeling, far more of the whole Turner, went into his tragic paintings. And we might say the same of Hardy: he is at his best when he is wholeheartedly and not romantically, but realistically, involved—and making us involved—with the fortunes of his people, with their happiness or their loss of it.

It is from this point of view that I find *The Trumpet-Major* the most difficult of all Hardy's books to take seriously. I was unable to attend Mr Johnson's lecture earlier in the week, and he might well have converted me. I imagine, however, that, if he had done this, he would have first brought me round to a new point of view, that at present he and I are looking for quite different things in a Hardy novel. If you are looking, as I am, for serious concern for the persons in the story, you will find *The Trumpet-*

Major lacking. Here is the opening sentence:

> In the days of high-waisted and muslin-gowned women when the vast amount of soldiering going on in the country was a cause of much trembling to the sex, there lived in a village near the Wessex coast two ladies of good report, though unfortunately of limited means.

Surely that is not the Hardy one knows? And what disturbs the reader is not just the phrase about the amount of soldiering causing 'trembling to the sex' and the other clichés; it is the odd tone, a tone we return to again and again. At the start of the second chapter we are told of Miller Loveday that his family history is—

> lost in the mists of antiquity. His ancestral line was contemporaneous with that of De Ros, Howard, and De La Zouche; but owing to some trifling deficiency in the possessions of the house of Loveday, the individual names and intermarriages of its members were not recorded . . . But it was known that the family had formed matrimonial alliances with farmers not so very small, and once with a gentleman tanner, who had for many years purchased after their death the horses of the most aristocratic persons in the county—fiery steeds that earlier in their career had been valued at many hundred guineas.
>
> It was also ascertained that Mr. Loveday's great-grandparents had been eight in number, and his great-great-grandparents sixteen, every one of whom reached to years of discretion . . .

Or again, the description of Oxwell Hall in Chapter VI:

> The hall was as interesting as mansions in a state of declension usually are, as the excellent county history showed. That popular work in folio contained an old plate dedicated to the last scion of the original owners, from which drawing it appeared that in 1774, the date of publication, the windows were covered with little scratches like black flashes of lightning; that a horn of hard smoke came out of each of the many chimneys; that a lady and a lap-dog stood on the lawn in a strenuously walking position; and a substantial cloud and nine flying birds of no known species hung over the trees to the north-east.
>
> The rambling and neglected dwelling had all the romantic excellencies and practical drawbacks which such mildewed places share in common with caves, mountains, wildernesses, glens, and other homes of poesy that people of taste wish to live and die in . . .

And so on. Often, when Hardy's style is attacked, I am happy to defend him. If he wishes to make a point, he is not deterred by its awkwardness: he battles through and makes it—awkwardly. As Julian says in *The Hand of Ethelberta,* 'Earnestness is mostly clumsy.' But it is not awkwardness or clumsiness that we find in *The Trumpet-Major.* It is something in the tone of the book: a facetiousness, almost, or at least a lack of the Hardyan earnestness which might have produced clumsy passages. The tone that pervades the book seems to be telling us that we need take none of the characters seriously, with the exception, perhaps, of the Trumpet-Major himself. Upon the unreliable and ambiguous actions of

Bob Loveday and Anne Garland and the stock comedy-coward Festus Derriman the ups and downs of Hardy's serial plot are perfunctorily constructed until finally the only responsible and reliable person is packed off—not casually, exactly, but with a piece of rhetoric which again seems to me quite uncharacteristic of Hardy—to his death.

I am not dismissing *The Trumpet-Major;* I am trying to make the point that it lacks those qualities which I find most impressive and valuable in Hardy. To the Hardy scholar it is of interest because of the historical background which Hardy was to use again—with such force—in *The Dynasts.* But when he says in the preface that the book is 'founded more largely on testimony than any other' he has written, he is accounting for the fact that he is less personally and imaginatively involved.

Admittedly there are good things in the book. There is a scene splendidly like an episode in the television series 'Dad's Army'; there is George III, poor fellow, forced to bathe to the strains of 'God save the King'; perhaps the most human scene in the book is where Anne and Matilda sink their jealous feelings in conspiring to save Bob from the press-gang (a scene which reminds one of some of those narrative poems of Hardy's where conventional feelings of jealousy or revenge give way to more generous and more truly human impulses); and there is the scene where Bob, in pursuit of Matilda, but less and less convinced of the wisdom of continuing, tosses a coin:

> 'Heads I go; tails I don't.' The piece of gold spun in air and came down heads.'
>
> 'No, I won't go, after all,' he said . . . .[1]

It is always liberating to choose firmly, instead of waiting and pretending that a choice is made for one; all the same the particular significance of this decision is that Bob is deciding to change his mind—as he so often does.

We are reminded of the incident in *A Pair of Blue Eyes* when Elfride tries to get her horse to choose for her.[2] The difference is that we are already deeply involved with Elfride and Stephen; her choice will affect the happiness of both; our involvement makes us take the whole matter more seriously, and makes *A Pair of Blue Eyes* (to my way of thinking) a better book.

The whole book is serious. There may be an occasional exchange of dialogue which is similar in its facetiousness to the tone which I find distressing in *The Trumpet-Major,* but in *A Pair of Blue Eyes* any such scene is but one element in a varied and balanced pattern. One example is when Stephen meets Martin Cannister and William Worm at his parents' house, but this is much more than is usually meant by the term 'comic relief'; it is an embarrassing reminder to Stephen of the distance between his world and Elfride's. Even Stephen's mother is embarrassed on his behalf when she remembers that Worm was once in Swancourt's employ. Such incidents begin by relieving, and end by increasing, the tension.

There are weaknesses in *A Pair of Blue Eyes;* but these are difficult to remember in the light of the book's merits. Hardy wrote better books, indeed, but until *The Mayor of Casterbridge,* none is so deeply felt; and several things in it are of particular interest.

First is the character of Knight. He is the first of Hardy's heroes whose superior and civilised qualities—for he is intellectual, sensitive, idealistic—seem to unfit him for some of life's encounters, especially encounters with women. He is monstrously cruel to Elfride, whom he loves, while convinced of his own tolerance and of the rightness of his reasoning and principles. If she loves him, why does she not confide in him candidly? That he is making such confidences impossible for her, and that her feelings of guilt could be a sign of her innocence,[3] he is incapable of realising till much later.

Basic themes in *A Pair of Blue Eyes,* as in many of Hardy's later novels, include the need to establish any human relationship on the truth; the importance—and the difficulty—of mutual understanding and communication; and the necessity of building life on reality and not on illusions: really three aspects of the same theme. 'There is enough poetry left in life,' as Hardy says elsewhere, 'after all the false romance has faded, to make a sweet pattern.'[4] Knight, too late, realises the truth of this. And the point, as in so many of the later novels, seems to be that all the raw material of happiness was there, but that Elfride with her lack of candour, and Knight with his fixed ideals of what a woman should be, threw away the chance of making that happiness a reality.

It has been said that 'sexual betrayal' was an obsessional theme of Hardy's. I cannot agree. By far the more important theme seems to me the misunderstanding which gives rise to betrayal and false accusations of betrayal.

Elfride's and Knight's need for each other is symbolised by the incident on the cliff, when a life-and-death problem was solved by their combined efforts. For the reader the incident is unforgettable. It resolves all the painful hesitations that have gone before; Knight and Elfride finally know, and accept the fact, that they are in love. It is ironical that in the growing misunderstanding that follows, Knight never once remembers that Elfride had saved his life.

At one point Elfride 'almost wishes' Knight 'had a grosser nature', and this foreshadowing of an oft-quoted reflection of Hardy's upon Angel Clare that 'with more animalism he would have been the nobler man'[5] opens our eyes to a number of parallels between *A Pair of Blue Eyes* and the later book. Elfride is very different from Tess, but she is like her at least in being a girl pure in heart, passionately in love for the first time in her life—despite earlier attachments—and rejected by her lover because his ready-made principles lead him to misunderstand her confession. Elfride is Hardy's first full-length portrait of a woman who possessed what seemed to him not so much weaknesses as essential and fascinating feminine traits. Elfride's odd mixture of vanity and modesty, evasiveness and integrity, folly—as when she writes so unguardedly to Mrs Jethway—and resourcefulness—as when she saves Knight's life—may not sound convincing, but Hardy makes it entirely so. In addition the portrait has considerable charm.

The production of such portraits is one of the novel's functions. Isobel Archer is not Henry James's only 'portrait of a lady', and if Elfride Swancourt is Hardy's first, she is certainly not his last. There are a number of other women, who are very different from Tess and Elfride, but who share one important circumstance with those two: each stands rather alone, and at a disadvantage in the world, because of her sex. Elfride is a victim, as no man could quite be, of family pressures; public scandal could be disastrous for her, and private report does indeed ruin her chances with Knight, and breaks her heart. And even more significant are the little things: Knight pounces upon Elfride's sex, when he reviews her book; when he first meets her he remarks that the best thing for any woman is for her to get married, and thereafter to be heard of no more. Even on the church tower, he issues orders as if she were a child; she 'feels like a colt in a halter for the first time', Hardy says. Even the way Stephen's mother talks about her as a possible daughter-in-law, maintaining that Stephen could marry a girl with better prospects, would suggest that a woman is not a free agent, but an object to be discussed and docketed. And Hardy makes all this clearer by giving Elfride a generous measure of independence and unconventionality. It avails her nothing.

In his next book, Hardy explores the possibilities of a woman's independence more positively. Bathsheba is more capable of looking after herself than Elfride, but after a few initial mistakes she has a hard struggle; and later in the book it is not only good management but a good deal of luck and help from Gabriel Oak that enable her to regain her freedom and balance. Freedom, for Hardy, was not synonymous with complete independence; Bathsheba is not independent when, at the end, she marries Oak and enters a farming partnership with him. Hardy is trying to suggest, rather, a dependence upon each other of equals.

I mention *Far from the Madding Crowd* for the support it gives my impression that from the time of *A Pair of Blue Eyes* Hardy was for many years concerned, on and off, with woman's part in life, the social and psychological difficulties which a woman encountered in finding herself, realising her potentialities. These explorations culminated in Tess, a woman of integrity ('a pure woman'), of good intelligence, of good looks, but without money or social position. For any such person fulfilment may be possible, but it is certainly difficult. However, *Tess of the d'Urbervilles* has a place in the literature of woman's emancipation which no one is likely to dispute. It is when we return to the minor novels of an earlier period that an awareness of this theme may be helpful.

It certainly helps, I think, with *The Hand of Ethelberta,* which until recently I had regarded as Hardy's least interesting book. Berta lacks the attraction of many of Hardy's heroines; her adventures arouse little feeling either for her or for any of her lovers. Perhaps we feel some sympathy for Christopher Julian, for whom Berta herself has some affection; but Hardy gives him little personality; and he shares one particularly irritating trait with several other young men in Hardy's early books: he tends to think of love-making as trying to get the heroine to tie herself up in promises. One of Hardy's axioms is that girls seldom like this.

Certainly the book is not a general favourite. I believe it was at one time disliked because of the sniping shots which the plot enabled Hardy to take at 'high society'. It was written, Hardy says in his preface, 'as an interlude between stories of a more sober design', and the lack of tension in the first half of the book bears this out; he goes on to say, however, that the word 'comedy' in the sub-title conveys his aim 'not quite accurately'.

It gains interest as it goes on, and as Hardy gets caught up in the story. There are certainly surprising scenes: for instance, when Berta and Picotee go looking for Neigh's country seat, and find a knacker's yard, adorned with horses' skulls and skeletons; or the odd scene at Corvsgate Castle when Ethelberta disowns the ass, and it looks at her with contempt; the scene where the maids and footmen have a silent romp and an almost silent waltz while the 'company' are dining below—a scene which must have shocked respectable *Cornhill* readers as much as it shocked little Picotee.[6] We suffer mild impatience to know how the secret of Berta's parentage is to be leaked to fashionable London; and it is significant that she should start to make the revelation herself to a crowded drawing-room through the medium of one of her stories; significant too that Lord Mountclere should cut her short—knowing the facts already. And when the revelation finally comes, who would have guessed it would be blurted out by Berta's own father, Mrs Doncastle's butler, horror-struck that his daughter is about to marry Lord Mountclere! It is typical of Hardy, I think, that the foundations of society are *not* shaken by the disclosure of Ethelberta's parentage after all. Admittedly Mrs Doncastle tries to sack Chickerel on the spot, but her husband countermands the dismissal very promptly and accepts the notion that his butler is about to be the father-in-law of a viscount quite as a matter of course. Finally there is the chase to prevent Ethelberta's marriage, with comedy arising from the very different motives of all concerned.

Politically, it is Sol who has the last word: 'Berta, you have worked to false lines. A creeping up among the useless lumber of our nation that'll be the first to burn if there comes a flare.'[7] The sentiments could have been Hardy's; but when Sol goes on to scold his sister more directly, Hardy is no longer quite behind him, nor is the book.

For the book is a provisional vindication of Ethelberta; not wholehearted, but a vindication all the same. There are plenty of comic situations, in addition to those already mentioned, and many of them are handled with subtlety; but they do not cohere. Such coherence as the book possesses comes from Ethelberta herself. She may not be a 'sympathetic' character; indeed, as someone describes the heroine of *A Laodicean,* she is rather 'a mixed young lady'; but much of the mixture is admirable. She is extremely talented and resourceful, and, having gained a position in society and some temporary independence through the death of her husband, she wants to use her position and her talents to help her very large family. Unfortunately her talents are her only permanent asset; her position is very precarious, for from her husband's family she has inherited almost no money and only a very short lease on a London house. How is she to ensure that her father and mother do not die in poverty, that her older brothers and sisters have better jobs and fuller lives, and that her younger brothers and sisters get a good education? A man with Ethelberta's talents, energy, and initial advantages might succeed; but what hope has Berta, unless she rejects her lover and marries a rich man? It is easy to condemn her as 'scheming' or 'hardhearted' in these days of well-paid jobs for women, old-age pensions for a woman's parents, and free education for her brothers and sisters; but for those days one must surely accord Berta some respect.

Of course that does not mean that one must admire the *book.* But it does help, I think, to see it from this point of view, to suppose that Hardy was creating different types of women, putting them in different situations, and seeing how they would make out. Ethelberta succeeded: her iron rule of Enckworth Hall and the estates, and her stern management of Lord Mountclere himself were not indeed the highest kind of self-realisation, but she did what she wanted to do for her family; and she was prepared to pay the price.

This, after all, is the important thing about Ethelberta: she knew what she was doing; she realised how her worldly course was affecting her character, and indeed the characters of her relations. When she received a letter from her mother urging her to bring one of her suitors to the point of proposing before it was too late, she condemned not her mother's unscrupulousness but her own dubious line of conduct which had so sadly affected her mother's honest nature. The Corvsgate donkey may not have been accusing her of snobbish and cowardly betrayal; Ethelberta got the message from her conscience.

Hardy treats Ethelberta, as he does several of his more interesting characters, with a mixture of compassion and criticism which contrasts with the self-criticism and *absence* of self-pity with which Berta treats herself. She acts deliberately, analyses her own motives, and knows what she is doing—with one notable exception: she has no idea that Lord Mountclere has a mistress living on the estate. It is significant, by the way, that this fact is known to all the men in the book, even to Ethelberta's father and brothers, but to none of the women—one of the many small indications that Ethelberta is living in a man's world.

'I thought honesty was the best policy?' said Picotee. And Ethelberta replies: 'So it is, for the man's purpose. But don't you go believing in sayings, Picotee: they are all made by men, for their own advantages. Women who use public proverbs as a guide through events are those who have not ingenuity enough to make private ones as each event occurs.'

So many things pleasantly surprised me in my recent re-reading of *The Hand of Ethelberta* that I am giving the book disproportionate space here. What surprises me most is that I intend to re-read it again. But in a way this is an adverse comment: the implication is that the good things (as I've said) don't cohere; they don't lend significance, to one another, or build up in the memory. There are, for instance, many of those vivid images which are sometimes so effective in Hardy, including a description of the opal halo which surrounds the head's shadow when moonlight is shining on dew or frost. The image turns up again in one of the early chapters of *Tess*, where the Trantridge villagers are walking back over the fields from Chaseborough.[8] The difference is that in *Ethelberta* the image is no more than a pleasant observation, read and forgotten, whereas in *Tess* the halo seen by each of the villagers seems a sort of beatification, a blessing on their tipsiness; it heightens the whole scene and, since the mood of the villagers affects Tess and her actions, it is an organic part of the plot, and unforgettable. But before I leave Ethelberta, may I point out two passages where the images are effective. The first comes at the very beginning of the book; while the ostler and the milkman at the Red Lion are still making Ethelberta the object of their male fantasies, she has walked out on to the Heath and is watching a hawk chasing a duck. By repeatedly diving below the surface of the pond, the duck eludes the hawk until the latter gives up the chase. The incident is not quite relevant enough to be a symbol or a 'proleptic image'; still, in so far as the book is about Ethelberta eluding predators and contriving to survive, it is memorable. The second is towards the end of the book, when the stormy weather is hampering the travellers hastening to stop the marriage, and the little boat from Sandbourne has turned back, unable to put in at Knollsea. Here Berta has voiced certain misgivings about her marriage next morning:

> 'I have had a thought—why I cannot tell—that as much as this man brings to me in rank and gifts he may take out of me in tears.'
>
> 'Berta!'
>
> 'But there's no reason in it—not any; for not in a single matter does what has been supply us with any certain ground for knowing what will be in the world. I have seen marriages where happiness might have been said to be ensured, and they have been all sadness afterwards; and I have seen those in which the prospect was black as night, and they have led on to a time of sweetness and comfort. And I have seen marriages neither joyful nor sorry that have become either as accident has forced them to become, the persons having no voice in it at all. Well, then, why should I be afraid to make a plunge when chance is as trustworthy as calculation?'
>
> 'If you don't like him well enough, don't have him, Berta. There's time enough to put him off even now.'
>
> 'O no. I would not upset a well-considered course on the haste of an impulse. Our will should withstand our misgivings. Now let us see if all has been packed, and then we'll sing.'
>
> That evening, while the wind was wheeling round and round the dwelling, and the calm eye of the lighthouse afar was the single speck perceptible of the outside world from the door of Ethelberta's temporary home, the music of songs mingled with the stroke of the wind across the iron railings, and was swept on in the general tide of the gale, and the noise of the rolling sea, till not an echo of a tone remained.[9]

We recall the night that Gabriel Oak was tending his sheep and the new-born lambs, all the sounds made by the wind over the hill-side contributing to the sensation of the whole earth moving beneath the stars, until this sense of vast impersonal motion was brought under control, given a human meaning, by Gabriel Oak's flute, dominating the other sounds and imposing a harmony. In *The Hand of Ethelberta* the human sounds are lost amidst those of wind and sea; the mood is different, sadder, embodying Ethelberta's misgivings despite her words of courage; but the scene is no less effective.

Further enquiry into Hardy's feminist leanings would include a consideration of Viviette Lady Constantine. Throughout *Two on a Tower* she is very much alone in a man's world and—it might be argued—took no more than her due revenge upon it. The turning-point of the book is her reading of Swithin's uncle's letter to find in it a ruthless picture of herself. The shock was the greater because it was not exactly a revelation: it tallied enough with her own secret verdict on herself to release her from possessiveness and self and all the other impurities of love, and to enable her to act—as we would all wish to act and so seldom do—in complete objectivity and freedom for the good of her young lover. It is true that when she found she was pregnant, she tried to recant; but Swithin was beyond recall, and her generous action had its due effect.

Two on a Tower seems to me seriously underrated. There are irritating things in the book, but these are outweighed by its merits. The plot is contrived—but surely *well* contrived—to bring out the subtleties of Viviette's and Swithin's relationship, and the good faith of her action. There is not much to him, perhaps, barring the single-mindedness of his aims, the devoted prosecution of which is an important factor in the plot—more relevant than with most of Hardy's heroes. But the book is certainly Viviette's, not Swithin's.

Paula Power, the 'Laodicean', must also have some mention; but it seems as though Hardy, in giving her the intelligence and talent that he had given to Ethelberta and, in addition, wealth and the further advantage of freedom from family ties and commitments, had deprived her of any chance of having an interesting story. We all know the difficulties under which the book was written: Hardy fell ill after the first few chapters and had to dictate the instalments from a sick-bed. Certainly the promise of the opening is not fulfilled: those encounters between the sincere but blinkered Baptist minister and the open-minded and open-destinied Paula lead one to expect more interesting psychological complexities. As it turns out, the only threat to Paula's freedom is the romantic past of Stancy Castle and the de Stancy name.

There is a truly remarkable chapter which initiates this theme. So far Paula has seemed a very modern young woman, with her telegraph (the telephone was still in the process of being invented) and her new clock:

> 'It tells the seconds [Charlotte de Stancy explains], but the old one, which my very great grandfather erected in the eighteenth century, only told the hours. Paula says that time, being so much more valuable now, must of course be cut up into smaller pieces.'[10]

But this afternoon Paula is at a loose end. She has made a great fire of logs to try to bring some cheer into the Long Gallery—the woodlice (a nice Hardyan touch) running out from under the bark, and the faces in the portraits (not her ancestors, of course, but those of the de Stancys) staring down at her. She is expecting Charlotte, but time passes and the light fades, and when Charlotte finally arrives she brings with her her brother Captain de Stancy, who has been abroad and whom Paula has not met. De Stancy has not been inside his ancestral home since he was three weeks old, when the castle was sold to pay his father's or grandfather's debts, but he has mugged up his family history, at Dare's instigation, and is well prepared:

> As they moved hither and thither, the various expressions of de Stancy's face made themselves picturesquely visible in the unsteady shine of the blaze. In a short time he had drawn near to the painting of the ancestor whom he so greatly resembled. When her quick eye noted the speck on the face indicative of inherited traits strongly pronounced, a new and romantic feeling that the de Stancys had stretched out a tentacle from their genealogical tree to seize her by the hand and draw her into their mass took possession of Paula.

Later, when candles are brought, de Stancy

> walked in advance, holding the two candles on high, his shadow forming a gigantic figure on the neighbouring wall, while he recited the particulars of family history pertaining to each portrait that he had learnt up with such eager persistence.

He also recites verses by a remote ancestor—verses said to have been written on some more-than-usually romantic and desperate occasion in that ancestor's own blood. He dons a suit of armour and finally, carried away by the occasion and by his own eloquence, he offers to run upon his sword. ' "Don't, Captain de Stancy, please don't!" cried Paula involuntarily.' And you'll be relieved to know that he does not. It is a scene when the narration shifts from the grim to the comic as oddly as the lights and shadows change.[11]

Has anyone, one wonders, analysed these scenes of phenomenological interest in Hardy: his many different uses of strange lighting effects, scenes of contrasted light and darkness, scenes lighted by anything from candles, log-fires, and burning castles (as in *A Laodicean)* to stars and glow-worms?

Paula manages not to be pulled in by the tentacles of the de Stancy romantic octopus. At all events the interest shifts from Paula to Somerset when the latter becomes the victim of Dare's fraud and misrepresentation, and, in so far as Dare and Captain de Stancy personify the twin Doomsters Chance and Time, it is Somerset's doom the reader is concerned with—not, I think, as a matter of great urgency. Except as a curiosity, one would hardly recommend the book. The greatest curiosity is the figure of Dare: a reminder of Hardy's lack of interest in real villainy.

The book lacks that strong sense of the Wessex scene which helps to give most of the novels reality and unity of tone; indeed much of the action takes place outside England, though Hardy succeeds well in subordinating the final scenes—those of Paula's pursuit of Somerset through the coastal towns of Normandy—to the general theme of the book, the rejection of the old and the romantic.

Rejection of the romantic, in a slightly different sense, is also the theme of a better book, *The Well-Beloved*, in which Hardy links his favourite idea of the absurdity of valuing what has been lost or is otherwise unattainable, of letting the beautiful dream or the unexpiable remorse, spoil the savour of reality—

> Nay, she was the woman I did not love,
> Whom all the others were ranked above,
> Whom, during her life, I thought nothing of.[12]

He links this idea with classical critical notions of Art's concern with ideal beauty. Keats's 'What the Imagination seizes as Beauty . . . ', Shelley's dreams, Sir Joshua Reynolds' *Discourses*, all go by the board in the sombre finale. Pierston's life is changed almost in an instant; and this time it is not an *unusual* trick of lighting, but the ordinary 'cold grey morning light' that unexpectedly reveals Pierston to himself, reveals him as he is going to be seen, for the first time in full daylight, by Avice III that morning. In Book III of the novel, there are many good things, well written and well planned. It is, of course, a planned book: its heroine is multiplied by three—one Avice for each of the stages of Pierston's life; the contrast between the rocky reality of the Isle of Slingers and the unreality—but artistic productivity—of Pierston's life in London symbolises the psychological theme of the book; and this contrast is buttressed by a nice detail in Book III: the appearance in Budmouth of the once liberal-minded and intelligent London beauty, Mrs Nicola Pine-Avon. She is now married to Pierston's former friend Somers, and has become a timid and conventional matron with no motive in life but that of protecting her daughters from any harsh truth, from the dire threat of any thought that is not a platitude. Her re-appearance sufficiently sets in relief the comparative realism, freedom, and honesty of our Portland protagonists. We forgive Hardy even when he overdoes his planning: when Marcia's attack of rheumatism entails her being married in a wheeled chair, we feel that crutches would have been enough! But at least we take Hardy's point.

More attention to Hardy's planning might sometimes enable us to take his point more readily. I should like to refer to *Desperate*

Remedies here; rather guiltily, because this book is packed with interest, and deserves much more than a single reference. Edward and Cytherea first discover and declare their love in a rowing-boat on Budmouth Bay. When, after a truly remarkable series of trials and tribulations they at last get married, Cytherea has inherited Miss Aldclyffe's house and estate, and she and Edward go rowing on the lake and re-enact, on the last page of the book, that early love scene. There is no special point in this: I mention it merely as evidence that Hardy saw the need for such devices. And the re-enactment is deliberate, so the reader cannot fail to notice it. But how many of us have noticed a similar piece of patterning in *The Mayor of Casterbridge*? At the beginning of our re-acquaintance with Henchard, the morning after we meet him as Mayor, he walks west, to 'top o' town', with Farfrae, to wish him well on his journey; but instead of parting with him, he brings the Scotsman back as his partner. Near the end of the book, the same man takes another walk, this time in the opposite direction, down the hill to Grey's Bridge, where he parts from Elizabeth-Jane and sets out on his lonely journeyings. He knows that within the hour she will be told of his lies and deceptions; he also knows that she is his last link with love and humanity. If he is not to break that link he must tell her the truth; or he must say at least, 'Forgive me: I lied because I loved you and could not bear to lose you.' He says nearly that, but not quite. He breaks the link 'for want of a word'; he goes off, and Elizabeth-Jane returns to meet Farfrae and her real father. To notice Hardy's design is to recall the earlier incident and the actual words from Henchard that led to the Scotsman's unexpected change of mind. The two men have already said good-bye; here are Hardy's words:

> Still holding the young man's hand he paused, and then added deliberately: 'Now I'm not the man to let a cause be lost for want of a word. And before ye are gone for ever I'll speak. Once more, will ye stay?'

It is warm and generous speech; I have quoted only the beginning of it: the part I need—'I'm not the man to let a cause be lost for want of a word.' What happened between that time and his parting with Elizabeth-Jane? Had those few years so changed him, so dispirited him? Or is Hardy saying that Henchard *could* have spoken? that he had a last card, and this time failed to play it? One thing Hardy is *not* saying is that the cruelty of chance or circumstance stood in Henchard's way.

To give this lecture some kind of design, I should perhaps go back and consider again the questions I asked at the start. But from what I have said you have, I hope, been able to infer the kind of answers I myself would give. At the same time I hope I have not suggested that your answers ought to be the same as mine. For the Hardy scholar none of his novels lacks interest; all are well worth reading. Two or three of those usually regarded as 'minor' works seem to me much better than is commonly supposed; worth the general reader's attention, and not just the Hardy scholar's: *A Pair of Blue Eyes*, certainly, and *Two on a Tower*, perhaps, and *The Well-Beloved.* Over *Desperate Remedies* I hesitate: it is full of a young man's—very characteristically Hardyan—aphorisms and worldly wisdom; full of good things and bad packed in astonishingly. *A Laodicean* and *The Hand of Ethelberta* are on a rather lower plane; different in kind, perhaps; thinner, less concentrated; stretched out to fit the bed of the procrustean serial and three-volume novel; and with the good things—as I've suggested—not always integrating well. All the same, good things are there, complementary to situations in the better books, and seeds, too, that are later to germinate and flower. Whether you take or reject assumptions I have made about Hardy's themes and attitudes is another question. I believe Hardy wrote with fairly definite ideas about some human problems. At the same time he would not be the great novelist we take him to be if he were moralising or prescribing. His books are truly, I believe, explorations or—to use Wordsworth's word quoted by Hardy for just this purpose—'questionings'.[13]

V

Maire A. Quinn:

THOMAS HARDY AND THE SHORT STORY

> Nor is there singing school but studying
> Monuments of its own magnificence . . .

To Hardy, the poet and novelist, many such monuments were available, but the practitioners of his craft with whom the short-story writer was most familiar were folk artists, local story-tellers of Solomon Selby's ilk. Hardy had been born into a community which had accumulated a 'vast mass of unwritten folklore, local chronicle, local topography and nomenclature'. Although this 'continuity of information' had been broken in his lifetime, he could

> recollect the time when the places of burial even of the poor and tombless were all remembered, and the history of the parish and squire's family for one hundred and fifty years back known. Such and such ballads appertained to such and such a locality, ghost tales were attached to particular sites . . . .[1]

Hardy's stories frequently are attempts to translate these oft-told tales with which he was familiar from childhood into a literary medium or to create new tales on the model of the old. His comparison of the story-teller to the Ancient Mariner *(Life,* p. 252) is perhaps even more apposite in his own case than he himself realized. The Mariner stops the wedding-guest with a tale cast in the traditional ballad form. Hardy, too, often attempts to interest the 'hurrying public' in stories whose origin is clearly the 'owre true tale' told 'by country-folks on winter nights'.

Although Hardy thought of the good story-teller as an Ancient Mariner with the power to divert a reluctant audience from other enjoyments, the story-tellers of his childhood had addressed themselves to a captive and uncritical local audience as does Selby in 'A Tradition of Eighteen Hundred and Four'. The audience within the short stories, unlike the wedding-guest, are offered no rival attraction to test their interest. They listen as they jog along to their destination in a carrier's van or as they loll beside a warm fire on a wet day. One of Hardy's problems as a purveyor of rural stories and traditions is that of interesting an outsider, a Fitzpiers, in a closed context like Little Hintock. The desire for an 'almost exhaustive biographical or historical acquaintance with every object within the observer's horizon' which fostered the rural habit of tale-telling is not necessarily the condition of a 'professional man who drops down into such a place [as Hardy's Wessex] by accident'. Hardy's reluctance to leave his comfortable fireside seat and his easy local audience has resulted in such delightful comic tales as 'Absent-Mindedness in a Parish Choir', but on occasion it beguiles him into telling stories as banal as 'Interlopers at the Knap', which does not rise above the level of village gossip. At other times awareness of the appeal of his material to the amateur folklorist tempts him to string together a series of superstitions and pass it off as a story. The interest in 'The Superstitious Man's Story' obviously lies in the superstitions recorded. The story itself is negligible.

The anomalies of Hardy's position as a writer emerging from an oral tale-telling context are revealed on several occasions in critical comments on his own work. Aware of a lack of contrast in his first collection of short stories, *Wessex Tales,* he is very ready with the excuse that the imbalance in favour of tales about capital punishment is due to the fact that 'in the neighbourhood of county-towns hanging matters used to form a large proportion of the local tradition'. Not only is he prepared to admit that two of the stories, 'The Withered Arm' and 'The Distracted Preacher' are based on fact; he actually deplores his own slight tampering with the truth of the original story in 'The Withered Arm'. He describes his 'misrelation' as a machine-made casting which lacks 'the sharp hand-work of the mould'. Towards the end of the preface, however, the conscious literary artist takes over from the culpable folk narrator, and attempts to extricate himself from the role of unreliable recorder of local events: 'the stories are but dreams and not records'. This ambivalence between creative dream and factual record, between the role of imaginative story-teller and local chronicler, is to be encountered once again in the 1896 preface to *Life's Little Ironies.* Here he begins with the rather startling pronouncement:

> A story-teller's interest in his own stories is usually independent of any merits or demerits they may show as specimens of narrative art; turning on something behind the scenes, something real in their history . . .

and continues:

> In the present collection 'The Melancholy Hussar of the German Legion' has just such a hold upon myself for the technically inadmissible reason that the old people who gave me their recollections of its incidents did so in circumstances that linger pathetically in the memory . . .[2]

Although as a sophisticated critic Hardy is aware that his stance is 'technically inadmissible', his opening gambit is based on the assumption that local gossip and oral testimony are the short story writer's usual sources. Again his reply to Howells relies on a similar presupposition as to the distinctively oral nature of the tale:

Howells and those of his school forget that a story *must* be striking enough to be worth telling. Therein lies the problem—to reconcile the average with that uncommonness which alone makes it natural that a tale or experience would dwell in the memory and induce repetition.[3]

The unease with which Hardy reaches out from the idea of a local audience and an oral art form to a wider readership and the story on the page may be glimpsed occasionally in the attitudes of some of his narrators. The story-teller's reliance on written notes is not too surprising, perhaps, in the case of the first narrator in *A Group of Noble Dames* since he is something of a pedant. The parenthetic—'said the narrator, turning over his memoranda for references'—which greets us in the first lines of the first story in that collection is possibly deliberately introduced by Hardy as an oblique acknowledgement of his use of authentic historical source material (i.e. John Hutchins' *The History and Antiquities of Dorset*). But what are we to make of the opening of 'A Committee Man of "The Terror"':

'I wrote it down in the shape of a story some years ago, just after my mother's death,' said Mrs. H. 'It is locked up in my desk there now.'
'Read it!' said we.
'No,' said she; 'the light is bad, and I can remember it well enough, word for word, flourishes and all.'

In part, Hardy, intent on verisimilitude, is accounting for the overly literary style of the narrative which follows. It is surely significant, however, that the story is no longer told spontaneously as by a Solomon Selby, but is a deliberate conjunction of art and artifice, the oral recitation of the written word. In this fusion of oral and literary narration, the story offers an interesting instance of Hardy's desire to achieve a compromise between these two rival modes. The unsuccessful 'Alicia's Diary' is probably another experiment in the combination of literary and spontaneous narration.

Hardy's belief that the short story form was primarily oral frequently resulted, as might be expected, in the employment of narrators in his tales. Narrators are used in all of the stories in *A Group of Noble Dames* and *A Few Crusted Characters*. They are also a feature of many of the stories in *A Changed Man*. The narrator for Hardy is merely a means of preserving the oral character of the tale. With the notable exception of the carrier's tale in *A Few Crusted Characters*, he is not concerned about correlating tale and teller. The carrier, aptly named Burthen, tells the returned exile, John Lackland, the tale of 'Tony Kytes, the Arch-Deceiver'. This has a peculiar appropriateness since Tony Kytes was himself a carrier, the very carrier who drove Lackland to Casterbridge on his outward journey. The story of Tony Kytes has for setting a carrier's van, for dramatis personae the carrier and his three female passengers; its crises are based on the collection of passengers; and its comic denouement is achieved by the eventful overturning of the van. In this tale Hardy is at his best in manipulating narrative and vocational roles. Elsewhere he does little with this, apart from such obvious gestures as having a surgeon tell the story of 'Barbara of the House of Grebe'.

The creation of a story-telling ambience occupied an important place in Hardy's art in the years following the publication of *Wessex Tales* in 1888. It is probable that the collecting of a number of stories for publication as a group provided the impetus for a ready-made collection, 'a tale of tales—a series of linked stories'. In any event his response to *The Graphic*'s request for a short novel in April of the following year was a unified group of six short stories entitled *A Group of Noble Dames,* which was to form the nucleus of the later volume of that name. That Hardy had begun to think in terms of collections of stories is confirmed by the appearance some months later of *A Few Crusted Characters*. The original title of this work, *Wessex Folk,* and its publication by Harper (who had handled the American serial rights of *A Group of Noble Dames)* prompts the conjecture that this was conceived of as a complementary set of tales. The Wessex nobles have had their hour; now it is the turn of the Wessex folk.

In his selection of stories for his *Wessex Tales,* Hardy had had to rely on the principle of diversity since the stories had little in common except their Wessex setting. The notion of a series of linked tales was not only intended to solve the problem of unity, however. After all, *A Few Crusted Characters* was too short to compose an independent volume. The vital distinction between *Wessex Tales* and the story collections of 1889 and 1890 is Hardy's preoccupation with setting up an oral narrative situation. Having exploited the traditional fireside setting in *A Group of Noble Dames,* he turns his attention to the snug interior of the carrier's van which he had already noted as a vehicle of gossip in *The Woodlanders* several years before.

When no narrator is introduced at the beginning of the story, the fact that the author is recounting a local tradition is sometimes mentioned, partly to preserve the sense of continuity with oral narration. 'The Withered Arm' and 'The Distracted Preacher', already mentioned, are cases in point. In 'The Grave by the Hand-post' Hardy claims that he is disinterring 'memories of village history'. In 'Master John Horseleigh, Knight', he retells a 'strange local tradition', and in 'The Duke's Reappearance' he recalls a 'family tradition'. The story of 'The Three Strangers' is well known in the country about Higher Crowstairs, while fragments of the story of 'The Melancholy Hussar' 'got abroad at the time and have been kept alive ever since'. In his preface to *Far from the Madding*

Crowd, Hardy had stated that for 'the preservation of legend, close inter-social relations, and eccentric individualities' the 'indispensable conditions of existence are attachment to the soil of one particular spot by generation after generation'. His own role as heir of the rural story-teller is the literary perpetuation of such 'traditions'. So attuned were his creative processes to those of the local tale-teller that he even found himself in the whimsical position of having apparently invented an existing 'tradition'. The story in question is 'A Tradition of Eighteen Hundred and Four', the traditional basis of which was finally disproved.

The convention of the narrated story or the 'tradition' sometimes resulted in a certain formal triteness on Hardy's part, particularly in the beginnings and endings of stories. The openings of many of the narrated tales in *A Changed Man,* for instance, bear a dreary similarity to one another:

> I lately had a melancholy experience (said the gentleman who is answerable for the truth of this story)—*'Enter a Dragoon'.*
> The genial Justice of the Peace—now, alas no more—who made himself responsible for the facts of this story, used to begin in the good old-fashioned way . . . —*'What the Shepherd Saw'.*
> The genial Justice of the Peace—now, alas no more—who made himself to fact of the following narrative . . . —*'A Mere Interlude'.*
> It was half-past five o'clock (by the testimony of the land-surveyor, my authority for the particulars of this story . . .)—*''The Romantic Adventures of a Milkmaid'.*

The weakness of the 'traditions', on the other hand, lies in the repetitiveness of their endings. In these tales Hardy has a habit of concluding at the graveside:

> The older villagers, however, who know of the episode from their parents, still recollect the place where the soldiers lie. Phyllis lies near.—*'The Melancholy Hussar'.*
> We who listened to old Selby that night have been familiar with his simple grave-stone for these ten years past.—*'A Tradition of Eighteen Hundred and Four'.*
> The grass has long been green on the graves of Shepherd Fennel and his frugal wife; the guests who made up the christening party have mainly followed their entertainers to the tomb . . .—*'The Three Srangers'.*

As soon as the carrier's van has deposited its 'human freight', John Lackland, as befits one who has listened to a series of 'traditions', heads for the cemetery.

When he relinquished the support of such narrative conventions Hardy frequently experienced difficulties, particularly in the business of launching his stories. The beginning of 'Fellow-Townsmen' makes the same point about the proximity of urban and rural life as Hardy makes in *The Mayor of Casterbridge.* The fact that Casterbridge is the 'pole, focus, or nerve-knot of the surrounding country life' is of vital significance for Hardy's artistic purposes in the novel. In the short story the inter-relatedness of town and country serves no useful function whatever, and one wonders why Hardy did not plunge straightaway into the second paragraph. 'The Fiddler of the Reels' opens with a paragraph on the Great Exhibition of 1851, followed by one on the year 1851 as 'a sudden bringing of ancient and modern into absolute contact'. The connection that all this has with the story which follows is rather tenuous. Car'line Aspent's husband-to-be assists at the preparations for the Great Exhibition and she thinks she glimpses Mop Ollamoor during her visit to it. The train which conveys her from Wessex to London possibly represents the conjunction of ancient and modern. None of these factors, however, is central to the story of Car'line's bewitchment by Mop's music.[4]

In 'For Conscience' Sake' there is much preliminary huffing and puffing as Hardy searches for a point of entry into his story. First there is the quotation from John Stuart Mill which seems intended to introduce a note of philosophical gravity. This is immediately followed by what is obviously a second attempt at beginning in a changed style and tone: 'There were few figures better known to the local crossing-sweeper than Mr Millborne's . . .'. Finally the story proper starts as a first person narrative related by Mr Millborne to his physician.

Some stories begin in a leisurely manner seemingly more suited to the novel than to shorter fiction. 'The Son's Veto', foı example, begins with a thorough survey of a woman's hairstyle and then proceeds to a detailed description of her general appearance and the wonder she excites in others, before launching into the narrative proper. The mystery of the character he is about to depict grips Hardy at the outset, and he wants us to share his wonder before setting about his task of dispelling it. The sense of place, too, takes priority over action at the beginning of some stories. The lane along which Farmer Darton rides to court his Sally, the ewe-leaze on which the cottage at Higher Crowstairs is built, such scenes absorb Hardy. This lack of a sense of relevance, of narrative economy, may possibly be attributed to the oral story-telling tradition. The night is always young, and time is needed to create narrative expectancy, to form a group of desultory conversationalists into an audience. A great deal is made of the business of getting under way in many of Hardy's stories, as it is in oral tales. When the right ambience has been created in advance, when the stories follow hard upon one another's heels as in *A Few Crusted Characters*, then the preliminaries are few and quickly disposed of.

The conclusions of Hardy's stories do not always form an ıntegral part of the story proper, although where there is no narrator or 'tradition' involved the tale usually ends where the story ends. In short stories like 'An Imaginative Woman', 'On the Western

Circuit', 'To Please his Wife', and 'The Grave by the Handpost', the ending is used to make a final ironic point, a last twist of the knife. However, as is often the case with oral story-tellers, Hardy does not like to finish his story abruptly, and usually takes some time to return from the fictional world to the world of normality, which generally means a transition from past to present. The consequent lowering of narrative temperature is used to best advantage in 'The Fiddler of the Reels'. In this story Hardy seems intent on preserving a note of drollery and curbing the mythic dimension of his subject. How better deflate the mythic pretensions of captivating musician and captured child than by referring to their present ages in the last lines of the story: 'he must be an old scamp verging on three score-and-ten and she a woman of four-and-forty'. The most powerful short story conclusion is perhaps that of 'The Son's Veto'. Instead of the usual device of a final paragraph placing the tale in its historical context this story ends with a scene which encapsulates all that has gone before, a final confrontation of the principal characters, the woman, her admirer, and her curate son who thwarted their union. At the woman's funeral her son usurps the place of chief mourner, while her grief-stricken lover is merely a bystander. Hardy points up the contrast between the two men by an almost Blakeian use of colour. In the lover's case black is the colour of mourning; in the son's, it signifies hatred. This splendidly visualized final scene is actually better than the story deserves.

Hardy once remarked, 'I have unconsciously the habit of regard-the scene as if I were a spectator not solid enough to influence my environment' (*Life*, p. 210). In his writings this stance of observation rather than participation has consciously or unconsciously given rise to a literary technique of spectatorship to which he frequently resorts in both novels and stories. 'The Son's Veto', for instance, begins with an onlooker's impression of a woman's hair; to the eyes of a man viewing it from behind the nut brown hair was a wonder and a mystery. 'The Waiting Supper' opens with a double observer motif: the spectator narrator surveys the scene and notes the presence of the yeoman, a 'watcher' within the story. For some time Hardy, as author, maintains a spectatorial attitude, deducing everything from the externals of dress, behaviour, and speech, but as this rather lengthy short story proceeds he gradually slips into the role of omniscient author and penetrates into the minds and hearts of his characters. In 'A Changed Man' he inserts an observer into the story and equips him with both motive and opportunity for taking an interest in the drama of other lives. He is an invalid, so that 'time hung heavily on his hands unless he maintained a constant interest in proceedings without'. To facilitate his observation of the passing scene Hardy provided him with an oriel window 'whence could be obtained a raking view of the High Street, west and east'. Having established this observer early on in the story, Hardy is at a loss to find something for him to see. His role changes from surveyor of the High Street to general confidant and focal point of unity in the story. Every so often the state of his knowledge of affairs is ascertained, but his presence becomes more and more cumbersome, and long before the story ends he has stopped earning his keep. In parts V and VI he is no longer consulted, and he reappears only to take his bow as the story concludes. 'A Changed Man' shows the problems Hardy was up against in his use of an observer. Either the spectator must be quite mobile, or the story must be quite static. As the plot of 'A Changed Man' necessitates Laura's removal from the 'raking view' of the oriel window, the invalid's incapacity cripples the form. 'A Changed Man' is a clear case of Hardy's failure to reconcile technique and theme. In most of the stories in which he resorts to the use of a spectatorial stance a similar failure occurs, and the transition to another mode usually involves a certain degree of technical clumsiness. One of the few occasions on which the technique is successfully applied is in 'The Melancholy Hussar of the German Legion', where it is used at a climactic moment in the story. The ritual of military execution by a firing squad is presented as a theatrical spectacle whose effect is heightened by Phyllis's presence as audience at her lover's death:

> What she beheld at first awed and perplexed her; then she stood rigid, her fingers hooked to the wall, her eyes staring out of her head, and her face hardened as if to stone.

A detailed description of the execution follows.

Such staging of a scene with the observer as audience at a remove from the dramatic action is successful but difficult to sustain. One of Hardy's rare attempts to construct an entire short story on this theatrical principle is 'What the Shepherd Saw'. It cannot be rated among his best stories because, as is so often the case in Hardy's depiction of aristocratic life, drama gives way to melodrama and the stilted dialogue becomes unintentionally comic: 'You are a Duchess, and I am Fred Ogbourne.'

The story, however, is an interesting experiment in the crossing of three of Hardy's short story modes, the narrated story, the 'tradition', and the story written from a spectatorial viewpoint. At the outset the tale is entrusted to a narrator and begun as he used to begin it 'in the good old-fashioned way'; Hardy inserts reminders of the continued presence of a story-teller in the second paragraph with the parenthetic 'he would say' and 'he said'. By the third paragraph the narrator no longer obtrudes, and interest is focused on the observer, the shepherd boy. In the early part of his tale Hardy labours to establish the shepherd in his role of spectator. When we first hear of him it is his 'eye' which is mentioned, and his first action is that of 'abstractedly looking . . . at the scene without'. Keeping watch is, in fact, the young shepherd's chief function, and the hut in which he is placed is a look-out post. What the young shepherd witnesses is presented as a drama (or melodrama) with a Druidical trilithon as backdrop. The two characters in the first scene, the Duke's wife and her former admirer, seem to be aware that they are playing dramatic roles. He accuses her of concealing her heart in 'made-up speeches', while she reproaches him for adopting a 'tragedy tone'. When they exit in opposite directions a third character, the Duke, appears 'upon the scene'. He, too, has been an audience at the previous encounter, but so remote from it that to him it appeared a 'dumb show'. Hardy's theatrical design is made absolutely explicit in his comment upon the Duke's exit: 'The boy remained in the hut confronting the trilithon as if he expected yet more actors on the scene, but nobody else appeared.'

The story is divided into four acts, referred to as four nights, and the young shepherd is placed in a position to observe all the action, even to become acquainted with the contents of a letter. ('I think I can repeat the exact words', says the Duchess.) On condition that the boy forgot what he has seen, he is promoted from his role as humble watcher to that of educated man of affairs. In the last act of the story the 'double entendre' of its title is revealed. There was a concealed member in the audience at the ducal drama, one not bound to silence. On his deathbed the old shepherd confesses what he saw. The Duke dies. The story is told by the former shepherd to the proper authorities and the fiction comes full circle as one such 'proper authority', a Justice of the Peace, now narrates it. In the final paragraph Hardy also links this tale to a local 'tradition', and shows how ghost stories became attached to a particular site. The story of the Duke's crime has given rise to ghost stories in which the murder is spectrally re-enacted with present-day shepherds as audience. A third possible layer of meaning in the title is revealed.

'A Tradition of Eighteen Hundred and Four' is another story of the 'what the shepherd saw' variety, but on this occasion there is a lengthy introduction to place the fiction in an historical context. The use of first-person narration like the use of semi-dialect in this story is a device to lend verisimilitude to an unlikely tale. 'Selby's manner of narrating the adventure' was to be the touchstone of its authenticity. How well it succeeded we already know.

The simulation of theatre in 'The Melancholy Hussar of the

Foreign Legion' and in 'What the Shepherd Saw' recalls Hardy's association of the 'play-shape' with the 'instinctive, primitive, narrative shape' in his defence of 'stage-form' in *The Dynasts*:

> this play-shape is essentially, if not quite literally, at one with the instinctive, primitive, narrative shape. In legends and old ballads, in the telling of 'an owre true tale' by country-folk on winter nights over a dying fire, the place and time are briefly indicated at the beginning in almost all cases; and then the body of the action follows as what he said and what she said, the action being often suggested by the speeches alone. This likeness between the order of natural recital and the order of theatrical utility may be accidental; but there it is; and to write Scene so-and-so, Line so-and-so, instead of Once upon a time, At such a place, is a trifling variation that makes no difference to the mental images raised . . .[5]

Whether it was the 'play-shape' of the 'owre true tale' that prompted Hardy to further theatrical experimentation in the short stories must remain conjectural. My guess is that his self-confessed habit of slipping into the role of observer rather than participant led him to assume an observer stance in the stories, and of this the observer/audience viewpoint was a logical extension.

Hardy seems to have sensed that a story written from the viewpoint of a spectator would have that formal shape and coherence which eluded him in so many of his stories, and he continued to toy with this technique into old age. The fifth of his misnamed *Plots for Five Unpublished Short Stories* is not a single plot-outline but a projected series of outlines for stories, some of which are entitled, significantly enough, 'Glimpse the First', 'Glimpse the Second', etc. From the handwriting and the dates on the backs of the papers used, Evelyn Hardy has concluded that these 'Glimpses' are a product of Hardy's old age.[6] Most of these tales were to be narrated in the first person by a sparrow, and here Hardy seems to have envisaged entire stories written from the viewpoint of an observer with no authorial intrusion. Even the conclusion of the story is to arise naturally out of this convention:

> The stories may be broken off at any convenient point by darkness closing in, and the sparrow being so sleepy that it tucks its head under its wing and sees no more: or by a boy or a cat frightening it away.

In the early story, 'What the Shepherd Saw', Hardy's most sustained use of the observer convention is presented in the context of the oral tale and the 'tradition'. His late bird's-eye 'glimpses' of the human drama represent a complete break with the subject-matter and techniques of the rural tale, but these stories were never written. Perhaps the emancipation was never fully achieved.

Perhaps Hardy did not want to achieve it. Possibly because it had helped in the formation of his aesthetic, certain features of the 'owre true tale' were well adapted to his artistic purposes. Hardy thought that the story must be concerned with the uncommon in human experience while preserving the common touch:

> The writer's problem is how to strike the balance between the uncommon and the ordinary so as on the one hand to give interest, on the other to give reality (*Life*, p.150).

> A story must be striking enough to be worth the telling. Therein lies the problem—to reconcile the average with that uncommonness . . . (*Life*, p.239).

The rural tales of his childhood achieved this combination of the ordinary and the extraordinary by telling of uncommon happenings in the lives of local people, how a young girl witnessed the military execution of her lover, how a rejected mistress blighted the beauty of a new wife. In these tales which Hardy retold and in others which he invented, uncommonness lies in the events and not in the characters. Simple shepherd boys observe ducal murders and Napoleonic exploits; a village child is kidnapped by a Mephistophelian fiddler.

The biographical bias in oral story-telling, in Solomon Selby's narrative, for example, was eminently suited to Hardy's 'idiosyncratic mode of regard'. His stories are leisurely chronicles, many of them covering a lifetime. They do not end with wedding-bells but follow their protagonists into the frequently unhappy ever-after. Netty Sargent is not left flushed with triumph at the success of her ruse to secure herself a husband and a home. She is pursued into the less than blissful future in which her husband takes to beating her. Hardy needed a lengthy time-span in order to explore his favourite theme, the satires of circumstance:

> As, in looking at a carpet, by following one colour a certain pattern is suggested, by following another colour, another, so in life the seer should watch the pattern among general things which his idiosyncrasy moves him to observe, and describe that alone . . . (*Life*, p.153).

As a short story writer Hardy is interested above all in patterns of irony. He likes to balance event against event, to reveal the relationships between seemingly unconnected happenings, to bring about strange conjunctions. 'A Mere Interlude' is entirely composed of a series of interconnected ironic situations. On her way home to be married to the elderly David Heddegan, Baptista marries a young admirer, Charles Stow, who is drowned the same day. Baptista proceeds on her way as if nothing untoward had occurred and marries Heddegan. This behaviour precipitates a series of ironic events which Hardy delights in exploiting. The first night of Baptista's honeymoon, for example, is spent in a room from which her previous husband's corpse has just been removed to be placed in an adjoining room:

> That night she lay between the two men she had married—Heddegan on the one hand, and on the other through the partition against which the bed stood, Charles Stow.

This is the kind of ironic situation in which Hardy loves to indulge in a poem like 'The Workbox' or in Elfride's courtship on Jethway's tomb. In 'A Mere Interlude' this situational irony is framed by the larger structural irony that Baptista who married in order to escape teaching, because of her guilty secret, is blackmailed into acting as governess to her husband's illegitimate brood.

'A Mere Interlude' lent itself to cheap verbal ironies like Heddegan's remark—'here 'tis quiet as the grave'. The ironies of 'The Withered Arm' are of a different order. This is a story in which the weight of the action is amassed towards the ending, but it is better than other stories which work towards an ironic culmination in that it is not merely glibly ironic. Its characters are three-dimensional, its superstitions have subtle psychological dimensions, its ironic repercussions verge on the tragic.

Hardy must not be blamed for his failure to write Joycean epiphanies, to seize on a significant moment and treat it with dramatic fulness. His art is concerned not with the isolated incident but with the connected series. 'The Waiting Supper' does not focus on one night's failure to achieve union but on the before and after, on the pattern of repeated failure which makes a couple into 'time's laughingstocks'. With the remarkable exception of 'The Three Strangers' life's little ironies rarely unfold themselves for Hardy in a single evening. Retribution is delayed. The Spirit Ironic may not even complete the pattern within one life-time, as in 'The Doctor's Legend'.

Hardy's ironic mode of regard demanded that he should have whole life-times in his keeping, and this is not a fact to be deplored. But it must be admitted that he has the defect we may expect of such a virtue. His weakness is a certain garrulousness. He is over-diffuse, and there are few stories which would not be improved by a little judicious pruning. However, better a little overgrowth than no growth at all. There are few of his stories that we would willingly be without.

VI

Lennart A. Björk:

PSYCHOLOGICAL VISION AND SOCIAL CRITICISM IN "DESPERATE REMEDIES" AND "JUDE THE OBSCURE"

Few readers of Thomas Hardy would disagree with J. Hillis Miller's observations that 'Love is Hardy's obsessive theme both in his fiction and in his verse' and that 'Hardy's sense of the quality of human existence is more important than his ideas.'[1] But to accept that Hardy's central theme is love, and that his work offers more of an emotional than of an intellectual stimulus, does not necessarily imply that one should neglect to examine whether his choice of an elementary emotion—love—as main theme has any definable intellectual basis as well as ideological purpose. To attempt such an examination with special regard to two of Hardy's novels, *Desperate Remedies* and *Jude the Obscure,* is the somewhat far-reaching aim of this paper. Obviously, all I can hope to do within the scope of a single lecture is to outline the basic frameworks only of Hardy's psychological vision and social criticism.

The special nature of Hardy's favourite theme—love—makes it reasonable to assume that its intellectual basis is to be found in his view of human personality, that is, in what is here called his psychological vision. My first step, therefore, will be to consider some external and internal pieces of evidence of this vision. The second step, dealing with the ideological purpose of his main theme, will be to try to define the major trend of his social criticism. This will lead on to a consideration of the interaction of Hardy's psychological vision and social criticism; I shall try to show how the theme of love—with love seen in its larger context of human emotions generally—is a key element, if not the key element, of Hardy's censure of modern society, as this is dramatized in *Desperate Remedies* and *Jude the Obscure,* the first and the last of his published novels.

In discussing Hardy's psychological vision in relation to his social criticism, I shall also propose to demonstrate that Hardy may have been rather profoundly influenced, early in life, by the French utopian socialist Charles Fourier. My analysis of Hardy's views on human nature and modern society does not, however, depend on this proposed influence, but draws, I believe, sufficient support from evidence in his fiction. And, as it is all too easy to become too uncritically partial in advocating a hitherto virtually ignored influence on Hardy, I should like to emphasize that I do not in any way wish to argue that Fourier was the only, or even dominating, influence in these matters. But on the basis of available evidence, both external and internal, I should like to suggest that Fourier may have played a significant role in that complex cluster of intellectual and emotional forces that reinforced those idiosyncrasies and concerns which Hardy's own nature and environment had made him particularly susceptible to.

I

To take my first step, then—to look at evidence of Hardy's psychological vision—I turn to his autobiography, that rich source of his preferences and prejudices. *The Life of Thomas Hardy* offers unambiguous evidence of Hardy's own temperamental predilection for, as well as his considered opinion on, an anti-rationalist view of human life and nature. I select here only a few examples. The earliest is from 1872. Having found that the income from his writing is insufficient, he feels forced to give up his imaginative work and turn to the financially more rewarding architectural profession. This is against his personal feelings, but he decides 'to stifle his constitutional tendency to care for life only as an emotion and not as a scientific game'; a few years later he reflects, again, 'that he was "up against" the position of having to carry on his life not as an emotion, but as a scientific game'.[2]

His anti-rationalism, or perhaps rather his awareness of his own anti-rationalism, seems to have grown still more pronounced later in life. In a letter on rationalism in 1901, he remarks that his 'own interest lies largely in non-rationalistic subjects, since non-rationality seems, so far as one can perceive, to be the principle of the Universe (*Life*, p. 309). In another letter from 1915 he denies being 'a hard-headed rationalist' (*Life*, p. 369). In a third letter written with the help of his wife in 1920, he again states his position unequivocally: 'He [Hardy] says he thinks that he is rather an irrationalist than a rationalist, on account of his inconsistencies . . . Moreover, he thinks he could show . . . that human actions are not ruled by reason at all in the last resort' (*Life*, p. 403).

It is not surprising to find the same psychological view permeating Hardy's relatively few aesthetic pronouncements. In harmony with his notion that 'in representations of the world, the passions ought to be proportioned as in the world itself', Hardy justifies in 1887 his appreciation of Shelley's *Lament* and Byron's *Childe Harold:* 'I know this is an old-fashioned taste; but it is a well-considered relapse on my part, for though in past years I have been very modern in this matter I begin to feel that mere intellectual subtlety will not hold its own in time to come against the straightforward expression of good feeling.'[3] Some sixteen years later Hardy evidences the same disparagement of intellectualism in literature. De-emphasizing the importance of the philosophy of *The Dynasts,* he writes: 'I am convinced that, whether we uphold this or any other conjecture on the cause of things, men's lives and actions will be little affected thereby, these being less dependent on abstract reasoning than on the involuntary intersocial emotions' (Orel, p. 146).

These psychological speculations from Hardy's later years complement the autobiographical notes from earlier years; they show the same anti-rationalist bias, and the same tendency to establish a dichotomy of emotion and reason, head and heart, which we shall see also characterize his novels. However, before turning to the evidence of the fiction, it may be helpful to look at some external evidence of his interest in psychology, and see whether it is possible to discern and characterize any particular sources of influence.

There is a good deal of such evidence in Hardy's *Literary Notes.*[4] Of particular interest are the entries from Charles Fourier and the positivist philosopher Auguste Comte. I shall, however, now have to restrict my comments to Fourier alone. On the fly-leaf of a notebook, labelled 'Literary Notes I', which Hardy started compiling in the spring of 1876, is pasted a chart of Fourier's system of the twelve passions. The chart itself, however, is dated 1863 and was, consequently, drawn when Hardy was 23. On the back of the sheet there is the heading 'Diagrams shewing Human passions, Mind, & Character—Designed by Thos. Hardy. 1863'. Below are four figures, one graph and three tree designs, illustrating the charts on the first page and some other Fourier ideas. The graph, top left on the page, indicates Fourier's division of life into four major phases. The first tree design, bottom left, shows the trunk of a tree growing out of a base called 'Humanity'; the trunk is labelled 'Passions'; two roots, or vines, grow up from the base on either side of the trunk and wind around it. The left vine is called 'Intellect', the right 'Will', and both are subdivided. The second tree design, top right, has no base indicated. There is, however, a horizontal line dividing the trunk into two sections. The lower may indicate the roots, as the trunk is here split vertically into three parts, named, from left to right, 'Intellect', 'Passions', and 'Will'; 'Intellect' and 'Will' are subdivided. The three parts unite shortly before the horizontal line, at the level of which 'Amalgamn.' is written. Just above there is also the notation 'Moral Harmony', before the tree again splits into three main branches, of which only the middle one is annotated. It is labelled 'Affectives dominant' before it subdivides into four minor branches called, from left to right, 'Friendship domin^{t}.' 'Love dominant', 'Familism dom^{t}.', 'Ambition dominant'. There is a cross-section of the second tree design bottom right. It shows 'Will' at the centre, divided into two parts but not annotated. The middle circle of the cross section is labelled 'Intellect' and subdivided into three parts; a dotted line projects from each part to an R, D, and S respectively, supposedly abbreviations for Retentiveness, Discrimination, and Similarity—the same division of Intellect as in the first tree design. The outer and largest section of the tree is called 'Passions'. To the left is a notation referring to the cross-section: 'Intellect—the *adviser* of P. & W.'.

This is not the place to go into any detailed interpretation of these charts and figures. What I should like to emphasize here is that this earliest extant piece of evidence of Hardy's interest in psychological speculations is based on Fourier's analysis of human nature in his book *The Passions of the Human Soul* (transl. into English in 1851), and that the charts and diagrams reflect Fourier's dogmatic assertion that 'thoughts are not the cause of life but the effects', and that 'the passions and attractions of the soul . . . [are] the motive springs'. Hardy's figures, that is, assign a similarly central role to the passions. This is particularly true in the first tree design in which the passions constitute the whole trunk. And, in spite of the different positions of the faculties in the two tree designs, there is no contradiction, at least not regarding the relationship between 'Passions' and 'Intellect'. The small notation to the second figure states that Intellect is only the 'adviser'—not the ruler, that is, of Passions and Will. The vines winding about the trunk in the first tree design may be seen as assigning a similarly restraining effect to Intellect in that design. What may seem more disturbing for my discussion of the polarity of head and heart in the psychological vision of both Fourier and Hardy is that both drawings, as well as the charts, show a tripartite division of the human faculties: Passions, Intellect, and Action or Energy ('Will' in Hardy). However, in Fourier's discussions of the role of the passions in human life, the adversary is always the intellect; Will is ignored. This is also the case in Hardy's novels, as I shall try to demonstrate below. It is to be noted here that the 'Will' of these notations is a psychological concept and thus different from the 'Immanent Will' of *The Dynasts,* which is largely a philosophical concept in a cosmic context and thus not of immediate relevance here. I am not arguing that Will in the latter sense is absent from the novels but only that it falls beyond the scope of this paper. Whereas, then, an interpretation of the details of these charts and figures must remain tentative, it seems possible to be more certain about the general trend:

in attributing a fundamental role to the passions, the diagrams of 1863 project an 'affective' psychology, or a psychology of feeling, from which the dichotomy of head and heart can easily emerge. In view of the potentially high significance of this evidence of Hardy's familiarity with Fourier, a brief synopsis of the Frenchman's thought may be helpful.

Charles Fourier (1772-1837) was an anti-rationalist; he believed that emotion or passion—not thought—was the motive power, the cause of human activity, and that 'the all-pervasive misery of mankind stemmed from the suppression of passions'.[5] It is not surprising, therefore, that his psychological vision, his theory of 'the passions of the human soul', is at the very centre not only of his highly complex system of the universe—which is of no relevance here—but also of his social criticism: 'I am the advocate of the twelve passions, and I maintain that, if these exist, social order ought to secure their enjoyment to the classes of all ages who may seek for it'.[6] Since, according to Fourier, modern Christian civilization did not allow a harmonious development of natural human passions, he launched what has been called the 'most circumstantial attack on the uses of civilization since Rousseau'.[7] Of this many-faceted attack we are here—in addition to his psychological vision—concerned only with his castigation of Christianity, in particular Christian morality as manifested in the sacrament of marriage; his views on the Christian attitude to sensual pleasures; and, his plea for a new social morality.

Fourier's censure of the institution of marriage is closely connected with his views on love, and one of his major objections to matrimony is that it corrupts the natural affection between the sexes. In a chapter on love he distinguishes between 'spiritual affinity' and 'material affinity'. Marriage, Fourier argues, encourages 'material affinity' only:

> There are not wanting in civilization those loves . . . in which the material and spiritual tie exists on both sides; but these attachments only spring up in the case of couples who do not love each other in a parliamentary fashion, by virtue of an act published and registered at the magistrate's office. All these loves are violations of the law . . . The conditions of marriage, and the pecuniary traffic which it imposes on love, scarcely leave any access to the sentimental tie, reduce the household *(ménage)* to a cold and mercantile union, the two principals of which soon become tired of each other, and from which there can only result a conflict of universal falsehood, neither of the parties being willing to adhere sincerely to the permanent fidelity required by this tie, which is so foreign to the wishes of nature (*The Passions*, I, 357-58).

In the hierarchy of different kinds of love and emotional bonds between man and woman which Fourier here recognizes, he clearly emphasizes the value and importance of sensual pleasures, and in his writings he consistently criticizes the Christian morality prevalent in modern civilization for vilifying them. Like Hardy, he points to pre-Christian attitudes as a healthy alternative: 'Antiquity, nearer to the true religious spirit than we are, deified the pleasures and made them objects of worship; it seemed to guess the intention of the Deity, which is to lead us to social harmony through the pleasures. The modern age thinks otherwise; it turns the pleasures into ridicule, or rather erects them into vices, even when they are free from excess' *(The Passions,* I, 247).

Fourier's utopian vision has, of course, a more comprehensive aim than to secure free indulgence in sensual pleasures. Perhaps the most important element of his social criticism is his insistence on the need for a radically new social morality. What seems to be the most vital component of this new morality he calls 'unityism'. Frank E. Manuel gives a helpful analysis of the meaning of the term: 'When unityism is treated as a distinct passion it is the one which links a man's happiness with all that surrounds him, with all of mankind . . . It is not alien to the benevolence of the Scottish moralists. When Fourier was at a loss for positive ways to communicate his meaning he defined unityism as the polar opposite of egotism, the all-pervasive emotion of the state of civilization.'[8] In this new moral atmosphere love would, as Fourier phrases it, be 'applied to universal unity' and not to small exclusive units of the family kind. To this I shall return when discussing *Jude.*

It would have been contrary to Hardy's well-documented eclecticism—and sound common sense—to adopt Fourier's dogmatic system of thought without modifications. It seems, in fact, probable that Hardy rejected more than he accepted in the Frenchman's thought. For instance, Hardy's fiction does not show any traces of Fourier's many distinctions between various groups and kinds of passions. But in focusing on the passion of love, Hardy follows Fourier. And, in spite of all differences, the general trend, as well as several details, of Fourier's ideas outlined above is, I suggest, recognizable in Hardy's novels.

Of course, similarity proves neither direct borrowing nor influence. Furthermore, the simple polarity of intellect and emotion in Fourier's psychological vision, his attacks on Christian morality and the sacrament of marriage for curtailing man's passions and social ethics, his advocacy of sensual pleasures, and his juxtaposition of pagan and Christian attitudes, are in no way original. Despite the necessary reservations of this kind, I believe there remain strong and valid reasons for suggesting the possibility of a profound influence on Hardy from the French utopian. For, in addition to the particulars of Fourier's ideas indicated above, it is important to keep in mind, when assessing the probability of Fourier's presence in Hardy's fiction, that all of Fourier's social criticism is inseparably linked to his view of human personality. Admittedly, this is to some extent true about most social critics, but it is rare to have the psychological basis so explicitly and purposefully stated. As I shall try to show, the same intimate relationship between a similar psychological vision and social criticism is to be found in Hardy's fiction.

II

Having thus briefly considered evidences of, and suggested a particular influence on, Hardy's psychological vision, I shall now proceed to explore what I find to be the main trend or direction of Hardy's social criticism.

The Poor Man and the Lady, Thomas Hardy's unpublished first novel, is not extant in its original form. From Hardy's own account, however, it was 'a sweeping satire of the squirearchy and nobility, London society, the vulgarity of the middle class, modern Christianity, church-restoration, and political and domestic morals in general, the author's views, in fact, being obviously those of a young man with a passion for reforming the world—those of many a young man before and after him; the tendency of the writing being socialistic, not to say revoluntionary' *(Life,* p. 61). The social criticism was in fact so one-sided, in addition to being evidently artistically crude, that Alexander Macmillan, to whom Hardy had first submitted the novel, felt obliged to point out to the young reformer that his 'chastisement' of the upper classes would 'fall harmless from its very excess', that 'nothing could justify such a wholesale blackening of a class', and that Hardy's 'black-wash' would not be 'recognized as anything more than ignorant misrepresentation'.[9] Hardy's exaggerated social criticism was also censured by none other than George Meredith, who read the manuscript for Chapman and Hall, the second publisher Hardy turned to. Meredith 'strongly' advised Hardy 'not to "nail his colours to the mast" so definitely in a first book, if he wished to do anything practical in literature; for if he printed so pronounced a thing he would be attacked on all sides by the conventional reviewers, and his future injured' *(Life,* p. 61). It would have taken a man of considerably more self-assurance than Hardy to neglect advice from critics of such status. Hardy took the manuscript away and later dismembered it; some scenes were incorporated in other novels, and presumably a major part of it was adapted as *An Indiscretion in the Life of an Heiress.*

The fact that Hardy did not engage in such explicit social criticism again until his last novel, *Jude the Obscure,* is, of course, open to various interpretations. It is quite possible, as Michael Millgate suggests, that 'the kind of emotions, opinions, and attitudes which had gone into *The Poor Man and the Lady*' were gradually repressed, not surrendered, until they surfaced again in *Jude.* And

Millgate's explanation of what he calls the 'element of circularity' in Hardy's writing of fiction may well be correct: 'Hardy's unhappy experience with his first book seems to have taught him not that the concept of the social instrumentality of fiction was invalid, but that it was commercially impracticable, at least for a new and unknown author.'[10]

Without denying the highly probable, and understandable, financial considerations behind Hardy's abandonment of his crusade for 'revolutionary' and 'socialistic' ideas, it is also plausible, it seems to me, to attribute some importance to other and less narrowly financial and pragmatic motives. Especially in view of Hardy's 'affective' psychology, it seems possible that he would have realized already at an early stage that his major concern as a writer, apart from his aesthetics, was more with man's emotional and spiritual situation than with his political or economic, a realization the more probable since, after all—and this must always be remembered in discussing Hardy—an elementary emotion, love, is consistently the primary subject of his fiction. Simply because his first novel was rejected largely on account of its biased social criticism, it is all too easy to exaggerate, I believe, the social commitment on Hardy's part. One should not perhaps read too much into his own statement in the *Life* that 'portions of the book apparently taken in earnest by both his readers [Macmillan and Morley] had no foundation either in Hardy's beliefs or his experience' *(Life,* p. 61), but it does suggest that the revolutionary urge that prompted the book might have been a temporary one. This is also the impression given by a letter from Hardy to Macmillan, as he waited for further comments on the first novel: 'As the days go on, and you do not write, and my production begins to assume that small and unimportant shape everything one does assumes as the time and *mood* in which one did it recedes from the present, I almost feel that I don't care what happens to the book, as long as something happens' (Morgan, p. 91). Again, the evidence is slim, but the tone of the letter is hardly that of an ardent socialist anxious for the world to partake of his radical views. To give up explicit social criticism of the kind found in *The Poor Man and the Lady* may not, therefore, have been a tactical step only, taken at great expense to Hardy's social conscience. It may also be true that the new kind of social criticism which we find in Hardy's published novels is the result, not of a change of his social views, but a change of focus of his social criticism, from what appears to have been primarily economic and political issues in his first novel to the prevailing religious, philosophical, and moral ideas of modern society and their effects on man's emotional and spiritual life; to concerns, that is, more intimately related to Hardy's psychological vision and to his preoccupation with love as his major subject matter.

It is in this sense, I believe, that Hardy's 'social' criticism can most profitably be discussed. This is not to say that Hardy failed to see the relationship between the overall social situation of a society and its intellectual and spiritual life. This connection he had found, if nowhere else, clearly stated in the positivist social psychology which the *Literary Notes* show that he had read. Nor do I mean to suggest that Hardy was aloof from political or economic problems either as a man or as a writer. There is abundant evidence of his sensitivity to social injustice and inequality—and such evidence will be considered below—but I suggest that these issues are not of the first importance in his novels.

As is the case with Hardy's psychological vision, the various aspects of his social interests—in economic and political issues on the one hand, and in emotional, intellectual, and spiritual on the other—are also well reflected in his *Literary Notes.* These notes, extending over so many years, establish, I believe, the potentially most important influences on Hardy's social thought and, consequently, also the essential frame of reference within which the nature of the social criticism of his novels is best understood. Again, I can here select only a few examples, and I shall give instances that at first may seem to contradict my thesis, in the belief, that is, that Hardy's fiction will provide sufficient support for my argument.

Many entries, then, in the *Literary Notes* testify to Hardy's concern for social injustices, inequalities, and suffering, both past and present. He took an interest, for instance, in J. P. Mahaffy's account of 'the conflict between rich and poor' in Ancient Greece and the cruelties perpetrated there by whoever was in power (entry 555), at the same time as he noted that 'Athenian society was not burdened with an aristocracy of mere birth, overriding that of intellect' (entry 573). In Hutchins' *History of Dorset* he observed how medieval villeinage deprived the sons of poor people of education (entry 594), and also from Hutchins he copied one of the most moving entries on social tragedies due to poverty and inadequate social organization, '*Whipped for Vagrancy*—Ed. Bayly wth a pale thin visage & light brown hair aged 10 years or thereabouts, & Mary Bayly wth a pale thin visage & light brown hair aged 12 or hereabouts were whippt as vagrants Oct. 6, 1697, & sent towards Boxell in Sussex, their last place of residence' (entry 599).

Class distinctions and tensions are also objects of considerable attention in the *Literary Notes*—as they are in Hardy's novels. The very first entry in vol. I of the notebooks proper reads: '*Subordination,*—"The grand scheme of subordination" [class to class] Boswell',—an ironic introduction, that is, to a great number of entries on the subject, ranging from the sweeping generalization that 'Privilege is illogical, unjust, & undesirable (i.e. class & wealth)' to more specific comments on the phenomenon of subordination inherent in the English political and class systems.

Whereas, then, Hardy entered many observations on social inequalities and injustices, the notes do not indicate much interest in political movements or individual persons engaged in alleviating such social problems. The notes show, and this is important to the overall picture of Hardy's intellectual background, that he read many writers with revolutionary social views, whether positivist, socialist, radical, or utopian, such as Balzac, Baudelaire, Bjornstjerne Bjornson, Victor Hugo, Charles Kingsley, Leopardi, William Morris, Alfred de Musset, Jean Paul Richter, Zola, and a great number of positivist writers. It is indeed probable that Hardy sympathized to no little extent with their views and concerns. The point here is, however, that Hardy studied social problems not in specifically social or political documents or movements but through the medium of literature, and often, as a great number of entries in the *Literary Notes* reveal, from the point of view of the humanistic idealism characteristic of Matthew Arnold's criticism of nineteenth-century society. Hardy's approach is, of course, understandable in a novelist and no cause for great excitement or far-reaching conclusions, but it is a fact to consider when we try to define Hardy's own kind of interest in social issues—and the nature of the social criticism conveyed in his novels. I should like to stress here, that it is far from my intention to depict Hardy as an anti-democratic or anti-socialistic ogre. On the contrary, I have drawn attention to evidence in the *Literary Notes* of his interest in, and implied compassion for, human suffering due to economic and political inequalities and injustices, for the specific purpose of emphasizing Hardy's awareness of these issues, despite the fact that he does not make them primary concerns in his fiction—to which I shall now move.

III

Desperate Remedies (1871), Hardy's first published novel, introduces themes and concerns—some of limited, others of uninhibited scope—that we have come to think of as typically Hardyan: the distressed love of two young people under temporary social and economic pressures; the problem of individual 'success' in relation to social status; and the all-embracing conflict between what Hardy considered natural human emotions on the one hand and traditionally accepted social and moral values on the other.

The young lovers Cytherea Graye and Edward Springrove are separated by accidents which involve dire financial results for both: the illness and consequent poverty of Cytherea's brother Owen, and the burning down of the uninsured cottages of Edward's father. Their situation is further aggravated by the unfortunate coincidence that both are financially dependent on the wealthy and strong-willed Miss Aldclyffe whose illegitimate son Aeneas Manston has fallen in love with Cytherea, and who has unscrupulously enlisted the support of his mother in his courtship. Thus, the natural attachment of Cytherea and Edward clashes with the interests of Miss Aldclyffe and her son, who do not hesitate to exert considerable pressure on the two lovers as well as on their families.

In this melodramatic course of events the simple basis of Hardy's pyschological vision is clearly manifested: the opposition of reason and emotion, of head and heart. As Cytherea finds that she cannot resist her love for Edward, she exclaims 'Ah Brain, there is one in me stronger than you', and when she tries to shift her affections from Edward to Aeneas she realizes that 'she must once and for all choose between the dictates of her understanding and those of her heart'. The same tension is felt by her two suitors. Edward's passions are so kindled by Cytherea that his 'judgment cannot keep pace with its [the emotion's] rise'; Aeneas's 'susceptibility of heart where feminine beauty' is concerned is so strong as to require 'all the ballast of brain . . . to confine [it] within reasonable channels'.

In *Desperate Remedies,* as in most later novels, it is the inner struggle of the female protagonist that is in focus. Cytherea, like some later Hardy heroines, finds that her freedom of choice between 'the dictates of her understanding and those of her heart' gradually becomes depressingly limited by external considerations. Owen, her sick and destitute brother, urges her to marry Aeneas: 'Act in obedience to the dictates of common sense . . . and dread the sharp sting of poverty'. Attempting to neglect her own feelings, Cytherea decides to follow Owen's pragmatic advice and marry for financial security. At the marriage ceremony, however, she catches sight of Edward, and her old passion reasserts itself. But her brother, speaking for himself and society, is soon there to impress upon her the necessity of disregarding her own feelings and, if need be, of practising hypocrisy for the sake of her social respectability: 'your duty to society, and those about you, requires that you should live with (at any rate) all the appearance of a good wife, and try to love your husband'.

It seems no coincidence that Cytherea's integrity is threatened by the institution of marriage; for, in *Desperate Remedies,* as in Hardy's later novels, marriage is one of the main tools or agents of civilization in suppressing individual liberty. In *Desperate Remedies* the threat is linked with the materialistic aspects of matrimony. There is, for instance, no doubt as to the financial motives behind Owen's urging that his sister marry Aeneas; and, realizing her situation, Cytherea exclaims, 'Marrying for a home—

what a mockery . . . '. Thus, facing her life-long union with the man she has been forced to marry by outside pressures, Cytherea points to the discrepancy between the professed high ideals of the sacrament of marriage and the actual base reality of it in her case.

In spite of these disparaging views of the Christian institution of matrimony, the strictures on Christian morality in *Desperate Remedies* are far from the overt denunciations in *Tess of the d'Urbervilles* and *Jude the Obscure.* Apart from the marriage question and a humorous discussion between Aeneas and the local postman, the criticism of the creed as a whole is rather oblique. The novel dramatizes, to be sure, the suffering which results from the violation of human emotions by the social and moral values here concentrated in the marriage contract, but it refrains from any outspoken and far-reaching conclusions.

The general socio-economic criticism is also less harsh than what *The Poor Man and the Lady* seems to have contained, or what *Jude* was to offer. Hardy conveys the idea, however, that the social values of modern civilization are compatible only with the single-minded devotion to social climbing. So, Edward explains to Cytherea, this is why, as a sensitive artist, he cannot expect any social distinction: 'the long and the short of the matter is, that men must stick to a thing if they want to succeed in it—not giving way to over-much admiration for the flowers they see in other people's borders; which I am afraid has been my case'. The reader is not expected to pity Edward for this, since the kind of success denied him—financial prosperity—is not necessarily a sensible aim in life, as Hardy implies in the somewhat ponderous conclusion to the very first chapter: 'But what is wisdom really? A steady handling of any means to bring about any end necessary to happiness. Yet whether one's end be the usual end—a wealthy position in life—or no, the name of wisdom is seldom applied but to the means to that usual end.' The rest of the novel argues that the wisdom of the means is equally questionable—if one applies the criterion of a harmonious development of human character: 'The man who works up a good income has had no time to learn love to its solemn extreme; the man who has learnt that has had no time to get rich.' Thus, although in relatively mild phraseology, *Desperate Remedies* rejects society's socio-economic values. It is to be noted that the ultimate reason for the rejection is the effect these values have on human emotions, especially love.

The relative ease with which the happy ending is finally brought about may at least partly be explained by the emphasis on economic matters in the novel. Once the immediate financial pressures are removed, there is no other major obstacle. The case is different in later novels, particularly, as we shall see, in *Jude*. In *Desperate Remedies,* however, the economic problems are seen primarily in relation to the love story, and do not serve any important overall function as social criticism.

In the conflict between head and heart in the novel, the heart is always at a disadvantage. No matter what the antagonistic side is called—Understanding, Judgment, Brain, Common Sense, Intellect, or Head—it is constantly supported by the economic, social, moral, and religious principles of modern civilization. So when Cytherea tries to follow 'the dictates of her understanding' it means assessing her actions in terms of possible material gain and according to accepted moral criteria. It is easy to see the interdependence of Hardy's psychological vision and his social criticism.

My brief discussion of *Desperate Remedies* implies important affinities between the novel and the ideas of Charles Fourier. These similarities are both general and specific. We find the overall psychological vision with its anti-rationalist view of human nature and the broad criticism of modern civilization as well as the detailed criticism of the ethics of marriage, with the objections to the marriage licence as a business contract and to the whole institution *per se* as an infringement on individual liberty. This is not to say, of course, that either the 'affective' psychology or the social criticism of *Desperate Remedies* is a dramatization in fictional form of Fourier's *The Passions of the Human Soul;* nor to claim that Hardy's ideas and attitudes are original, or to deny other influences. But, since the major psychological and sociological ideas of *Desperate Remedies* are all to be found in the works of Fourier that Hardy read before writing the novel, it seems legitimate to claim that these analogies—in connection with the conspicuous evidence in the *Literary Notes* discussed above—are indeed significant, and deserve attention in any attempt to distinguish the various influences in Hardy's intellectual background.

IV

Jude the Obscure (1895) marks the clearest and most poignant rendering in prose of Hardy's psychological vision with its twofold division of emotion and intellect. The novel describes, as Hardy explains in the Preface, the 'deadly war waged between flesh and spirit'. With its religious overtones, the terminology is new, but the psychology and the theme are obviously the same as before. In *Jude,* however, despite its high-pitched tone, Hardy seems to have acquired a sophisticated perspective on the polarity of emotion and intellect which the earlier novels, with very few exceptions, do not show. The opposing forces are now arraigned in armour of elaborate intellectual design: there is the conspicuous effort to attire the powers of the heart in Hellenic or Pagan and those of the head in Christian suits. Also, and to a larger extent than before, the arguments on both sides are supported or refuted by associations with, and quotations from, diverse moral, religious, and philosophical sources: Matthew Arnold, Gibbon, Newman, John Stuart Mill, Milton, Humboldt, Voltaire, and the Bible.

The sinister psychological battle also entails a more detailed and outspoken social criticism than in Hardy's earlier fiction. As before, one of the main targets is the institution of marriage; but now the scrutiny probes deeper, and the findings are both harsher, more extensive, and more explicitly stated. There is also a new dimension to the criticism in that Hardy, although very tentatively, suggests possible future alternatives to the existing social organization, alternatives that would make man's psychological make-up less of a liability than at the present. As I shall try to show, these social speculations have certain Fourierist overtones.

The social criticism in *Jude* rests firmly on Hardy's psychological vision as it is dramatized in the characterization of the male protagonist. Being a 'ridiculously affectionate fellow', Jude shares the liability of a highly emotional constitution with most of Hardy's heroes, and the battle between head and heart is as much fought within his own character as between him and the other *dramatis personae* on the one side and society on the other. Hardy shows very clearly that Jude's intellectual ambitions are not hampered by society alone. The duality of his character is also responsible, and the incompatibility of head and heart, spirit and flesh is strongly emphasized.

This incompatibility is painted with ironic, but heavy, symbolic strokes at a very early stage of Jude's intellectual endeavours. On his way home from work one day, Jude anticipates the pleasures of his ecclesiastical future as a bishop; as he enumerates the classical works he has to study before taking possession of his see, he is, however, suddenly and rudely smacked on the head by a pig's pizzle. As Jude catches sight of the thrower of the pig's organ, the buxom Arabella ('a complete and substantial female animal'), the significance of this literal clash is soon clarified. As their eyes meet, there is 'a momentary flash of intelligence, a dumb announcement of affinity *in posse*' between the two, and a Darwinian selection by sexual attraction is swiftly concluded. As Hardy somewhat despondently explains, Jude senses the 'unvoiced call of woman to man', and he singles out Arabella among her friends 'in commonplace obedience to conjunctive orders from headquarters, unconsciously received by unfortunate men when the last intention of their lives is to be occupied with the feminine'. 'Headquarters' is thus of an emotional rather than a rational nature, and very early in the novel, then, the basic thematic opposition of head and heart, flesh and spirit, is conspicuously established.

Jude quickly experiences the conflict between the affectionate and the rational sides of his personality; he senses that the frank and coarse sensuality in Arabella is 'quite antipathetic to that side of him which had been occupied with literary study and the magnificent Christminster dream'. What he does not realize at this point is that he is himself endowed with the same strong sexual instincts which will prove incongruous both to his intellectual expectations and to his later more modest hopes of ecclesiastical service. It is to be noted that when Jude first becomes aware of the conflict it is free from philosophical and moral overtones. It is simply a clash between frank sexual feelings and intellectual ambitions. In yielding to his sexual interest in Arabella he only temporarily neglects his studies, and it is clear that the temporary sexual impulses would not have been fatal without society's standards of morals—concretized in the sacrament of marriage: but for his sense of the demands of society, Jude would not have married Arabella.

Jude's further adventures clearly show that Hardy in this novel engages in an overall attack on modern civilization and its norms and values. Nevertheless, he again singles out marriage as one of the most damaging institutions of nineteenth-century Christian society in its enslavement of man in general and of human emotions in particular. Several unhappy marriages are presented: those of Jude's parents, Jude and Arabella, Sue and Phillotson; even Arabella and Cartlett are described in their 'antipathetic, recriminatory mood of the average husband and wife of Christendom'. The most interesting aspect of the criticism of matrimony in *Jude,* however, is the explicit scrutiny—unparalleled in Hardy's earlier fiction—of the ethics upholding the institution as it is practised in modern socety. It is interesting to note in this context that Hardy's censure of marriage is based on ethical considerations very similar to those of Fourier in *The Passions of the Human Soul.* Like Fourier, Hardy objects on the following grounds: the sacrament of marriage is tainted by financial motives; it infringes on personal liberty; it distorts and corrupts both physical and spiritual love; it co-operates with inadequate socio-economic criteria, thus preventing the emergence of a more far-reaching and humane social morality.

As we have seen above, Fourier objects to the 'pecuniary traffic' attached to marriage and the reduction of the household 'to a cold and mercantile union'. Hardy expresses the same viewpoint through Arabella and Sue. As her homespun philosophising as well as decisive actions demonstrate, Arabella accepts marriage mainly because of its potential social and financial expediences. Sue rejects marriage for, partly at least, the very same reasons.

Feeling 'proof against the sordid conditions of a business contract' herself, she explains to Jude that 'fewer women like marriage than you suppose, only they enter into it for the dignity it is assumed to confer, and the social advantages it gains them sometimes—a dignity and an advantage that I am quite willing to do without'.

An equally important argument of both Fourier and Hardy against marriage is that the laws of matrimony infringe on individual liberty, especially for the woman. Fourier bitingly points out how even modern female education is directed towards the inevitable subjection of women in marriage: 'education forms, and must of necessity form, woman to entertain servile sentiments out of respect for conjugal slavery, which is her destiny. It is proper that she should be prepared beforehand to serve the caprices of a master whom she does not yet know. Thus woman being very early imbued with prejudices on the score of her inferiority, inclines to submission, which is necessary in the civilized order' (*The Passions*, I, 351). Sue strives against her conjugal enslavement for a long time. Individual liberty being one of her main arguments, she appropriately calls on the support of John Stuart Mill in pleading with Phillotson to be let free to join Jude: 'She, or he, "who lets the world, or his own portion of it, choose his plan of life for him, has no need of any other faculty than the ape-like one of imitation". J. S. Mill's words, those are. Why can't you act upon them? I wish to, always.' Sue obtains her liberty but only temporarily, and it is with bitter irony that Hardy through Jude shows how futile her wish is to live according to Mill's principles, and how, gradually, her individuality is frittered away. Thus even before she has elicited her release from Phillotson, Jude can admire her for having preserved her own personality: 'Wifedom has not yet squashed up and digested you in its vast maw as an atom which has no further individuality.' At the end of the novel, however, Sue is reduced to a cowering wretch, meekly submitting her personal notions and preferences to the strict and, in Jude's opinion, demeaning Christian views on love and marriage: 'You make me hate Christianity, or mysticism, or Sacerdotalism, or whatever it may be called, if it's that which has caused this deterioration in you. That a woman-poet, a woman-seer, a woman whose soul shone like a diamond—whom all the wise of the world would have been proud of, if they could have known you—should degrade herself like this!'

In *Jude the Obscure* Hardy also criticizes, like Fourier, marriage as a manifestation of society's inadequate concept of love. It is Sue especially who argues this point, as, for instance, when she tells Jude that they cannot continue meeting as good friends because of the restricted views of their environment: 'Their views of the relations of man and woman are limited . . . Their philosophy only recognizes relations based on animal desire. The wide field of strong attachment where desire plays, at least, only a secondary part, is ignored by them . . . '. Some of Sue's respect for Phillotson is for the very reason that he has a broader view than society; explaining why she comes to visit him during his illness, she refers to his recognition of 'other feelings between man and woman than physical love'. Granting that some allowance must be made for Sue's rather frigid sexual feelings and her consequent de-emphasis of their importance in human relationships, there is little doubt that Hardy wants the reader to recognize the validity of her account of civilization's distortion of love.

Hardy's attitude is also evident in Phillotson's spirited defence of Sue's and Jude's relationship against the view of his clergyman friend Gillingham, a spokesman of Christian civilization. Gillingham is shocked at Phillotson's permission to let Sue join her cousin, but Phillotson defines their attachment in moral terms: 'to the best of my understanding, it is not an ignoble, merely animal, feeling between the two. . . . I found from their manner that an extraordinary affinity, or sympathy, entered into their attachment, which somehow took away all flavour of grossness. Their supreme desire is to be together—to share each other's emotions, and fancies, and dreams.' It might be objected that Hardy merely intends to show Phillotson interpreting their relationship in as acceptable a manner as possible to his ecclesiastical friend, if it were not for the frank and independent character of Phillotson's thoughts and actions on several occasions. Phillotson is, in fact, himself a rebel against various accepted moral and social views in the greater part of the novel, and he becomes a spokesman for certain revolutionary notions on social re-organization which are quite similar to those of Fourier. Phillotson's theories and practice—for the greater part of the novel—are in harmony with the concept of a new social morality which is so central to the all-comprehensive moral concerns of the novel.

This is the case, for instance, when Phillotson argues in favour of Jude's and Sue's way of life, that is, living together unmarried. Gillingham objects that such behaviour might lead to 'a general domestic disintegration' in which the 'family would no longer be the social unit'; Phillotson then advances the radical idea of matriarchy: 'I don't see why the woman and children should not be the unit without the man'; in the light of the general psychological framework it is hardly a coincidence that Phillotson reminds Gillingham that the idea of matriarchy—which, assumedly, is more in accord with natural human emotions, according to the novel's criteria, than is the traditional family unit—comes from him only as 'a feeler, not a reasoner'.

Granting that Hardy may have acquired the idea of changing the family structure in several ways and from diverse sources, it nevertheless seems significant that abolition of the traditional family unit is fundamental also in Fourier's scheme of a future social organization that would be more in harmony with human nature than the present social structure. Fourier, for example, argues sharply against allowing 'familism' (one of his four groups of passions) to remain the ruling principle of modern society: 'If . . . philosophy makes any account of honour, it ought not to constitute familism the presiding passion over social relations; since the mean-spiritedness which this passion engenders proves that it requires a counterpoise, and that it is highly irrational to wish to make it a predominant lever in social mechanism'; and, in another context, Fourier warns against giving familism an important function in the social system, because, he argues, this passion is 'essentially false' (*The Passions*, I, 364, 253).

In order to be able to dispense with the traditional family unit, however, a new social morality is needed. As we have seen above, Fourier calls this new morality 'unityism', and in this love should be applied to 'universal unity' and not to small sects or groups such as the family. Hardy seems to approach the same concept as he argues in *Jude* that children, irrespective of parenthood, should be the collective responsibility of adults: 'The beggarly question of parentage—what is it, after all? All the little ones of our time are collectively the children of us adults of the time, and entitled to our general care. That excessive regard of parents for their own children, and their dislike of other people's, is, like class-feeling, patriotism, save-your-soul-ism, and other virtues, a mean exclusiveness at bottom.' It is obvious that Hardy's call for a less selfish attitude towards children is part of a more comprehensive concept of social morality, a concept which, with perhaps a touch of irony, Hardy makes a point of summing up in the traditional term 'charity', which is repeatedly used in the novel. In insisting on this very term, it seems, he attacks the morality of institutionalized Christianity with one of its own professedly key virtues.

Jude the Obscure is, then, a novel with a decidedly moral concern. It has, as Hardy approvingly quotes from a reader in his Preface, some characteristics of a 'religious and ethical treatise'. Its ethical attack is directed against Christian social morality in general and its manifestations in the sacrament of marriage in particular. As in his previous fiction, Hardy's sociological/moral criticism is inseparable from his psychological vision. For, the main purpose of his social and moral speculations in the novel seems to be to demonstrate that 'it is none of the natural tragedies of love that's love's usual tragedy in civilized life, but a tragedy manufactured for people . . .'.

V

The psychological vision in Hardy's novels, as here discussed, is obviously not that of a professional psychologist. For a man of Hardy's wide and serious reading, his juxtaposition of head and heart may, in fact, seem surprisingly simple. Nevertheless, this is, I believe, the basic psychological framework for Hardy's dramatization of the human situation, the purpose of this dramatization being—according to his often stated opinion—to give adequate representation of the elementary human passions. As we have seen, this aim is in harmony with his anti-rational view of human personality, his belief that the motive springs of human actions are to be found in the emotional rather than the rational faculty.

As I have attempted to show, the antithesis of passion and intellect is also an essential element in Hardy's social criticism in which the intellect becomes the agent of those norms and attitudes of civilization which eventually chasten, distort, or destroy the natural human emotions. In all its crudeness, this simplification indicates, I hope, an important aspect of Hardy's social criticism: its indistinct, visionary character. Hardy is not a sociologist and is not much concerned with concrete details of politics or economics, nor with sociological ideologies. He offers us remarkably little constructive criticism and is free from any optimistic utopian visions.

In a novelist the hesitation to embrace or profess any specific social scheme should be neither disqualifying, nor disconcerting. Above all, it should not be taken as an indication of any constitutional inability to reason clearly. It seems more rewarding, and perhaps fairer to Hardy, to take the avowed purpose of his craft into consideration in this context. For Hardy appears to have shared Conrad's notion that the aim of art is not 'in the clear logic of a triumphant conclusion'; rather it is found in 'unadjusted impressions' which, as Hardy modestly puts it in the Preface to Jude, also 'have their value'.

In the absence of any explicitly formulated psychological or sociological principles in Hardy's novels, it may seem questionable to attempt to single out the utopian socialist Fourier as a specific source of influence. And, taken individually, some details of Hardy's views on human personality and modern society may be said to have been current; others may be traceable to other sources of known impact on Hardy—John Stuart Mill, Carlyle, Arnold, Swinburne, the Romantics, to mention only a few. Yet, in addition to the significant external evidence in the *Literary Notes,* there remains a conspicuous internal similarity by no means in all details but in enough details to produce the same cause and effect theory which characterizes their overall analyses of the human predicament: on the basis of their anti-rational view of human personality they conclude that the pervasive unhappiness of modern man stems from the suppression of his natural passions by modern western civilization.

Hardy's psychological and social ideas here considered are, then, neither original nor very profound, and J. Hillis Miller's observation, that Hardy's sense of the quality of human life is more important than his ideas, remains true. But Hardy's main theme, the theme of love, emerges from these psychological and social ideas; and they deserve attention, for they constitute, after all, the raw material by the dramatization of which Hardy conveys his sense of the quality of human life.

VII

Melvyn Bragg:

THOMAS HARDY AND "JUDE THE OBSCURE"

The first page of the first notebook of Thomas Hardy dated 1863—in the Dorchester Museum—is given over to a diagrammatic tree showing the inter-relations between 'Human Passion, Mind, and Character'. The idea of three interconnecting strands had taken me to Dorchester in the first place: to use the notebooks to discover correspondences between the life of Hardy in his fifties when he wrote Jude; the life of Hardy as a young man, particularly in respect of his education and expectations in his early twenties, when Jude's great struggles occur; and the life of Jude himself. To be met with this triple-tongued tree on page one was a welcome coincidence; but attempts to use it for neat divisions—Passion=Jude; Mind=The Older Hardy; Character=The Young Hardy—soon fell down. The notebooks themselves, however, contained enough to provide evidence for the notion that in *Jude the Obscure* there was a most intense and painful collision of Hardy's past, his present, and his fiction; a collision which produced a novel full of unintentional revelations from his past, a bitter commentary on his present state—particularly his marriage—and the decision, perhaps because of the forces which were now working themselves out in his fiction, to seek the refuge of poetry.

Robert Gittings uses annotations in Hardy's Prayer-Book and Bibles to very good effect. I shall concentrate on the notebooks which, amazingly, are only now being edited and published. Yet there they are, five books in his own very clear hand, survivors of those gloomy bonfires at Max Gate where Hardy threw his life on the flames. We must be suspicious of the notebooks *because* they survived. Like the 'biography' attributed to his second wife, they could be a plant. Yet like that elaborate autobiography they are just as interesting in ways in which Hardy may not have intended as in ways in which he did. They begin in 1863, when Hardy is 23 and about the same age as Jude on reaching Christminster; for the 1890s, when Hardy is working on *Jude,* they are thin but, I think, significant, especially as the official biography is quite gossipy in that period. One of the chief preoccupations of the notebooks is the listing of reading-matter and comments on other authors and books, and so they seem particularly useful in connection with Jude, the archetypal autodidact.

The acknowledged origin for *Jude* is to be found in the notebooks and in the official life five or six years before the writing itself was undertaken. 'A short story of a young man—"who could not go to Oxford" ', it reads.—'His struggles and ultimate failure. Suicide . . . There is something [in this] the world ought to be shown, and I am the one to show it to them—though I was not altogether hindered going, at least to Cambridge, and could have gone up easily at five and twenty.'[1] It is remarkable how closely Hardy stuck to this. Most importantly, however, is the instant relationship Hardy sets up between himself and the 'young man'. Not only 'There is something in this the world ought to be shown, and I am the one to show it to them', but also, immediately following, 'though I was not altogether hindered': first the association with the fictitious young man and then the defensive distancing.

Like many of Hardy's novels, *Jude* was first printed as a serial story, this time in Harper's new monthly magazine, from December 1894 to November 1895; in November 1895 it was published as a complete novel. Hardy, ever willing, officially, to please the publisher, had soothed Harper's anxieties (brought on by the protest over *Tess)* by declaring that he was writing 'a tale that could not offend the most fastidious maiden'. Then, as happened more and more the greater his confidence grew, he went on and did as he wanted—though we can never be quite sure with Hardy in the novels that he did exactly as he wanted. He wanted respectability as powerfully as he wanted fame, and disclaimed both only when he had achieved both and was unshakable. There are too many examples of his re-writing to order and even to prescription for us to be certain that he was not in some way impressed by the judgement of Harper's—that the novel should he 'in every respect suitable for a family magazine'.[2] In the past, the voice of editors, publishers, and friends—George Meredith, Morley, Leslie Stephen, Horace Moule—had caused him to make the most radical changes. He was used to being humble about his novels.

Even so, *Jude,* like *Tess,* had to be extensively bowdlerised for the serial version. He found it very tiresome having to restore it to his original conception. 'On account of the labour of altering *Jude the Obscure* to suit the magazine, and then having to alter it back, I have lost energy for revising and improving the original as I meant to do', he wrote.[3]

As always, Hardy did his homework; he went to Oxford with notebook and sketch pad and got to work. Certainly Jude's double entry into Christminster by touch and by those ghostly voices is a very vivid fictitious translation of the spiritual and tactile way in which Hardy himself approached Oxford. Whether or not the place moved him as it moved Jude, we can say that the Idea of the place moved him very greatly, just as the architecture did. The novel is full of references to stone, to shapes and forms of stone, to terms and descriptions of stone—cull it carefully and it would provide a stout dossier of architectural terms and observations. It is also cram-packed with names and quotations from previous Oxford eras and with awe at those names—the spirit and the structure of the place entrap both the author and his hero, and both idealise it.

The spirit, the idealisation, came from Newman; to go back to 1865, when Hardy was a young man, the first quotation of all in the notebooks is from Newman's *Apologia*—'The notion that my calling in life would require such a sacrifice as celibacy involved . . . strengthened my feeling of separation from the visible world'. This sentence could be the motto of Sue, the spiritual quantity in the novel.

Having been to Oxford, Hardy nearly thirty years on from Newman sat down to write out his Christminster. By this time, Newman's idealisation is very outdated. Yet, it is the idealisation which comes first in the novel and sets the dominating standard. As a young boy, Jude wants to see the city, and waits until at last in the distance, it appears: 'Some way within the limits of the stretch of landscape, points of light like the topaz gleamed. The air increased in transparency with the lapse of minutes, till the topaz points showed themselves to be the vanes, windows, wet-roof slates, and other shining spots upon the spires, domes, freestone-work, and varied outlines that were faintly revealed. It was Christminster, unquestionably; either directly seen, or miraged in the peculiar atmosphere.' The heavenly Jerusalem was what it looked like to Jude, quickly bringing in the Christ-life analogy which accompanies much of Jude's pilgrim's progress.

Immediately after that, Jude is warned by a convenient carter that he would have to get his head 'screwed on t'other way' before he could read what they read there. Thus, from the start, Jude is suspended between longing and dread. At about the same age in his own life, Hardy was being fought over by Mrs Martin, who promised wealth, luxury—a shimmery mirage; and Jemima, his mother, who gave him solid literature and sent him from home altogether to break the grip of the adoring and idealising Mrs Martin.

In 1892, before he started Jude, Hardy's father died. It is surely interesting that the next hero who pops up is, like Hardy's father, a stone-mason, a man who can job around in a country manner, an artisan. Hardy later elevated his father's status, just as he ignored his thirty-one working-class cousins in the genealogy he worked out for himself, preferring to hunt down the fragile connection with Hardy of Trafalgar. However, he was a dutiful son and it is significant that he should take up his father's trade—for his fiction—so very soon after the death. On the one hand, it would no longer embarrass his father nor could it be contradicted by him; on the other hand the world of childhood facts and emotions could clearly be tapped.

Yet another to join the queue of coincidences which stretch up to and well into this novel is that, after a twenty-year lay-off, Hardy took up an invitation to be in charge of the restoration of West Knighton Church. A chore he had turned down many times before; the sort of job his old firm in Dorchester would have undertaken and his father carried out; and West Knighton the sort of church—perhaps the model for the church—in which Jude and Sue are, like Adam and Eve of course, to be made conscious of their 'nakedness' and shamed out. West Knighton, moreover, was precisely the sort of modest local church which Hardy had worked in so happily as a young apprentice architect and attended so devotedly for most of his adult life. The connections here, between the older Hardy, Jude, and Hardy the younger, though they are chiefly relevant only to the background of the novel, provide a clear case of the intertwining of the three strands. The old stone-mason dies; Hardy reaches back to work he did as a young man, and invents a young stone-mason who is to lead a life patterned on the Gothic revival such as Hardy himself was engaged in.

And it could be said that the ballast of the book is in the stone. Here Hardy uses the word 'illumination' almost as the anonym of 'vision'. The truth as opposed to the idealised. Soon after he arrives in Christminster, Jude goes to find work and goes to a stone-mason's work-yard which was 'a little centre of regeneration'. 'He asked for the foreman, and looked round among the new traceries, mullions, transoms, shafts, pinnacles, and battlements standing on the bankers half worked, or waiting to be removed. They were marked by precision, mathematical straightness, smoothness, exactitude: there in the old walls were the broken lines of the original idea; jagged curves, disdain of precision, irregularity, disarray. For a moment there fell on Jude a true illumination; that here in the stone yard was a centre of effort as worthy as that dignified by the name of scholarly study within the noblest of the colleges. But he lost it under stress of his old idea.' This is surely an example of the author talking through his hero—praising his past, possibly paying a tribute to his father—and then rejecting it for the fiction.

Yet the identity of Christminster was always to perturb him a little. In the introduction to the Wessex Edition of his novels he firmly marks down Oxford beside Christminster as he gives the list of place cross-references, and yet he was forever finding it necessary to qualify this. In the official biography, through Florence, he writes, 'At a party at Sir Charles Tennant's, to which Hardy and his wife were invited to meet the Eighty Club, Lord Rosebery took occasion in a conversation to inquire "why Hardy had called Oxford 'Christminster' ". Hardy assured him that he had not done anything of the sort, "Christminster" being a city of learning that was certainly suggested by Oxford, but in its entirety existed nowhere else in the world but between the covers of the novel under discussion.'[4] He was more explicit elsewhere. 'The description of these backgrounds has been done from the real', but, he goes on, 'no detail is guaranteed—the portraiture of fictitiously named towns and villages was only suggested by certain real places and wantonly wanders from inventorial descriptions of them'. This is plain enough, and yet Lord Rosebery had a point.

For Christminster shows the strain, as I believe it had become for Hardy, of labouring under the sort of lightly disguised realism which had been the most praised element in his earlier novels, never entirely absent from any of them but increasingly irksome to his literary taste and ambitions. He wanted to use Christminster, he said, as he would have used 'war, fire or shipwreck, for bringing about a catastrophe'. But the trouble with the place was that he had followed the conventions of the realist and gone there first. The tension between realism and idealism which had been so well held for so long was becoming less flexible, less useful to him as a writer.

Probably the most important fact about his life at this time was his despair at his relationship with his first wife, Emma, which appears to have been worsened considerably during the writing of *Jude*. It had been bad for some time. In 1893, Hardy and Emma went to Dublin where he met Mrs Henniker. They collaborated on a short story, and it seems reasonable to assume they fell in love. Emma appears to have thought so, and there are poems to confirm their affinity. Yet Hardy in the official version refers to Mrs Henniker in the same style as he refers to others in his social life: in a spirit of conscientious vanity and snobbery mixed up with justifiable pride in his own elevated existence and a real appreciation of quality wherever he met it. This, though, can be said: the having of two women in his sight was very like the emotional situation confronting or sustaining him when he wrote *Far from the Madding Crowd,* which was such an important breakthrough not only for his career but, more importantly, for his self-confidence as a novelist. Then it was Emma and his cousin Tryphena Sparks. And we are again reminded of the struggle over the boy Tommy between Jemima and Mrs Martin—whom he never ceased to dream about even into his old age. The despair over Emma then was accompanied, perhaps balanced, by the elation over Mrs Henniker. Jude, also, has two women—Arabella and Sue: and there is some evidence—in Robert Gittings' book—that, when he was in London, young Hardy had a relationship with a woman as well as continuing to pay court to the appropriate

Sparks—he was to fall for all three sisters in turn.

Superficially in the 1890s Hardy's life had settled down to that of the literary squire. He was well-off—on the way to being wealthy. He was well-known—on the way to being famous. Max Gate was built and staffed. London trips were organised. Parties were given and invitations taken up most eagerly. It is useful to be reminded of what Hardy himself considered to be worth saying about his own life at this time, for this again indicates some of the tension which was present in the writing of *Jude*. The chasm between the life and the work was perhaps a deeper part of the fatigue with the work than he would ever have cared to admit. Certainly the life, as reported by his conjugal amanuensis, was unflaggingly busy, social, and gay.

In the first notebook—after the Diagram of Human Passions etc., and after Newman, the first entry in the notebook proper reads '*Subordination*—"The grand scheme of subordination" (class to class)—Boswell'. Though Hardy's anger at natural injustice comes through—in *Jude* for example, he is bitter against the complacent conspiracy of the privileged which ignores those, like Jude, for whom the idea of a university was engendered—and it is easy to see why Marxists apply a class-conflict reading so confidently; yet he contradicted himself. His notes often read like the 'Diary Of A Somebody'. Look at me, they say, with touching self-delight, I'm here! This, then, is how he wanted his life to be seen, and what he thought worth showing as he was working on *Jude*.

April 1893. 'Lady Winifred Gardner whispered to me that meeting the Royal Family always reminded her of family prayers. The Duke confused the lady who introduced me to him by saying it was unnecessary, as he had known me for years, adding privately to me when she was gone, "That's good enough for her: of course I meant I had known you spiritually".'

April 27, 1893. "A great lack of tact in A. J. B., who was in the chair at the Royal Literary Fund dinner which I attended last night. The purpose of the dinner was, of course, to raise funds for poor authors, largely from the pockets of the more successful ones who were present with the other guests. Yet he dwelt with much emphasis on the decline of the literary art, and on his opinion that there were no writers of high rank living in these days.'

The chief interest for me in those entries is what is left out. No mention of brother Henry who spoke in dialect all his life and told the time by the sun. No mention of the vast families of Heads and Hands—what better Hardyan names could be thought up for Hardy's real grandparents?—which flitted in and out of the careless stratifications of working-class life. The past was to be buried. But it found a seed-bed in Jude, for there indeed is the pigsty: in one way the book can be read as the nightmare of what Hardy feared might have happened to himself.

The inwardness of the book is confirmed, I think, by the almost total lack of any of those landscape descriptions put in for the sake of the description. Description in *Jude* is symbolic: nothing is described which is not part of the intellectual pattern of the book. The landscape here is the landscape of the mind. All the miles walked by Jude are virtually untouched by the scenic appreciation which was previously part of Hardy's pleasure and his stock-in-trade.

At the time of writing *Jude,* Hardy looked like a bit of a Burlington Bertie—not the man who, on first glance in a South Kensington drawing-room, you would expect to be writing a rural melodrama full of biblical and classical lore and Gothic passions. The gap between the cosmopolitan life he led and the provincial life he fed on for his fiction was growing—and there are indications that he felt that each was endangered by the other. In his introduction to the Wessex novels he defends himself against a charge which only he himself has brought against himself—that his works 'cannot be so inclusive in their exhibition of human nature as novels wherein the scenes cover large extents of country, in which events figure amid towns and cities and even wander over the four quarters of the globe'. He gives his reasons for staying 'within [his] frontiers when it would have been easier to overleap them and give more cosmopolitan features to the narrative'. Despite comparing Wessex in size to that of Ancient Greece, he was still uneasy enough to find the point worth emphasising.[5] And it seems to me that Wessex was endangered by London because the attraction of that greater sophistication threw into high relief the simplicity, even the crudeness, of his rustic material (seen in Victorian terms), while London was endangered by Wessex because in the novels Hardy's own past was coming out more and more urgently, likely, he would think, to upset the tastes of those whose invitations he valued so highly. There were even direct threats: Jude, for instance, rails violently against the very class and type of person with whom Hardy was sunning himself. Moreover, his determined interest in *ideas*—and Hardy was an anthology of popular science and philosophy—meant that they were willy-nilly superimposed on people and scenes which could not bear them. He was going deeper in his fiction and opening himself to all that was around him; having wound himself up as an *autodidact* with such care and tenacity, he had, to a certain extent been a Frankenstein to the monster of his own willed drive to write; but the creature now threatened to evade the grip of the master and take on worlds which would destroy it.

As he is writing *Jude,* Hardy notes that he reads *The New Spirit* by Havelock Ellis, Lambroso on *The Insanity of Genius,* Myers' *The Meaning Of Life,* Peer Gynt, Carlyle on the German Metaphysicians, as well as Zola, Tolstoy, Euripides, and the Doomsday references to Dorset. This listing is par for the course.

He was proud of his learning and he had every right to be. He was also most conscientious about it. Here he is listing what he had read in 1887: 'Milton, Dante, Calderon, Goethe, Homer, Virgil, Molière, Scott, The Cid, Nibelungen, Crusoe, Don Quixote, Aristophanes, Theocritus, Boccaccio, Canterbury Tales, Shakespeare's Sonnets, Lycidas, Malory, Vicar of Wakefield, Ode to the West Wind, Ode to Grecian Urn, Christabel, Wye above Tintern, Chapman's Iliad, Lord Derby's ditto, Worsley's Odyssey'. It is a very strong and touching compulsion which makes a man of Hardy's age and reputation note down the actual short poems he read during the year. Nothing was too prosaic—he would read *The Times* leader column to improve his style; nothing too poetic—the long connection with Virgil is only one instance of that. If there is not quite the unabashed love of Keats's discovery of Chapman's Homer, neither is there the grim diet of Jude. Hardy's own love of learning is firmly set in the time and world of Samuel Smiles, earnest but full of delight and fun.

Fun is forbidden Jude. When, in his twentieth year, Jude sums up his achievements—and here he is on the crest of his self-confidence, full of hope—he lists his learning—'an average student's power to read the common ancient classics, Latin in particular', he goes on to add . . . 'two books of the Iliad' . . . 'a lot of the Greek Testament . . . Euclid . . . algebra . . . the Fathers . . . Roman and English history'. It would be interesting to use one of those sampling laboratories to discover whether, totally unaided, a boy *could* achieve so much in such a little time—not a niggle this, but yet another sign, I would guess, of Hardy's lack of interest in paying his former attention to the constraints—as he saw them by then—of realism and naturalism. That apart, though, we might compare the austere regimen Jude got with the more varied nourishment enjoyed by the author himself at about the same age—when he was three years older than Jude. Here are a few consecutive entries from the notebooks. At the age of twenty-three he copies out from Macaulay: ' "The finest gentlemen of the age"—Wyndham; "and the great Scoffer-mocker"—Voltaire; *immediately* after this, he notes, "The large scale of Modern doing"—it will take 28 miles of carpeting the ordinary width to carpet the Hotel San Francisco'. Followed by '*Paradise* (underlined) (Mohammed's—in the Koran) No old women—six dozen houris to one man—river flowing over gravel of rubies and emeralds'. "The *damned*", he goes on (in ditto) wear shoes of fire—drink boiling water.' Hardy must have enjoyed these juxtapositions, but, more than that, they show a mind thankfully capable of working in many ways and on many levels. Jude was in a scholastic strait-jacket by comparison. Hardy was also here, capable of seizing on humorous instances—he was, later in life, especially in his biography, it seems to me rather testy on the subject of his sense of humour, and made a serious point of insisting on it. But in the notebooks we can see some of the lighter-hearted bubbles which were to be transmitted into his earliest public pieces. 'Isocrates' he notes, from the Classical Dictionary, 'put an end to his life—from patriotism—at the age of 98.' Followed by 'Cost—the Suez Canal cost about £19,000,000' and then 'Ardour Damped'—from *The Graphic*. 'The Ardent Philhellene, M. Alphonse Kerr, went to Greece overflowing with sympathy for its suffering people but was rather hurt in his affections by losing his portmanteau at Marathon, being robbed of his watch at Salamis, and stripped naked by three Brigands at Thermopylae.' Jude does not appear to have taken *The Graphic* or *The Times*.

Still the weight of the notebooks is high-minded; and if there is a guiding principle it could be said to be in those lines transcribed from Matthew Arnold: 'Matthew Arnold's advice is to take lines and expressions from the great masters and apply them as a touchstone.' Both the author and his character long to be in connection with the great dead. And this preoccupation sometimes does them no good; Jude could have benefited from the fresh air of *The Graphic,* and Hardy, too, could have thrown away his learning—every now and then.

Jude's great moment when Sue leaves Phillotson to be with him is severely diminished by Hardy's insistence that he burst out in Browning (unacknowledged, of course, like most of the quotations), and Sue's great moment of decisive action just before that meeting is surely flawed in the exchanges with her schoolmaster husband by a pedestrian reference to primitive Christianity. Or take the occasion when Jude first comes to Christminster. In the gloom the 'worthies' of the place come out as ghosts, and the incantation begins. 'There were poets abroad, of early date and of late, from the friend and eulogist of Shakespeare down to him who has recently passed into silence; and that musical one of the tribe who is still among us.' Soon we meet 'the founders of the religious school called Tractarian; the well-known three, the enthusiast, the poet, and the formularist . . . ', and so on. This is the apotheosis of the autodidact—to invent a character learned enough to discover ways of paraphrasing descriptions of such worthies of learning as most educated people would puzzle to recognise. Why not mention, in order, Ben Jonson, Matthew Arnold, Swinburne, and

Newman, Keble, and Pusey?

Yet, just as this can destroy the surface of the prose and the plot, so it indisputably binds in the roots. When Jude is in the pub, for example, in despair with his prospects, and, incidentally, getting drunk on the very little which Hardy considers is enough to make drunkards of us all—then, after a realistic setting up of the scene as good as anything in the book, he has Jude show his colours and recite the creed in Latin. Culture crashes in; awkwardly, baldly, with that gleam in its eye which alerts us to the arrival of the old obsession; but yet, it has to be said, it is just that very thing which makes the scene unforgettable. The paradox of Hardy—the naïvety *and* the learning, the awe *and* the cynicism, the gaucheness *and* the grandeur—it is this which is his strength. Even the absurd quibble over the Nicene or the Apostles' Creed becomes powerfully memorable.

What Jude is given all too little of, though, are the human qualities which fill out many other Hardy heroes and heroines. He is a real hero—his power in my mind carries into life—and, perhaps, from his reading of the Greeks, Hardy wanted less of a man than an idea of a man. But it is worth pointing up the character of Jude, I think, and comparing him with Hardy himself, because there is so very much of Hardy's life in Jude—and that is part of the reason why the novel-writing had to go.

There is a photograph of Hardy 'as a young man with forcible, meditative, and earnest rather than handsome cast of countenance. He was of a dark complexion, with dark harmonizing eyes, and he wore a closely trimmed black beard of more advanced growth than is usual at his age.' The description of course is of Jude as he enters Christminster, but the resemblance is certainly striking. It is offered not as hard evidence but as the merest indication of the pull this book exercised on its author despite his fiercest efforts to evade autobiography.

Yet how deeply he seems to have dug for Jude. Not only do we learn that there was a baker's boy in Hardy's own childhood, who used to deliver the bread around the villages in the same literary way as that adopted by Jude, but again and again, examining those parts of Hardy's past which he so fiercely wanted to blot out, we find attributes of this fictional character presenting themselves. We find that Hardy had an uncle, John Antell, a cobbler, who lived in the High Street. He, too, like Jude taught himself from scratch; he, too, dreamed of going to university; he too found that poverty and the hard work of everyday life was a bar; he too took to drink. He even had 'a great mass of black curly hair' and, although his actual death was not that of Jude, it was very like the moment when we know Jude will die, walking back along that road from seeing Sue for the last time, exposed to the elements: Antell's death too was said to have been hastened by exposure through having spent the night in a ditch after a drunken bout. There was also Horace Moule, son of the local vicar, just a few years older than Hardy, a brilliant classical scholar, we are told, and more than that, a real 'friend'; 'friend' was how Hardy spoke of him in his poems. When, late in life, Horace Moule went into the downward spiral not uncommon with literary men—dissatisfaction with work—drink—depression—recovery with work-dissatisfaction—depression—drink—he would take off to have an anonymous low-life and perhaps even, in his despair and in his cups, recite the creed in Latin to some who might mistake it for the ballad of the rat-catcher's daughter in Double Dutch. It was again a powerful incident from Moule's own desperate life which relates to Jude's strange son 'old father Time' brought up in Australia. Moule had an illegitimate child by a Dorchester girl, brought up in Australia and, to pile probability on coincidence, hanged there. Moule, as Jude threatened and virtually did, also killed himself.

For a writer as determined to shut himself out of his material as Hardy was, these facts already, from the bits and bobs he left scholars to work on, are an impressive haul. And he was prepared, even, to risk his own precious—I am using the word in no way satirically—family. The great shadow on the Hardy hearth at Bockhampton was paternal grandmother Mary Head Hardy. In her rumoured background were stories of illegitimacy and betrayal and brutality—all at the very lowest level of rural working-class life—and yet Hardy first thought of calling Jude—'Head'—the connection between family and symbol too powerful to resist. As it turned out he gave Sue Bride the 'Head' and found 'Fawley' for Jude. But Fawley was the place—near the Ridgeway—where the grandmother had hailed from. Hardy went to visit it while starting Jude: 'At Great Fawley, Berks. Entered a ploughed vale which might be called the Valley of Brown Melancholy. The silence is remarkable . . . Though I am alive with the living I can only see the dead here, and am scarcely conscious of the happy children at play.'[6] A couple of entries on, I noticed 'The best tragedy—highest tragedy in short—is that of the WORTHY encompassed by the INEVITABLE. The tragedies of immoral and worthless people are not of the best.' And of course Jude was given the profession of Hardy's grandfather and father and the aspiration, in learning, of himself. So Hardy was pulling up much more of his past than usual.

Take education. Hardy got what many might call an ideal education. His mother, contradicting her lowly origins as Victorians might phrase it, was a great reader, and her favourite work to which she returned regularly was Dante's *Divine Comedy.* There was the glamorous Mrs Martin, who intellectually and to some extent emotionally adopted the precocious boy, and set up a school under the auspices of the National Society for Promoting the Education of the Poor in the principles of the Established Church; and here Hardy did well in mathematics and geography, while at home, his mother, Jemima, fed her boy Dryden's translation of Virgil and Dr Johnson's *Rasselas*. When he was twelve, business being good enough to afford it, he was taught Latin as an extra. Alone he is reading romance, adventure, Dumas and *The Pilgrim's Progress*. Then again he fell on his feet—it is as if schools were especially built for him, because when he was thirteen and needed further education, Isaac Last, an ambitious teacher whose ill-health kept him from making his way in the wider world, was appointed to look after a school set up by the powerful non-conformist group in the Dorchester area. Under normal conditions Hardy would have had to leave school at thirteen. Now he could stay on with Isaac Last at what Hardy afterwards referred to as 'The Academy'. He stoutly denied that he was solely self-taught, and when someone said as much later in life he wrote that it was 'impertinent, and untrue, as he was taught Latin and French in School and College'. He left school at sixteen but only to land in the safe and understanding lap of John Hicks, a local Dorchester architect . . . and then, when he was seventeen, Horace Moule, to quote Robert Gittings, 'took virtual control of Thomas Hardy's life'. It is impossible to imagine a more sympathetic teacher. He gave Hardy books, reading-plans, ambitions, tutorials, standards, friendship, and a taste for and introduction into the world of modern thought in *The Saturday Review;* and there is no doubt whatsoever that Horace Moule also supplied that personal emotional tie which was essential to Hardy's connection with learning. It is almost painfully apt that his first school should have come from a woman who was so jealous of her little Tommy that she was prepared to fight the natural mother for the child's loyalty and affection; to have had two grown women struggling over him must have been the most enormous and fearful flattery; to have had two such stimulating women working on him was clearly of greatest possible benefit. Similarly, to have the distinguished son of the distinguished and local hero, the Reverend Henry Moule, in an attitude of real friendship must have stimulated the social glands of the Hardys and caused a feeling of satisfaction and gratitude which, though later decried to some extent, would undoubtedly fertilize the intellectual connection.

All this, then, which he, looking back, spoke of as 'a life twisted of three strands—the professional life, the scholar's life, and the rustic life combined in the twenty-four hours of one day'. In one way it can be seen as a quite perfect seed-time: 6-8 a.m., the *Iliad* in Greek and Latin; a healthy walk to work and architecture and talk; off in the evening with uncle James and the fiddle, all supervised by Moule who, in Hardy and another young Dorset scholar, found the vocation he could never settle on elsewhere. And besides this, the steady pulse of the Church, the hymns and Bible passages known and marked and stored away—few of our authors besides Bunyan knew their Bible as well as Hardy. What more could a university possibly provide? For later his luck was to hold: in London, he was at the office of the brilliant Arthur Blomfield, the young president of the Architects' Association, who took him up as many did; in his apprenticeship to fiction he was fortunate to be helped by George Meredith, John Morley, and the scrupulous Leslie Stephen. Hardy was supremely well learned and well taught.

Alas, poor Jude! No schools, no mother, no Isaac Last, no help with the Latin, no friendly contemporaries, no Horace Moule; no Morley, no Blomfield, no Leslie Stephen, only Phillotson, who —incredibly—forgets all about his star pupil in a few years, and Vilbert who exploits him, helps him not at all and then claims all the credit, and the man who writes the hymn, which moves Jude to a pilgrimage, but who speaks only of royalties.

But if, in these ways, Jude is given less, in other ways he gets more than enough. Later in life, Hardy was concerned to stress his early immaturity—'greater than common for his years', he dictated to his wife, adding, 'A clue to much of his character and action throughout his life is afforded by his lateness of development in virility while mentally precocious.' This immaturity was linked with a great susceptibility. Jude's susceptibility over learning and Arabella ruins him. Similarly, while there is a delightful and invigorating dedication about the young Hardy's devotion to learning, it is never far from shrewdness. His career as an apprentice is admirably well-managed. When he decided to tackle poetry seriously at twenty-five, he was out buying a Pronouncing Dictionary, a Rhyming Dictionary, a Manual of English Literature, and so on. Jude has all the devotion and not a scrap of the shrewdness. The 1870 Education Act, let us assume, had not begun to work satisfactorily in time for Jude, but this was the time of Winwood Reade, the South Place Ethical Society, the beginnings of the W.E.A.—surely, one keeps saying, someone would pick Jude up, or he would have the iota of common sense necessary to put this great vessel of his on a slip-way. But no, Hardy lets him build it far from the ocean and leaves him land-locked.

It was not only on Jude, though, that Hardy was pawning his life and fortunes. Sue Bridehead came in for her share of the family treasures. 'Sue is a type of woman who has always had an attraction for me,' he writes to a friend, 'but the difficulty of drawing the type has kept me from attempting it till now.' Sue is a recognisable 'modern woman' of the sort becoming common among European writers of the day—while we know that Hardy saw Ibsen's *Rosmersholm* shortly before writing *Jude* (whether intentionally or not there is very marked similarity between Sue's story and that of Rebecca West). It is undoubtedly true that Hardy wanted to create a type, a representative figure and a symbol in Sue as much as he did with Jude, but despite D. H. Lawrence's understandable howl of anger at the intellectual strip-tease which Sue plays upon the panting Jude and the parched Phillotson, she does emerge as in some way human: not much, not enough, for a naturalistic novel, not enough for many readers—but, if we regard her as a cross between an idealist, a Simpleton (Hardy's first of three titles for the book was *The Simpletons),* and a woman uninterested in and unreliant on or afraid of sex, then she makes sense. But in order to give her even *that* fictional weight, Hardy had to take great risks with his past—risks because he hated the secret past coming into what he rightly saw to be the particularly exposing and vulnerable affair of the novel. Leaving aside Emma, his wife, and their lack of children; leaving aside Mrs Henniker and her zithern—both of whom play their part in the character of Sue; I should like to refer briefly to his sister Mary, and Tryphena Sparks, his cousin. Both went away to training colleges very similar to Sue's, and both were indisputably loved by Hardy.

Aged twenty-one—the same age as Jude when he was to-ing and fro-ing with Sue—Hardy visited his sister Mary, who had tenaciously fought her way into a training college for teachers at Salisbury. He first saw Salisbury Cathedral then—to figure in *Jude*—and he notes in his Prayer-Book, 'Wherewithal shall a young man cleanse his way: even by ruling himself after thy word.' Jude could have written that after his forbidden meeting with Sue. 'Ruling Himself' is underlined, but so is 'my soul breaketh out . . . my soul melteth away' later in the psalm. Jude would have underlined that, too. There is also some evidence (alas, too bare to furnish more than a footnote) that a great love of Hardy's youth in London was a young 'modern' woman who accelerated his loss of religious faith—as Sue worked on Jude—and she also seems to have been called up in the writing of this book. A young woman who would, at that time, in the 1860s, have the ideas of the 1860s which Sue has—ideas carried boldly in *The English Woman's Journal,* which was saturated in the notions of J. S. Mill; Sue quotes him a great deal. The Positive Philosophy of Auguste Comte—favourite reading for Hardy at this time—was available for modern women in Harriet Martineau's translation of the 1850s.

The little known London love apart, however, one is tempted to say that the deepest root for Sue, stronger even than Mary, was Tryphena Sparks. A great deal of speculation has gone into this relationship, and what it was in terms of a sexual relationship we are not likely to know of here any more than with Hardy's other women. Little if any, probably; but a great deal of that frustrated passion in the mind which teases out this novel unbearably. Tryphena, though, looked like his mother Jemima; she also looked like her two elder sisters, both of whom in their time, Hardy had fallen passionately in love with—the three cousins seem to mark the three stages of his maturation; *and* she was very like the London woman and Mary in her life's pattern and perhaps in her ideas. Her own sister went into domestic service but, like Mary—and Sue—Tryphena got herself to college—Stockwell College where the first eight precepts were—I quote them to show how much in detail Hardy took from this situation for that tricky and crucial area of plotting in which Sue was *got* out of college and then *put* out:—

1. Never go out alone.
2. Do not speak at dinner time.
3. Never speak after 10.10 p.m.
4. Always wear a bonnet on Sunday.
5. Never go upstairs without asking.
6. If you go for a walk with a young gentleman—always leave at the corner.
7. Never leave a square inch of dinner on your plate.
8. Take a constitutional daily either between 12 and 1 o'clock or 6 and 7.

The real rules were much tougher.

We know that Hardy had an intense love affair with Tryphena: we know that he was strung between Tryphena and Emma for months before his marriage, so stymied by the decision he had to take, that he appears to have gone home to his mother and sister and the novel and waited for it all to roll away like thunder. It did, and Emma won—only to be, at the time of the writing of *Jude,* clearly thought of as a jailer, a bind, and an obstacle to the love for Mrs Henniker. Out of all this came Sue, whom the author alternately loves and detests; whose passionate inviolability he cherishes and damns; whose marriage gives him the occasion to be so bitterly eloquent against that institution, a woman born out of the clash between desire and necessity, mistress and wife, ideal and actual, satisfaction and respectability.

These oppositions are, in my opinion, part of the drive towards symmetry and coincidence which increases in pace and energy as the book progresses, until by the end we feel that plot is approaching the formality of metre. Lord David Cecil in his Clark

Lectures points out how often the plot strays from probability; but whereas he sees that as a weakness, I do not. However, we must concede that Hardy breaks all the rules of naturalism. For naturalism must obey certain inner injunctions of probability; if the author is saying, believe me, there *is* someone who walks, talks and *is* like Jude, then he has an obligation to prove it. He must not break the spell of that relationship. Pedestrian calculations about ages, dates, distances, wages, clothes, food, views, backgrounds etc., these must all have been considered even if they are then hidden from the eyes. And this is true of all—except someone of such intensified powers that, to save paragraphs of explanation, we call him a genius. Hardy certainly had genius, and it is that which allows him to defy the laws of probability. There is no need, I trust, to list here the literally hundreds of coincidences: from the major affairs of Jude and Sue being alter egos ('twins' they could be and are called), with her leaving the spirit of Christminster as he entered it, his first marriage matched by hers, or rather opposingly proposed, Vilbert and Arabella's perfect re-entries, Jude, of course, taking Sue to the hotel to which he has taken Arabella to whom he first committed himself before a portrait of Samson and Delilah, and so on. Proust pointed out that *Jude* was architectonic in the sense of being full of names of and allusions to buildings and parts of buildings. It seems to me that it would be comparatively easy to lay out *Jude* as a structure, Gothic of course; and, apart from minor planned disorders, the shape would fall out as balanced and symmetrical as the church which Hardy was restoring at the time.

There is much, much more one could say of *Jude*—about the themes—suicide, for example, which so interested Hardy in his book of facts and so intrigued him that he copied down—I assume with approval, though I could be wrong—the remarks of Cato, Pliny, Marcus Aurelius and Seneca on the subject. Stoicism indeed is a central part of the book's inner theory, as of course is sex—the morals of the time forced the book to be less explicit as you could expect, but not, as sometimes happens through imposed limitations, the better for it—Hardy had as much to praise about sex as he had to damn about marriage, and it is a pity that the picture comes over as just a problem.

The most important question about *Jude* is, why was it the last novel he wrote? The *Well-Beloved* was published after *Jude* but written before it. Hardy's top-of-the-head reason was that the reviews cured him of all further interest in novel-writing. Critical comment was indeed, in places, harsh; and Hardy was undoubtedly upset. He tried to pretend in his older and more revered years that his cosmic view of the world and of his own work gave him all the distance he needed to be out of reach of praise or blame.

But the latter bothered him right up to the end. He had begun by taking instruction from Horace Moule and continued by taking notes from all the great writers and educators whom he thought could help him; he was precisely the sort of man to be aware of his lacks and to hate the thought that others would be made aware of them. Success was not security enough: his marriage undoubtedly helped over some years, but not just before or after *Jude*. There was always refuge in the memory of his mother's early comfort and her presence continued, though this aid was bound to be less effective. It was in poetry that he sought and found sanctuary.

In this, too, of course he was re-inforced by his standard literary guide Matthew Arnold, who wrote, 'The future of poetry is immense because in poetry, where it is worthy of its high destinies, our race, as time goes on, will find an ever surer and surer stay.' This was duly transcribed. And Hardy would undoubtedly remember what Aristotle and Plato had written on poetry, or Shelley, Sir Philip Sidney, Francis Bacon. 'Poetry is . . . a kind of learning . . . truly belonging to the imagination'—and perhaps we should leave it there, with Hardy setting out to join those he considered immortal on the book shelves of his copy-book study at Max Gate.

On the other hand, the burden of this piece is that a great deal more happened in and about *Jude* than Hardy ever wanted publicly acknowledged. The image of the grand old man of letters drawing the first half of his career to a close or casting off the vulgar rocket which has launched him so that he can cruise in the ampler space—this is a good one, and Hardy had the time and the interest to cultivate and refine this picture as his long life went ever more sagely on. However, I do not believe it was as neat as that at the time. He had grumbled at reviews before—over *Tess* particularly—but been driven back to fiction. Of course he wanted to bring out his poetry, but I would guess that if *Wessex Poems* had been less of a success, he would have returned to fiction instead of using that energy for *The Dynasts*. One tiny fact here—trivial but possibly important: he had the habit of taking up a different pen for a different book and carving something of the title on the pen's shank—so there is a '*Tess*' pen and a '*Dynasts*' pen and so on—squarely, neatly carved in black. And a '*Jude*' pen too, of course; but on the other side of the '*Jude*' pen, he carved 'Poems'. Was he not sure enough at that stage to give them a pen to themselves?

No, I think he made *Jude* his last novel only partly for the reasons which he gave us. Clearly the drive towards poetry was strong and the manipulations in *Jude* are as abrupt as they are in the *Iliad*. But I believe that there was another and more powerful reason; and that was that he grew aware and afraid that fiction might reveal too many of his secrets, on the one hand, and, on the other, might force him into a confessional mode which he feared. When Emma read *Jude* she was very upset by the attack it contained on marriage; understandably. And though Hardy was at odds with her (perhaps he even hated her), we know that there was also a reservoir of love, however deeply buried under the crust of disappointment or frustration, which was to spring out in those poems following her death. For though there is expiation and remorse in those poems, there is also, clearly, great love. He would not enjoy upsetting her and might well fear where the next novel would take him. For though he denied, repeatedly, that there was any autobiographical element in *Jude,* he must have known how much, consciously or unconsciously, he had been forced to push out of his life in order to give the novel the force he wanted it to have: those who were most used (Tryphena Sparks—incredibly not mentioned in his official biography—his father, Horace Moule) were *dead,* or (John Antell, the London woman) *gone,* or (Mary, himself, Emma) part of his private and secret life and loyal to it. But, he must have wondered, how long could it go on? If his characters demanded so much of his personal life for nourishment, wasn't it dangerous? The next stop from Sue was Ursula Brangwen. The poet stood in a grander and safer relationship to his material: though he spoke personally, though he gave confidences, there was less risk of characters running away with ideas, for the only character need be the poet, and the control he could exercise and indeed needed to exercise was very different from the loose rein he needed to give characters in a novel.

There was also the division mentioned when referring to his notes on society, his awareness that he might have to move on to society novels, his comparative failure to handle this material in *The Hand of Ethelberta* and *A Laodicean,* Jude's expressed contempt for the churchmen and bishops and those with inherited wealth. Again this, as it were, slipped out; yet these were the very people whose company the older Hardy sought out and enjoyed. He was not part of the Joseph Wright dialect-revival movement. London was his centre now. The class-anger which was undoubtedly there was as liable to emerge in this demanding form—fiction—as the anger about marriage and the frustration about sex and the *obsession* with hanging. And what would happen to his life in London then?

In a sense *Jude* is the battle-ground where, according to your view on Hardy, he won or he lost. Whichever it was, he left that particular field. In the book naturalism collides with formalism, the Gothic with the old English, the flesh, as Hardy himself said, with the spirit, in a deadly struggle. The struggle was over the body of his future work. My guess is that the course Hardy saw before him was the course which D. H. Lawrence took—something involving the exposure of personal life, the very private feelings, the testing of the fiction in the circumstances of his own adventures. In short, there would have to be fewer secrets, none perhaps, if the thing were to be done fully, and less preoccupation with the old patterns and forms of novel-writing which gave him so much comfort. I think he saw that, and decided against going on because of those risks.

What he wanted to hide still, largely, remains the secret he has so carefully concealed. That he did want to conceal a great deal can scarcely be denied. In *Jude,* at a point of the utmost creative strain and fertility, he saw that fiction would not be ordered; that the things inside him could get out in ways which disturbed his sense of secrecy, propriety, and perhaps even survival. It was this, I think, which cured him of novel-writing. Though the poems are more than enough compensation, and in some ways the better part of his work, those who were caught up by the adventure of the novel-writing, where like Jude, he built himself up from the bottom to very near the top in terms of what he achieved, must regret that when he came to his Christminster he too saw, like Jude, that there was a wall between himself and the fulfilment of his journey—and turned away.

VIII

F. B. Pinion:

HARDY AND MYTH

Myth has become such a mazy academic subject, and the term is used and misused with such a variety of meaning that it is essential at the outset to state its implications for the present subject. I assume that myths are religious in origin, and relate to gods or similar personalized powers, that they were thought to reveal inescapable truths about the universe and nature, and that, even though their narrative features are fictitious, they can be used imaginatively by virtue of their original significance to reinforce or symbolize aspects of life.

I propose to discuss the functioning of images from four mythologies in four of Hardy's novels: Greek mythology in *The Return of the Native,* Norse in *The Woodlanders,* Christian in *Jude the Obscure,* and Hardy's own mythology in *Tess of the d'Urbervilles.* The question which Greek mythology reinforces in *The Return of the Native* is revived in *Tess* and *Jude,* but the use of Norse mythology with non-literal, human overtones is confined to *The Woodlanders,* and that of the Christian story to *Jude the Obscure.* Though Hardy did not make his own mythology explicit until he renounced prose fiction for poetry, he alludes to it several times in his novels. He refers to the First Cause under one name or another, and once, rather egregiously, to Nature as 'the great Mother'. It is only, I believe, in certain episodes of *Tess of the d'Urbervilles* that Hardy's mythical interpretation of the universe assumes a creative role, becoming indissolubly linked with narrative, or directing and permeating a dramatic action.

I

Eustacia Vye's Greek associations are well known. Much is made of them in that overcharged, extra-dimensional chapter 'Queen of Night'. We are told that her father was Greek by birth, a native of Corfu:

> Where did her dignity come from? By a latent vein from Alcinous' line, her father hailing from Phaeacia's isle?

In a dimlight her 'general figure' recalled Greek goddesses:

> The new moon behind her head, an old helmet upon it, a diadem of accidental dewdrops round her brow, would have been adjuncts sufficient to strike the note of Artemis, Athena, or Hera respectively, with as close an approximation to the antique as that which passes muster on many respected canvases.

She was 'the raw material of a divinity' and, with a little preparation, would have done well on Olympus.

Unfortunately she is on Egdon, and Edgon is her Hades. Eustacia's second misfortune is that she lives in a world of day-dream, and falls in love with Clym Yeobright before she sees him. The 'iris-hued embowment' with which she envisions him (to use Hardy's later expression for the illusion of a lover's dream) proceeds from the perfervid hope that he will be her means of escape to the gaiety and splendour of Paris. As she has no other choice for the fulfilment of her aspirations, it is a confounding irony of chance that the imaginary saviour returns to his native heath completely disillusioned with the vanity and flashiness of city life, and haunted by a sense of 'the whole creation groaning and travailing in pain'. All for 'plain living and high thinking', he is happy on Egdon, and wishes above all to be of service to his fellow-men. The altruism of Clym Yeobright conflicts with the hedonism of Eustacia.

Eustacia's protest against the restrictions of circumstance is manifested symbolically in her bonfire, the brightest of all those lighting up the heath as the pagan ritual is renewed at the onset of winter. This ritual is described as 'Promethean', and its parallel in Eustacia is clear: she has 'Pagan eyes, full of nocturnal mysteries'. Her essence is 'flame-like'; her 'smouldering rebelliousness' against Egdon gives her a 'true Tartarean dignity'. Not until her marriage to Clym does she realize that there is no hope of changing his purpose. When she is stung to protest against his submission in adversity, he replies:

> 'Now, don't you suppose, my inexperienced girl, that I cannot rebel, in high Promethean fashion, against the gods and fate as well as you. I have felt more steam and smoke of that sort than you have heard of. But the more I see of life the more do I perceive that there is nothing particularly great in its greatest walks, and therefore nothing particularly small in mine of furze-cutting. If I feel that the greatest blessings vouchsafed to us are not very valuable, how can I feel it to be any great hardship when they are taken away? So I sing to pass the time.'

The result is that Eustacia battles against depression, and goes to a gipsying, an outdoor dance, with Wildeve; she floats round and round on his arm in pagan ecstasy.

In the theme-chapter which introduces the novel, Hardy tells us that Egdon spells endurance, and that only a 'most thorough-going ascetic' (like Clym) could feel a 'natural right' to wander there. The heath is one of those places 'wearing sombreness distasteful to our race when it was young' but appealing to 'a more recently learnt emotion' than 'that which responds to the sort of beauty called charming and fair'. With thoughts akin to these Hardy wrote in January 1887: 'Nature is played out as a

Beauty . . . The "Simply natural" is interesting no longer . . . — it is . . . the style of a period when the mind is serene and unawakened to the tragical mysteries of life.' The pagan ecstasy which Eustacia savours with Wildeve is a reminder of an earlier civilization to whom the sombreness of 'haggard Egdon' would have seemed repugnant. The main theme of *The Return of the Native* is the irreconcilability of Hellenism with the modern Positivist philosophy which Hardy hoped would form the basis of 'the new religion': an alliance between Christian ethics and the best of modern science, its intellectual aim truth, its moral aim altruism.

There can be little doubt that Hardy was much influenced by the essay on Winckelmann in Walter Pater's *Studies in the History of the Renaissance* (1873). He, and Arnold after him, contrasted Greek sensuousness and Christian asceticism, but the deep impact which Pater made on Hardy was due to his success in formulating the dilemma of the modern artist. In the 'bewildering toils' of immutable laws operating throughout the universe and within the individual, how could one attain the Greek ideal of 'balance' and 'serenity' in presenting tragic issues? *Jude the Obscure* shows that the tragic consequence of natural laws may be inherent (from the chance of heredity and circumstance), or may arise from their incompatibility with the *mores* of a particular society. This is the kind of context which explains why the contrast drawn by Pater between Hellenic and advanced modern philosophy found a permanent lodgement in Hardy's mind. He alluded to it not long before his death in the introductory note to his last volume of poetry.

The latent dichotomy of a note made by Hardy in 1876 from John Addington Symonds on the Greek philosophy of life, 'What Clough described as a "stoic-Epicurean acceptance" of the world', probably gave greater emphasis to Clym's thematic role as the protagonist who endures. Arnold's essay 'Pagan and Mediaeval Religious Sentiment' undoubtedly influenced Hardy's modification of Eustacia. When he read this essay, fifteen chapters of *The Return of the Native* had been completed, but he replanned and rewrote much of what he had written before he produced the novel as we know it. Its first seven chapters were not finished until the end of August 1877, nearly five months after he had completed the fifteen chapters of the first version.

When Arnold writes on the 'ideal, cheerful, sensuous, pagan life' that is not 'sick or sorry', or the 'gay sensuous pagan life' that had gone when St Francis stirred 'the heart and imagination' of the poor, he comes nearer the hedonistic side of Hardy's subject than Pater does; and it is significant that, in speaking of Heine's reaction against Christian asceticism and his championship of 'the warm and glowing motions of sense', he comments: 'That is Heine's sentiment, in the prime of life, in the glow of activity, amid the brilliant whirl of Paris'. Paris and 'the warm and glowing motions of sense' cannot be dissociated from Eustacia.

Clym's asceticism is not Arnold's 'medieval sentiment'. In his face could be seen 'the typical countenance of the future' as Hardy foresaw it. He thought that the view of life 'as a thing to be put up with, replacing that zest for existence which was so intense in early civilizations', must ultimately change the facial expression of advanced nations. This view of life, in attuning Clym to Egdon, makes him incompatible with Eustacia; his humanitarian aims soon make him impatient with her 'sentiment on the wisdom of *Carpe diem*'.

> The truth seems to be that a long line of disillusive centuries has permanently displaced the Hellenic idea of life, or whatever it may be called. What the Greeks only suspected we know well; what their Aeschylus imagined our nursery children feel. That old-fashioned revelling in the general situation grows less and less possible as we uncover the defects of natural laws, and see the quandary that man is in by their operation.

The reference to 'natural laws' shows the writer's philosophical kinship with Pater. Clym's views coincided with Hardy's. The 'Sermons on the Mount' which he delivered on Rainbarrow were not restricted to Christian ethics; sometimes they were secular, sometimes religious. He was a preacher of the religion of the future, 'a John the Baptist who took ennoblement rather than repentance as his text. Mentally he was in a provincial future, that is, he was in many points abreast with the central town thinkers of his date.'

Here Hardy was probably thinking of men like John Stuart Mill, to whom he had listened in London. There can be no doubt that Hardy had thought seriously of what he could do for mankind. He had been interested in political reform; he was interested in education; before being converted to Mill's 'religion of the future', he had aspired to be a country parson like William Barnes; and his later writings show more and more openly the critical boldness of his altruism. Toward the end of his life, when he was losing faith in mankind, he asked himself why he went on writing, and decided that he must continue to write as long as he lived in a world of pain.[1] That is how Clym Yeobright felt; he could not live for his own ease and pleasure in a world 'groaning and travailing in pain'.

If therefore Eustacia's self-seeking may be regarded as in any way Promethean (as Hardy suggests) it is polarized by the idealism of Clym as a Promethean light-bringer to a people in darkness. Yet he fails to carry conviction. Clym like Eustacia is a dreamer, but they live in two different dream-worlds. Her wish to escape from the harsher realities of life is dramatized in the storm scene on the night of her death. The storm is Egdon's lover, and the wind its friend (such imagery recurs with tragic personal associations in Hardy's poem 'During Wind and Rain'). Clym is too sanguine about man's readiness for enlightenment, and fails to realize that most people prefer material advancement to 'plain living and high thinking'. Hardy had noticed that the 'religious sincerity' of Mill's speech 'was jarred on by his environment—a group on the hustings who, with few exceptions, did not care to understand him fully, and a crowd below who could not', though they were not wholly unimpressed.[2] Nor does Clym quite convince the reader; and the reason for this, I believe, is that, while the pagan and hedonistic Eustacia appealed to Hardy's imagination, his response to Clym was primarily intellectual. In the gathering gloom at the beginning of the novel Eustacia makes a more impressive figure on Rainbarrow than Clym in the daylight at the end. A degree of anticlimax was inevitable in the conclusion of *The Return of the Native,* whatever happened to Diggory Venn.

II

The theme of *The Return of the Native* is summed up in the words, 'That old-fashioned revelling in the general situation grows less and less possible as we uncover the defects of natural laws . . . '. They could serve as the epigraph to *The Woodlanders.* This novel, like Yell'ham Wood, signifies a 'thwarted purposing'; 'Life offers—to deny!'[3] The key to the dominant idea and feature of the novel is supplied in this passage:

> On older trees . . . huge lobes of fungi grew like lungs. Here, as everywhere, the Unfulfilled Intention, which makes life what it is, was as obvious as it could be among the deprived crowds of a city slum.

Hardy argued that, as man's awareness has evolved so far by natural law, it is unfortunate that the Creator has not mended matters 'by a second intent and execution', the elimination of evil in nature. If natural law had consciousness, 'how the aspect of its creatures would terrify it, fill it with remorse!'[4] In *The Woodlanders* he continually presents glimpses of the outer Darwinian world to reinforce the tragedy in the human situation:

> They halted beneath a half-dead oak, hollow and disfigured with tumours, its roots spreading out like claws grasping the ground. A chilly wind circled round them, upon whose currents the seeds of a neighbouring lime-tree, supported parachute-wise by the wing attached, flew out of the boughs downwards like fledglings from the nest. The vale was wrapped in a dim atmosphere of unnaturalness, and the east was like a livid curtain edged with pink.

Here we have description at three levels. The descent of the winged lime-seeds shows the observation of the poet; the distant scene is premonitory, hinting at disaster (Grace realizes, and her father is beginning to suspect, Fitzpiers' treachery); and the consumption at the heart of the oak (sharpened by the image of roots 'like claws') accentuates the cruelty of fate.

Grace Melbury is the victim of circumstances, of her father's ambition particularly, and of her own inherited weakness of will. Both characters are central to the suffering of the novel, but in the end one's sympathies remain unequivocally with Giles Winterborne and Marty South, both thwarted and unfulfilled in their lives, the stoic victims of chance. It is with them that images from Norse mythology are significantly linked.

The novel presents sunny woodland scenes and one particularly bright landscape, but its prevailing tone is sombre. Characteristically it opens in a 'tomb-like' silence on a winter's day. The first dawn has a 'bleared white visage' which emerges 'like a dead-born child'; soon 'the regular dripping of the fog from the plantation boughs around' is heard. In addition to images which reveal the cruelty of nature, sunlessness, fog, winter, decay, and death are important features of scenes which mirror the human situation.

The network of chance or causality is particularly elaborate. If there had been no American Civil War, and if Marty South had not had beautiful hair, Mrs Charmond would not have died as she did. Hardy seems to make a point of showing that the 'lonely courses' of Little Hintock inhabitants 'formed no detached design at all, but were part of the pattern in the great web of human doings then weaving in both hemispheres from the White Sea to Cape Horn'. It was 'but a cast in the die of destiny' that Marty South should be cutting spars late into the night. When she finished at three in the morning, she looked out:

> The night in all its fulness met her flatly on the threshold, like the very brink of an absolute void, or the ante-mundane Ginnung-Gap believed in by her Teuton forefathers.

The 'ante-mundane Ginnung-Gap' (the void before the earth was created, according to Norse mythology) expresses the emptiness or bleakness of Marty's life.

After hearing that Giles Winterborne is not for her, she cuts off her long locks of hair for the guineas and her invalided father. She has accepted her self-sacrificial role. Her hair lay on the 'pale scrubbed deal' of a coffin-stool table like 'waving and ropy weeds over the washed white bed of a stream'. She would not turn to the looking-glass, 'knowing what a deflowered visage would look back at her, and almost break her heart; she dreaded it as much as did her own ancestral goddess the reflection in the pool after the rape of her locks by Loke the Malicious'.

The next Norse reference occurs after the Unfulfilled Intention passage. Giles follows Melbury and Grace in the wood.

> They dived amid beeches under which nothing grew, the younger boughs still retaining their hectic leaves, that rustled in the breeze with a sound almost metallic, like the sheet-iron foliage of the fabled Jarnvid wood.

Hardy may have been familiar with the Jarnvid wood image in Arnold's *Balder Dead,* a poem which probably suggested the symbolical application of the last and most important Norse reference in *The Woodlanders.* This is to Niflheim, Hela's gloomy realm, where the sad spirits of those who had died of sickness or old age, the unfulfilled, as opposed to those who lived and died heroically, were doomed to remain.

One strangely fascinating feature of Hardy's story arises from the tree which appears to have a hold on John South's life. The source of this animistic belief seems to be more than local tradition:

> 'The shape of it seems to haunt him like an evil spirit. He says that it is exactly his own age, that it has got human sense, and sprouted up when he was born on purpose to rule him, and keep him as its slave. Others have been like it afore in Hintock.'

South had intended chopping it down when it was small and he was a boy. It had never forgiven him, he believed. 'And at last it got too big, and now 'tis my enemy, and will be the death of me.' This mania is driving him demented: 'As the tree waved South waved his head, making it his fugleman with abject obedience.'

To spare his torments and save his life, Giles is persuaded to lop off the lowest boughs. As he worked upwards one afternoon it grew dark and misty. In the evening gloom and thickened fog, he was no more than 'a dark grey spot on the light grey zenith' when Grace returned to tell him they were still close friends despite her acquiescence in her father's will. Giles, however, had accepted his fate like Marty. He remained aloft till the fog and the night completely obscured him from her view. If only he had come down immediately, 'something might have been done' (Hardy says) which would have raised his hopes. 'But he continued motionless and silent in that gloomy Niflheim or fogland which involved him, and she proceeded on her way.'

It might be thought that the fog represents the ignorance in which Giles works. He does not know how Grace feels; he does not know that by lopping off the boughs to save South's life he is helping, in Hardy's proleptic phrase, to fray it away. Nor is he aware that his action is the first step towards his own doom. Yet the narrative content suggests the blanketing-out of Winterborne's hopes, and the loss of Grace; this is confirmed by the synonymous linking of 'fogland' with 'Niflheim', to express the resignation or gloom of one who remains unfulfilled, like the spirits of Hela's realm.

III

Although he returned to it time and time again over a long period, Hardy never seemed quite satisfied with his plan for *Jude the Obscure*. Perhaps he was attempting too much; perhaps at the crucial period he had neither the time nor the calm of mind to achieve all that he aimed at. It contains some of his most dramatic and poignant scenes, probably not a far cry from his own matrimonial dilemma. Undoubtedly the idealization of Mrs Henniker and her refusal to be emancipated by his arguments against 'ritualistic ecclesiasticism' and 'retrograde superstitions' had much to do with the final recasting of the plan for this novel.

Paradigmatically, taking the unformalized marriage of Jude and Sue as the point of intersection, it is a cross. Disaster makes Sue give up her modern emancipated outlook for 'ritualistic ecclesiasticism'. Jude's course is the reverse; after studying for the Church, he burns his books and adopts contemporary rationalistic views, regarding Sue's return to conformity and Phillotson as the effect of 'retrograde superstitions'.

When Hardy told Edmund Gosse that 'the plot is almost geometrically constructed', he seems to have had this cruciformity of design in mind. It was not consciously planned; 'the characters necessitated it, and I simply let it come'. In choosing to call Oxford 'Christminster', however, there can be no doubt that he was thinking of the Crucifixion, and it is significant that the doomed sufferers first meet in Christminster 'at the cross in the pavement which marked the spot of the Martyrdoms'.

The name 'Jude' is linked with Judah and Jerusalem. When the boy Jude first sees Christminster, distance lends it enchantment; it is a city of light like the New Jerusalem. Heaven lies about us in our infancy, but the 'gleam and glory' of its lights seem dubious at close view. Allusions to 'Intimations of Immortality' link experiences which are years apart. There is no moonshine when Jude finds the colleges; they are decrepit, with unillumined corners, and many shadows cast by contemporary lights around them. This is the first step of disillusionment towards the prospect of Sarcophagus College, 'silent, black and windowless' with 'four centuries of gloom, bigotry, and decay'.

Merged dramatically in this story is the debate between Hellenism and Christian asceticism. Sue's views are Heine's, and when Jude rejects Christian theology, the two resolve 'to make a virtue of joy'. When they are happy, she says, 'I feel that we have returned to Greek joyousness, and have blinded ourselves to sickness and sorrow'. 'The ideal, cheerful, sensuous pagan life is not sick or sorry', Arnold wrote.

When Jude reaches Christminster with Sue and his children it is 'Remembrance Day'. The parallel between Commemoration Week at Oxford and the week of the Passover is made evident when Sue speaks of coming up to 'Jerusalem' to see the 'festival', and describes 'leaving Kennetbridge for this place' as 'like coming from Caiaphas to Pilate'. She loses her children, is smitten with a sense of sinful indulgence in the past, and decides to mortify the flesh ('the terrible flesh—the curse of Adam'), take to ritualistic ecclesiasticism, and accept conformity and (as Jude sees it) a 'fanatic prostitution' to Phillotson.

Both Sue and Jude are crucified. We are reminded of the Crucifixion when Jude first accepts her loss: 'Then let the veil of our temple be rent in twain from this hour', he says. And when she is faced with the duty of self-sacrifice to her licensed husband, she does not wish the cup to pass from her but will drink it 'to the dregs'. As Mrs Edlin says, her re-wedding is like a funeral. So too is Jude's. When he realizes that Sue still loves him, he makes no effort to live. His request for water recalls the Johannine account of the Crucifixion. The sounds of 'Remembrance games' from the direction of the river as Jude is dying are another reminder of the Passover festival.

References to the Crucifixion and events leading up to it are not mythical in themselves, yet, as one quotation has already hinted, they are ancillary to the myth of Adam and sin and Redemption. Twice Sue asserts that her children have died to save her from sin, and in fact Little Father Time takes the lives of the other two children and his own to spare their parents. The sight of the three hanging children is a ghastly travesty of the Crucifixion.

> The boy's face expressed the whole tale of their situation. On that little shape had converged all the inauspiciousness and shadow which had darkened the first union of Jude, and all the accidents, mistakes, fears, errors of the last. He was their nodal point, their focus, their expression in a single term. For the rashness of those parents he had groaned, for their ill-assortment he had quaked, and for the misfortunes of these he had died.

Here matrimonial incompatibilities and their hereditary effects are vaguely linked to the Christian myth of sin and redemption. 'For the rashness of those parents he had groaned' alludes unmistakably to Milton's *Paradise Lost*[5] and to the Crucifixion. Hardy seems to be obsessed to the point of morbidity with this imaginative motif. He prepares us for it very slightly by presenting Little

Father Time as a 'Divinity', though 'enslaved and dwarfed by his mortal condition'.

> A ground swell from ancient years of night seemed now and then to lift the child in this morning-life, when his face took a back view over some great Atlantic of Time, and appeared not to care about what it saw.

This seems to hint at hereditary disposition and outlook, but there is nothing in the presentation of the story to make the murder of Sue's children convincing, or to explain it completely with reference to Hardy's statement that the novel was 'concerned . . . with the tragic issues of two bad marriages, owing in the main to the doom or curse of hereditary temperament peculiar to the family of the parties'. What we hear on this subject in the novel is almost peripheral, and altogether too slight to validate this particular castastrophe. If this is so, it is unfortunate: the major tragedy or 'crucifixion' of both Jude and Sue is the direct consequence of an event which cannot be regarded as inevitable.

The hanging episode, whenever it occurred to him, seems to have originated, like 'The Church-Builder', in one of Hardy's 'In Tenebris' moods when his belief that our nursery children feel what Aeschylus imagined coincided with thoughts on abnormal heredity and perhaps on Malthusianism. This horror seems unacceptable on realistic grounds, and achieves little imaginative coherence with the remainder of the novel. It seems to have been introduced for the sake of the myth, but the mythical context of the Crucifixion parallel (with its overtones of sin and redemption) is out of proportion to the circumstances of this tragical climax, and an example, it seems to me, of that 'mental bombast' which Coleridge defined as 'thoughts and images too great for the subject'—adding, 'This, by the bye, is a fault of which none but a man of genius is capable.'

IV

Almost at the end of 1875 Hardy noted in Schlegel, 'The deepest want and deficiency of all modern Art lies in the fact that the Artists have no mythology.' This means, I suppose, a set of beliefs or a religion which is regarded as the key to life and the universe. Hardy's own philosphy was rooted in Comte's Positivism. In a world of imperfection created by natural law, no God could be regarded as omniscient or omnipotent. Since 'man is entirely subordinate to the world', progress depends on education and co-operation for the common good. Such is the theme of 'A Plaint to Man'. Comte stresses the importance of altruism. In Hardy it appears also as 'charity' or 'loving-kindness'.

Its spirit animates some of his finest characters, none more than Tess:

> she sought not her own; was not provoked; thought no evil of his treatment of her. She might just now have been Apostolic Charity herself returning to a self-seeking modern world.

It was, I think, predominantly with this spirit of self-sacrifice for others in mind that the Positivist Frederic Harrison described *Tess* as Hardy's 'very beautiful book'. 'To me it reads like a Positive allegory or sermon', he wrote to Hardy.

Hardy described Positivism as 'the new religion'. He agreed with J. S. Mill that Jesus was 'excellently fitted to aid and fortify that real, though purely human religion, which sometimes calls itself the Religion of Humanity'. In *The Positive Evolution of Religion* (1913) Harrison said that the acceptable part of Christianity was in no way higher than the religion of humanity, but that the religion of the future could not be limited to it, for Jesus was only one of many Messiahs. Hardy's thought is similar in his poem 'Unkept Good Fridays'.

There are incidental echoes of Comte in *Tess of the d'Urbervilles* (in references to fetishism, for example). More interesting, however, are two passages which are not so much allegorical (in Harrison's moral sense of the word) as the blending of the human narrative with the mythology which Hardy constructed on the basis of scientific humanism. In this he was considerably helped and fortified by the writing of intermediaries, J. S. Mill in particular. Hardy's mythopoeic period begins very early with the poetry he wrote in London from 1865 to 1867. The opening lines of 'Discouragement'—

> To see the Mother, naturing Nature, stand
> All wracked and wrung by her unfaithful lord

—contain the essence of many poems in *Poems of the Past and the Present* (1901) which Hardy intended as a kind of preparatory course for the religion of the future and, more immediately, for the great mythological presentation of *The Dynasts*.

The first of the passages in *Tess* which relate the human situation to the universal 'Cause of Things' is less effective, probably because it contains little action. It occurs after Tess's arrival at The Slopes. Mrs d'Urberville is kindly and well-meaning, but ineffective. She is blind and remote, unaware of what is going on; and she makes only one, brief, appearance. In her secondary, mythic role, she is 'The Lacking Sense' or Nature, working to immutable law:

Ah! knowest thou not her secret yet, her vainly veiled deficience,
  Whence it come that all unwittingly she wounds the lives she loves?
That sightless are those orbs of hers? which bar to her omniscience
  Brings those fearful unfulfilments, that red ravage through her zones
    Whereat all creation groans.

She is also 'The Sleep-Worker':

When wilt thou wake, O Mother, wake and see—
As one who, held in trance, has laboured long
By vacant rote and prepossession strong—
The coils that thou hast wrought unwittingly;

Wherein have place, unrealized by thee,
Fair growths, foul cankers, right enmeshed with wrong,
Strange orchestras of victim-shriek and song,
And curious blends of ache and ecstasy?

Appropriately the image we associate with blind Mrs d'Urberville is the 'large, four-post bedstead hung with heavy damask curtains' in the room where Tess performs the strange task of whistling to her caged bullfinches. She is absent when danger threatens:

Once while Tess was at the window where the cages were ranged, giving her lesson as usual, she thought she heard a rustling behind the bed. The old lady was not present, and turning round the girl had an impression that the toes of a pair of boots were visible below the fringe of the curtains.

The interloper is, of course, Alec d'Urberville. The caged birds are a reminder of the human condition: all people are caged birds, Hardy wrote in 1885. For 'the Mother' we turn to the poem 'The Bullfinches':

  All we creatures, nigh and far
  (Said they there), the Mother's are;
Yet she never shows endeavour
  To protect from warrings wild
  Bird or beast she calls her child.

  Busy in her handsome house
  Known as Space, she falls a-drowse;
Yet, in seeming, works on dreaming,
  While beneath her groping hands
  Fiends make havoc in her bands.

Alec has already been associated with the arch-fiend Satan in the scene which is carefully placed before the suggestion of menace in the bedroom. The old house and garden which are the home of his blind mother's pet poultry are surrounded by a wall, with only one door for entrance. Thick ivy conceals Alec before he springs from the coping of the wall into the plot, as Milton's Satan entered Eden:

> One gate there only was, and that looked east
> On the other side: which when th' arch-felon saw,
> Due entrance he disdained, and in contempt
> At one slight bound high overleaped all bound
> Of hill or highest wall, and sheer within
> Lights on his feet.

The Satanic role of Alec d'Urberville is reinforced later, when he is seen in the smoke of the bonfire in the Durbeyfield garden at Marlott, and quotes from the Tempter's speech in *Paradise Lost*, a less convincing technique than the allusive one I have just sketched.

After Tess's 'fall' there came her spring revival, happiness and love in the summer, a marriage mockery, and a cruel winter at Flintcomb-Ash. So we come to the second scene. 'It is', as Hardy writes, 'the threshing of the last wheat-rick at Flintcomb-Ash Farm' on a March day. By the stack stands 'the red tyrant' that the women have 'come to serve'; a little way off is the engine which is to act as 'the *primum mobile* of this little world'. It has a sinister, Tophet-like or Plutonic appearance. By Farmer Groby's orders Tess has to stand by the man who feeds the thresher, unfasten the sheaves, and pass them in steady succession so that the machine can be fed evenly and continuously (an indescribably hard task when sheaves were fastened with tough bands of corn):

> for Tess there was no respite; for, as the drum never stopped, the man who fed it could not stop, and she, who had to supply the man with untied sheaves, could not stop either, unless Marian changed places with her, which she sometimes did for half an hour in spite of Groby's objection that she was too slow-handed for a feeder.

As Tess could not turn her head, she did not observe the arrival of Alec d'Urberville.

When dinner-break came she 'left her post, her knees trembling so wretchedly with the shaking of the machine that she could scarcely walk'. She would avoid d'Urberville by having her meal out of sight, alone, on the stack. He came up the ladder, and they talked. Sensual and selfish he may have been, but he was in love with Tess, and would have done anything to save her from servitude; his protest to Farmer Groby showed the courage born of conviction. There is justification in his jibe against Tess's legal husband Angel Clare. But she has been plagued by Alec long enough, and the taunt is too truthful for her endurance. The ancient d'Urberville temper flares up and, without the slightest warning, she picks up one of her leather gloves, and swings it by the gauntlet hard in his face. Hardy emphasizes the effect of heredity:

> It was heavy and thick as a warrior's, and it struck him flat on the mouth. Fancy might have regarded the act as the recrudescence of a trick in which her armed progenitors were not unpractised.

The blow fetches blood:

> 'Now, punish me!' she said, turning up her eyes to him with the hopeless defiance of the sparrow's gaze before its captor twists its neck. 'Whip me, crush me; you need not mind those people under the rick! I shall not cry out. Once victim, always victim—that's the law!'

Here there is an allusion to Clarissa Harlowe and Lovelace's intent, 'Once subdued, and always subdued'. Alec is angered by Tess's ingratitude, and warns her that he will be her master. By force of circumstances, he is; Tess has to submit for the sake of her family. She admits that he is good to her and to them, but spiritually she is dead, a corpse drifting with the current.

To the Positivist in Hardy here was Tess, her one life ruined. Analyse the poem 'Discouragement' and the novel carefully, and you will find that she is the victim of chance—of heredity, physical and temperamental; of the position she was born into, and all the other factors that impinge on her life. She could not be held responsible for them; she was, in Hardy's words, 'a pure woman'.

Her victimization by chance is expressed in the threshing scene. In the pre-Copernican era, the universe was imagined in terms of concentric spheres. It was created for man, and he was at the centre. Round the earth turned the sphere to which the moon was fixed; beyond that, in turn, the spheres which held the sun and the planets; beyond them, the sphere containing the stars. Outside, giving movement to all within, was the Primum Mobile, which was inseparable from the Empyrean and God. Just as the Primum Mobile connoted God in medieval philosophy, so the term was used for the Prime Cause in Positivist philosophy. In *The Positive Evolution of Religion* Frederic Harrison describes the 'first Cause' as 'a kind of Primum Mobile'. Tess has no choice; she is the victim of chance; she is a slave to a machine driven by an engine, and that engine is the *primum mobile* of her little world. In the words which open the After Scene of *The Dynasts:*

> Thus doth the Great Foresightless mechanize
> In blank entrancement now as evermore.

Ultimate causes are indefinable; they need a mythology to express them. In the last scene Hardy has succeeded in expressing his view of life through the dramatic integration of narrative and myth. *The Return of the Native* presents two opposing points of view, one in some respects Hellenic; mythological references reinforce the antithesis, but they never endow action with a concurrent symbolical import as in the threshing scene; they are no more than incidental illuminations of a theme. The Norse references in *The Woodlanders* are much rarer, but they are just as incidental, providing a slight reinforcement of mood, outlook, and theme. The hanging of Jude's three children lacks sufficient credibility to support a myth which has universal significance; nor do the major features of the novel give coherence to the myth of sin and redemption as it applied to this scene. Whether it was part of Hardy's plan when he began the writing of *Jude* is not known, but it is certain that, after more than two years' delay, he embarked on its composition with no great enthusiasm or confidence, and finally regretted his inability to revise it as much as he wished. The threshing scene in *Tess* shows Hardy's imaginative thought working harmoniously and powerfully; the hanging scene in *Jude* suggests either a failure in critical judgment or a failure to raise performance to the level of earlier imaginative thinking. As Hardy's unresolved matrimonial discords began after the completion of *Tess*, he was probably unable to give *Jude* as much attention as he had devoted to the former novel. Something more than false modesty lies in his remark to Gosse, 'You have hardly any idea how poor and feeble the book seems to me, as executed, beside the idea of it I had formed in prospect.'[6] When we consider why Hardy abandoned novel-writing, we are apt to forget conditions at Max Gate. They were not conducive to that 'balance', that 'unity with one's self' which Pater thought a prerequisite for art, particularly in the 'perplexed light' of the modern world.

IX

John Paterson:

THE CONTINUING MIRACLE: NATURE AND CHARACTER IN THOMAS HARDY

No wonder Lawrence went, in his emergency as man and artist, to the fiction of Thomas Hardy. Who among his contemporaries offered a conception of life and art more satisfactory to his sense of the world as a 'religious' place, as an abiding miracle and mystery? For James and Conrad, for Ford and Joyce, reality was comprehended by the human, by the merely social and moral, and constituted as such the only proper province of the novelist. 'Fiction', as Conrad put it, 'is history, human history, or it is nothing.'[1] For Lawrence, however, neither life nor art was supportable on such meagre terms. Man was not after all the chief environment of man. Man was 'related to the universe in some "religious" way, even prior to his relation to his fellow man'. It was not enough that the novelist be 'a writer of books of manners'. He had 'to realise the tremendous *non-human* quality of life', the existence of a nature cosmos that had more to offer of glory and of glamour than the vulgar world of men and things. 'I am tired of life being so ugly and cruel', Lawrence wrote. 'How I long for it to turn pleasant. It makes my soul heave with distaste to see it so harsh and brutal.'[2]

If Hardy had a special appeal for Lawrence, then, it was because he felt the same divine dissatisfactions with life and art. For him as for Lawrence, it did not suffice to be 'a writer of novels proper'. 'He took no interest in manners,' Hardy said of himself, 'but in the substance of life only.'[3] For him as for Lawrence, too, it didn't suffice to register the merely human or material realities: 'the material world is so uninteresting, human life is so miserably bounded, circumscribed, cabin'd, cribb'd, confined. I want another domain for the imagination to expatiate in.'[4] For him as for Lawrence, that other domain was the domain of Nature. To define reality as a function of the merely human and social was to define it as ordinary and commonplace. But to define it as a function of a natural universe independent of and infinitely greater than the human creature and his cities and societies was to define it as the continuing repository of marvel and magic. Darwin may have demolished Wordsworth's kindly Nature as a fit and friendly habitation for mankind, but in the process he had also established a Nature whose terrifying integrity, whose terrifying independence of man, had made it a stranger and more miraculous place than Wordsworth had dreamed of. 'Nature [was] played out as a Beauty,' as Hardy put it, 'but not as a Mystery.'[5] Hence his special importance for Lawrence. By reinstating the natural cosmos as a real existence and man as an organic part of that existence, by creating concepts of life and character left unacknowledged by James and Joyce, by Conrad and Ford, Hardy in effect restored the possibility of the wonder and the miracle of things.

I

As Hardy liked to think of it, Nature was its own excuse for being. It was what his Angel Clare would call 'actualized poetry', a poetry whose beauty and splendour were expressions not of an eccentric art or imagination but of natural objects in themselves. Hardy has accordingly been celebrated, and justly so, for the preternatural acuteness of his eye and ear, for the precision and particularity with which he registered the sights and sounds of nature. Nevertheless, he never accepted the novelist as realist, never accepted himself as a novelist in this sense, and hence, as pictures of Nature, his novels are ultimately less remarkable for their representational force, for their equality with the rude substance of Nature, than for their imaginative force, for their transformations of that rude substance. In keeping with his dictum that 'the seer should watch that pattern among general things which his idiosyncrasy moves him to observe',[6] Hardy's habit was to observe in Nature precisely what his idiosyncrasy, what his predilection for the weird and the wonderful, moved him to observe. Indeed, the same idiosyncrasy that made him single out what was unusual and surprising for the actions of his plots also made him single out what was surprising and unusual for the data of his natural scenes and settings.

Hence, to begin with, his fascination with the extra-human realms of outer space. It is not alone in *Two on a Tower* that 'the stupendous background of the stellar universe' is acknowledged. Attesting as it does to the non-human, to something that by virtue of its sheer disconnection from the world of man and things seems weird and wondrous, the same stupendous background is acknowledged elsewhere in Hardy's novels. In *Far from the Madding Crowd,* for example, Hardy recites with Miltonic pleasure the majestic names of distant stars and constellations:

> The Dog-star and Aldebaran, pointing to the restless Pleiades, were half-way up the Southern sky, and between them hung Orion, which gorgeous constellation never burnt more vividly than now, as it soared forth above the rim of the landscape. Castor and Pollux with their quiet shine were almost on the meridian: the barren and gloomy Square of Pegasus was creeping round to the north-west . . .

Later, in *The Return of the Native,* he gives the geography of a moon (surely never before in fiction rendered more closely and fantastically), Clym's eye travelling

> over the length and breadth of that distant country—over the Bay of Rainbows, the sombre Sea of Crises, the Ocean of Storms, the Lake of Dreams, the vast Walled Plains, and the wondrous Ring Mountains—till he almost felt himself to be voyaging bodily through its wild scenes, standing on its hollow hills, traversing its deserts, descending its vales and old sea bottoms, or mounting to the edges of its craters.

Even those skies placed in a closer and more human relation to the earth are no ordinary skies. They are heightened or sublimed in a way that makes them as magical and unearthly as Gabriel's strange stars and Clym's even stranger moon. In *The Woodlanders,* Giles and Grace

> see far into the recesses of heaven . . . the eye journeying on under a species of golden arcades, and past fiery obstructions, fancied cairns, logan-stones, stalactites and stalagmite of topaz. Deeper than this their gaze passed thin flakes of incandescence, till it plunged into a bottomless medium of soft green fire.

The same partiality for the exotic and the extraordinary governs Hardy's selections from the sublunary, more familiar world of earth below. It is a world of birds, beasts, and flowers all right, but of birds, beasts, and flowers of no common garden variety. The wasteland of Flintcomb-Ash in *Tess* is dreadful enough in itself, but it becomes dreadful in a more spectacular way by the apparition of strange birds from the north that have no community whatsoever with a cosy English nature or with any experience remotely human:

> gaunt spectral creatures with tragical eyes—eyes which had witnessed scenes of cataclysmal horror in inaccessible polar regions of a magnitude such as no human being had ever conceived . . . which had beheld the crash of icebergs and the slide of snow-hills by the shooting light of the Aurora; been half blinded by the whirl of colossal storms and terraqueous distortions . . . [and] of all they had seen which humanity would never see, they brought no account.

Again, the world of Egdon Heath is remarkable enough in itself but it becomes even more remarkable with the apparition of a wild mallard from 'regions unknown to man' who, too, brings with him 'an amplitude of Northern knowledge': 'Glacial catastrophes, snowstorm episodes, glittering auroral effects, Polaris in the zenith, Franklin underfoot—the category of his commonplaces was wonderful.' Even the categories of creatures native to the Heath are rare enough and otherwise wonderful, so that the common flies are 'huge flies . . . quite in a savage state', the grasshoppers are 'tribes of emerald-green grass-hoppers', and the butterflies 'which Egdon produced, and which were never seen elsewhere' are called 'strange amber-coloured butterflies'.

Such, indeed, is the glamour of Hardy's natural universe that when a thing or creature is not in itself something rich and strange, it is likely to be converted by some cause or freak in nature into something rich and strange. In *Under the Greenwood Tree,* for example, fuchsias and dahlias are laden 'with small drops and dashes of water, changing the colour of their sparkle at every movement of the air', and in *Far from the Madding Crowd* 'the creeping plants . . . [are] bowed with rows of heavy water drops, which had upon objects behind them the effect of minute lenses of high magnifying power'. It is in the light of sun or moon or star, however, that natural objects in Hardy achieve their strangest transmutations. At times the effect, as with the waterdrops, is to bring the human eye abnormally close to the natural object, so that in *The Return of the Native* otherwise ordinary rabbits are weirdly altered in the sun, 'the hot beams blazing through the delicate tissue of each thin-fleshed ear, and firing it to a blood-red transparency in which the veins could be seen'. More usually, however, the effect is to bring the human eye abnormally far from the object, and to produce less a distortion than a transformation. In *The Return of the Native,* the wings and thighs and breasts of a heron are 'so caught by the bright sunbeams that he appeared as if formed of burnished silver'. In *Tess,* gnats wandering across the shimmer of the morning sun are 'irradiated as if they bore fire within them', while even more remarkably 'the huge pool of blood' that spills from the slain body of the heroine's humble work-horse is amazingly transformed by the same natural agency: 'when the sun rose a hundred prismatic hues were reflected from it'. In a Wordsworth or a Tennyson, in a Scott or George Eliot, Nature and the objects of Nature seem to be regarded from the same angle and from the same distance, from, that is, a human angle and a human distance. In Hardy, however, they are regarded from an angle or a distance either more or less than human, from an angle or a distance so near or so far as to make them unfamiliar and surprising.

Hardy was not content with such 'natural' alterations as were worked on things by sunlight and moonlight. In his idiosyncratic regard for the odd and the grotesque, he delighted in selecting from nature what was paradoxically 'unnatural', in catching her in those freakish moments when she inverted or reversed or otherwise contravened her own 'natural' order. In the opening page of *The Return of the Native,* the heath at twilight grows incongruously darker than the sky itself: 'darkness had to a great extent arrived hereon, while day stood distinct in the sky'. In *Far from the Madding Crowd* 'the pale sheen [of the moon] had that reversed direction which snow gives, coming upward and lighting up [Boldwood's] ceiling in an unnatural way, casting shadows in strange places, and putting lights where shadows had used to be'. These preternatural inversions of nature, as Hardy would have called them, occur most frequently and most variously in the great pages of *Tess* when Hardy celebrates the 'non-human hours' of dawn in the Valley of the Great Dairies. Here the yellow gleam of the buttercups gives the shaded faces of the dairy-people 'an elfish, moonlit aspect, though the sun was pouring upon their backs in all the strength of noon'. Here, too, the lovers see 'tiny blue fogs in the shadows of trees and hedges, all the time that there was bright sunshine elsewhere', and here again 'the reflected sun glared up from the river, under a bridge . . . though the sun itself was hidden by the bridge'. No wonder that words like 'strange', 'peculiar', and 'preternatural', and figures of speech like 'aqueous dawn', 'luminous gloom', 'vast pool of odour', and 'pollen of radiance' should recur in Hardy's pages. Such words and such figures could alone define the weird incongruities and strange anomalies of a world that was other than human and at times even other than natural.

Hardy's habit was not only to select from the matter of nature those things that in themselves were rich and strange. Consistent with his dictum that art was not just 'the thing' itself but 'a view of the thing', he acted to transmute the matter of nature in the crucible of his art or imagination. In his earlier novels he was indeed excessively fond of anthropomorphizing the natural world, of rendering its appearance and behaviour in the most melodramatic human terms. Trees writhe 'like miserable men'; boughs are 'beaded with the mist to the greyness of aged men'; a pool glitters 'like a dead man's eye'. Under the spell of a hectic imagination, nature in Hardy becomes at times positively Gothic, as it does in the storm scene of *Far from the Madding Crowd:* 'A hot breeze, as if breathed from the parted lips of some dragon about to swallow the globe, fanned him from the south, while directly opposite in the north rose a grim misshapen body of cloud.' Later, lightning flashes 'with the spring of a serpent and the shout of a fiend' and 'the forms of skeletons [appear] in the air, shaped with blue fire for bones'. Even in the later novels, Hardy's imagination will betray him. In *The Woodlanders,* trees have 'spreading roots whose mossed rinds made them like hands wearing green gloves'; in *Tess,* when seen against the moon, 'the pollard willows, tortured out of their natural shape by incessant choppings, [becomc] spiny-haired monsters'.

This is not to say that Hardy's anthropomorphizing never achieves its effect. To describe fungi in *Far from the Madding Crowd* as 'marked with great splotches, red as arterial blood' or, in *The Woodlanders*, as 'huge lobes' growing 'like lungs' may be extravagant, but it contributes to the strangeness of the natural object without compromising the integrity, the otherness, which is also the condition of its strangeness. Indeed, there are many moments in Hardy's novels when the dramatic situation calls not for the magic enhancement of nature but for the realistic definition and even for the realistic reduction of it. This is certainly the case when natural phenomena are compared with human artifacts and manufactures. So, in *Far from the Madding Crowd*, 'withered grass-bents, encased in icicles' can suggest 'the twisted and curved shapes of *old Venetian glass*' and in *Tess* the face of a 'tarnished moon' can suggest '*the outworn gold-leaf halo of some worm-eaten Tuscan saint*'. So, too, in these same novels 'a wasting moon' can hang over the west 'like tarnished *brass*, and a 'reflected sun' glare up from a river 'with a *molten-metallic* glow'. In imagery even more modern and industrial, a sun sinks in *Tess* 'with the aspect of a great forge in the heavens', while in *The Woodlanders* a western sky glows 'like some vast foundry wherein new worlds were being cast', and inside the trees of the forest the sap begins 'to heave with the force of hydraulic lifts'.

In the main, however, Hardy is at his best when he can make the ordinary in nature extraordinary in ways that do not draw attention to themselves, in ways that heighten and intensify reality without extravagantly rearranging it, and thus increase rather than decrease the glamour of it. Just so, the natural in his novels is often beautifully changed to precious stones and jewels. In the enchanted country of *Tess*, the mist gives off 'minute *diamonds* of moisture', the air of the fore-dawn is '*pearly*', and boughs are seen against 'the pale *opalescence* of the lower sky'. In the enchanted country of *The Woodlanders*, the heavens are hung with 'stalactites and stalagmite of *topaz*', and the bark of a tree after rain is 'coated with a lichenous wash as green as *emerald*'. In the even more ravishing cider-country, the air is as 'blue as *sapphire*', and the apple-trees are 'bossed, nay encrusted, with scarlet and *gold* fruit'. Indeed, if things in Hardy are more than merely things and creatures more than merely creatures, it is because they are so highly or so strangely coloured, so that in *The Woodlanders* mist becomes 'lavender mist', and fire 'green fire', and in *Tess* the dawns become 'violet or pink' dawns, and the fogs 'blue fogs'. For Hardy as for Lawrence, for Hardy, indeed, as for post-impressionists like Van Gogh and Gauguin, the natural world was not at all what the eye saw. It was what the imagination saw.

Natural phenomena seldom appear lovelier or stranger in Hardy than when they are juxtaposed with phenomena not outside nature but, more curiously, inside nature itself. The results are eccentric and surprising but without the shock and violence of 'arterial blood' or 'hydraulic lifts'. So, in Hardy, flower-bells can become as craters, showers as grain; a star can be compared to a flower, meadows to seas and trees to rocks. In *The Return of the Native*, 'each of the tiny trumpets [of the mummified heath-bells] was seized on, entered, scoured and emerged from by the wind as thoroughly as if it were *as vast as a crater*', and in *The Woodlanders* 'little showers had scattered themselves *like grain* against the walls and windowpanes'. In the summer fog of *Tess*, 'the meadows lay *like a white sea*, out of which the scattered trees rose *like dangerous rocks*', and later in the evening sky the planet Jupiter hangs '*like a full-blown jonquil*'. In Hardy's extraordinary cosmos, even the sun undergoes peculiar alterations. In the dark dense world of *The Woodlanders*, it is never seen whole but only 'in the form of *numerous little stars* staring through the leaves', and later, as Giles and his man return from their cider-making, one of the sun's stray beams alights now and then '*like a star* on the blades of the pomace-shovels'. In *Tess* a pasture can seem like a sea and sunshine like moonshine in one remarkable stroke, so that when Tess and Angel look one morning 'over the damp sod in the direction of the sun, a glistening ripple of gossamer webs was visible to their eyes under the luminary, *like the track of moonlight on the sea*'. For Hardy as for Lawrence, man and his society might not be magical and marvellous enough but the natural cosmos and its figures and forms most certainly were. For him as for Lawrence, the merely human world may not have sufficed for his imagination to expatiate in, but the non-human world of sun and moon, of sky and sea, of bird and beast, most certainly did.

II

If Hardy was dear to Lawrence, it was because he rehabilitated not only Nature as a source of mystery and miracle, but Man himself. By restoring the ancient heavenly connection between the human creature and the natural world around it, by establishing what Lawrence called 'the true correspondence between the material cosmos and the human soul',[7] Hardy sought, like Lawrence after him, to make the human character more wondrous and surprising than traditionally realistic novelists had dreamed of in their philosophies. To make people in novels the functions of their merely social values and conditions, to make them participants in a merely human drama, was to condemn them at once to the ordinary and the predictable. But to make them functions of wholly natural values and conditions, to make them participants in some larger non-human drama, was to create fascinating creatures too amazing to be understood, too mysterious to be predicted. 'That which is physic—non-human, in humanity, is more interesting to me', as Lawrence would put it in the most famous of his statements, 'than the old-fashioned human element.'[8] 'If one is to do fiction now,' he liked to think, 'one must cross the threshold of the human people.'[9]

Hardy was not of course free, any more than Lawrence was, to cross this threshold on a permanent basis. His Clyms, his Henchards, his Tesses, belong after all to the category of the human people, of perfectly ordinary characters with their roots in the substance of human and social history. But they are rather remarkable creatures, too, creatures who achieve at moments a transcendent power. As creatures rooted in the strange substance of Nature, as creatures persistently compared with natural forms and phenomena, they assume at times a magic, a majesty, that makes them something more than human.

This is first of all because what they are or do or feel invites comparison with the immensities and intensities of the universe, with the elemental forms and forces of sun and moon, of sky and sea, of wind and fire and water. Eustacia's form is 'soft to the touch as a cloud'; Clym's influence penetrates her 'like summer sun'; indignation spreads through her 'like subterranean heat'; when 'the calm fixity of her features sublime[s] itself to an expression of refinement and warmth', it is 'like garish moon rising to the dignity of sunset'. It is not otherwise with Michael Henchard. A powerful psalm-tune can make his 'blood ebb and flow like the sea'; the 'strong, warm gaze' he fixes on Lucetta is, in comparison with Farfrae's, 'like the sun beside the moon'; he is governed by 'the volcanic fires of his nature'; in his distress he moves 'like a great tree in a wind', and when he and Farfrae wrestle together, they are described as 'rocking and writhing like trees in a gale'. When Hardy's people are not made larger than life by being placed in the same continuum with the spectacular nature of suns and seas and gales, they are made stranger than life by being placed in the same continuum with the sublunary nature of birds and beasts and flowers. So, the rapidity of Bathsheba's movement is 'that of a kingfisher—its noiselessness that of a hawk'. 'All similes and allegories concerning her began and ended with birds', Hardy writes of Thomasin Yeobright. 'When she was musing she was a kestrel, which hangs in the air by an invisible motion of its wings. When she was in a high wind her light body was blown against trees and banks like a heron's. When she was frightened she darted noiselessly like a kingfisher.' Elsewhere and more remarkably, their similes begin and end with trees and plants, so that in death Eustacia's loose black hair surrounds her brow 'like a forest', and in the presence of Angel Clare's relentless love, Tess flinches 'like a plant in too burning a sun'. Indeed, there is often no disparity in Hardy's world of wonder between human psychology and natural physiology, a 'fevered hope' growing up in Boldwood 'like a grain of mustard-seed', Grace Melbury's heart rising from its sadness 'like a released bough', and a new spirit mounting in Tess 'as the sap in the twigs'. Hardy's men and women can be marvels, can be mysteries, because they rehearse the marvels and mysteries of the most elemental natural processes.

When they are not made stranger than life by their community with birds and trees and plants, they are made lovelier and more glamorous by their community with flower and fruit. In *Far from the Madding Crowd,* for example, the heroine's face is 'red and moist from her exertions, like a peony petal before the sun dries off the dew', and in *Tess* the heroine's mouth is a 'flower-like mouth', her lips parting, as she sleeps with her recovered husband, 'like a half-opened flower near his cheek'. Indeed, if figures like Gabriel Oak and Giles Winterborne suggest nature-gods or wood-gods, if they become at moments larger than life and more beautiful, it is because their human bodies and even their human clothing become so stuck and starred with the magic flowers and fruit of the earth that they are, as it were, trans-humanised. So Giles 'looked and smelt like Autumn's very brother, his face being sunburnt to wheat-colour, his eyes blue as corn flowers, his sleeves and leggings dyed with fruit-stains'. So, too, with Michael Henchard: in the days of his youth and innocence, before the crime that parted him from nature and made him a gentleman, he had worn 'leggings yellow as marigolds, corduroys immaculate as new flax, and a neckerchief like a flower-garden'.

Though all similes in Hardy begin with birds, beasts, and flowers, they don't end with them. The same instinct for the grotesque that governed his selection of natural objects also governed his selection of natural similes. It is surely strange enough that he should see his woodland folk attacking the bark of trees 'like locusts', or his Sue Bridehead entering a room 'like the flitting in of a moth'. But everywhere his people evoke analogies with things in nature even stranger to the human imagination, with things like dead herons and tiger-beetles, seaweed and mushrooms, toads and snakes. When the hitherto wholly comic Uncle Benjy dies in *The Trumpet-Major,* he leaves behind him a carcass 'dry and fleshless as that of a dead heron found on a moor in January', and when Eustacia appears in her winter clothing, she's 'like the tiger-beetle, which when observed in dull situations, seems to be of the quietest neutral colour but under a full illumination blazes with dazzling splendour'. In the rain Tess's hair becomes no 'better than seaweed', and when her cheeks are kissed by her betrayer, they are 'damp and smoothly chill as the skin of the mushrooms in the fields around'. More weirdly still, when she bends forward on the terrible night of her marriage, 'each diamond on her neck gave a sinister wink like a toad's', and even more weirdly, when she yawns in the morning she discloses 'the red interior of her mouth as if it had been a snake's'. Even Marty South, that least ostentatious of human creatures, is transposed into something at once marvellous and sinister: as one of the crew stripping the bark off the trees, 'she stood encaged amid the mass of twigs and buds like a great bird, running her ripping-tool into the smallest branches'.

If otherwise ordinary men and women in Hardy are magically metamorphosed, it is not only because they are *like* the marvellous and mysterious presences of Nature. It is also because, in the natural environment, they themselves *are* or *become,* such presences. In the sylvan setting of *The Woodlanders,* the normally commonplace heroine can become 'a sylph-like greenish-white creature, as toned by the sunlight and leafage', and the hero, for all his mildness and meekness, can become 'the fruit-god and the wood-god in alternation: sometimes leafy and smeared with green lichen . . . sometimes cider-stained and starred with apple-pips'. In *Tess,* too, the humblest folk are actualized into poetry by the very nature they inhabit, so that when the dairy-maids walk to Sunday-church, 'their gauzy skirts [brush] up from the grass innumerable flies and butterflies which, unable to escape, remained caged in the transparent tissue as in an aviary', and when the dairy-workers creep along the pasture in the morning in search of the garlic plant, 'a soft yellow gleam [is] reflected from the buttercups into their shaded faces, giving them an elfish, moonlit aspect'. Even more commonly, Hardy's people are sun-changed or moon-changed. Like other objects in Nature, they undergo, in the solar or lunar lights, rather remarkable transfigurations. So, in *The Mayor of Casterbridge,* the sun warms Farfrae's head and face 'to a complexion of flame-colour', and in *The Trumpet-Major* the sad young hero 'blaze[s] in the rays [of the sun] like a very god of war'. In *Tess,* the 'plump neck, shoulders, and arms' of the lowly and vulgar Car appear touchingly in the moonshine 'as luminous and beautiful as some Praxitelean creation', and as, on the same occasion, the intoxicated folk move homeward, there moves with them, 'around the shadow of each one's head, a circle of opalized light, formed by the moon's rays upon the glistening sheet of dew'.

In effect, Hardy dehumanizes his characters. Like the Cézanne Lawrence loved, Hardy paints out of them 'the so-called humanness, the personality, the "likeness", the physical cliché'.[10] This is partially because the human figure becomes, in the light of sun or moon, a head or a face, a mouth or an eye, a nostril or a lip. But it is even more because in the same strange light, that feature of head or face, of lip or mouth, is surprisingly changed into the non-human, into some aspect of nature eerily and incongruously other than human. Susan Henchard's lips become *fire:* 'the strongly-coloured sun . . . made transparencies of her eyelids and nostrils and set fire on her lips'. With Eustacia, a mouth becomes *a tulip scarlet with fire:* 'the sun shone into her mouth as into a tulip, and lent it a similar scarlet fire'. Elizabeth-Jane's hair becomes *a hazel copse* ('the rays [of the sun] streamed into its depths as into a hazel copse') and Grace Melbury's *a brake* (the firelight shone 'through the loose hair about her temples as sunlight through a brake'). Elsewhere, the features of the human figure, like the features of any natural object, are variously metamorphosed into precious metals or jewels to produce the same effect of the non-human. In *Tess,* the fog rests on the lashes of her eyes 'like *crystals*', and drops of moisture hang upon her hair 'like *seed pearls*'. In *Far from the Madding Crowd,* Boldwood's 'Roman features . . . [glow] in the sun with a bronze-like richness of tone; in *Tess,* the faces and hands of the heroine's pursuers at Stonehenge appear in the growing light of the dawn 'as if they were *silvered*'; and more weirdly yet, in *The Return of the Native,* Clym's face shows its shape in the light of the eclipsed moon, 'as if it were cut out in *gold*'.

It is the human eye, however, that registers most astonishingly in Hardy the strange unity and continuity of man and nature. The same fantastical imagination that turned lips into fire, mouths into tulips, and faces into silver and gold, also turns eyes into the mysterious shapes and weird colorations of the natural universe. When Hardy says of Boldwood that 'the impending night appeared to concentrate in his eye' or of Grace Melbury that her eyes were 'deep and mysterious as interstellar space', he translates the human creature at a single stroke into something more or other than the merely human. Indeed, Hardy does more. The human eye is not just *like* something vast or strange in nature; it *is* something vast or strange in nature. So it is when Marty South is visualized in *The Woodlanders* 'with the vermilion light of the sun in the pupils of her eyes' or when Anne Garland is visualized in *The Trumpet-Major* with 'each of her eyes having a little sun in it, which gave her glance a peculiar golden fire'. So is it, too, when Clym flings himself 'down upon the barrow, his face towards the moon, which depicted a small image of herself in each of his eyes' or when, as with Tess, 'the miniature candle-flame inverted in her eye-pupils shone like a diamond'. The eye which *is* the human being is suddenly no longer human. It—the eye, the expression, the being—*is* a moon or a diamond, a vermilion light or a golden fire. Only that and nothing more. Indeed, the image so bedazzles the human imagination that for the moment everything stops. The character is the eye and the eye is the image, and the image is arrestingly non-human.

Nothing but the astonishing is beautiful, the surrealists would eventually declare. And, in fact, if Hardy's characters are often astonishingly beautiful, it is because they are like figures in a surrealist dream. This is partly for the reason that their look or situation is in itself manifestly surreal, as when Clym appears with the moon in each of his eyes or Marty South with the vermilion light of the sun in hers. Elsewhere, however, the surreal is a function not of *what* is seen but of the *way* it is seen, not of the human features or objects observed but of the weirdly non-human similes and metaphors they inspire. So Diggory's eye is 'keen as that of a bird of prey, and blue as autumn mist', and Clym's face, as we have seen, appears in the light of the moon 'as if it were cut out in gold'. In such cases as these what the human thing is like, what the head or face or eye is compared with, is so powerfully and dramatically different that it totally transfigures the human thing itself. Diggory's eye is obliterated as an eye by the startling images of bird of prey and blue autumn mist; Clym's face is obliterated as a face by the even more startling image of a shape cut out in gold. The merely human creature is changed, changed utterly, into a terrible beauty, into a beauty otherwise strange and surreal.

The effect is even stranger and more surreal when the relationship between the human subject and the image it suggests is not logically explained, as it often is in the simile, but is left mysteriously unexplained. It is wonderful, surely, that Henchard should have worn 'leggings yellow as marigolds', but it is even more wonderful that he should have worn 'a neckerchief like a flower-garden', for where the logical resemblance between leggings and marigolds is specified by the term 'yellow', the logical resemblance between neckerchief and flower-garden is not specified at all. It is left entirely to the better magic and mystery of the imagination. Indeed, if the surrealist characteristically replaces the logical order with a dynamic flow of images, then he best achieves his effect when he expresses the association between the human subject and the image not as a simile but as a metaphor, when the human subject is not just *like* but *is* the image it evokes. It is wonder-working that Bathsheba's face should be 'like a peony petal', but it is even more so that Tess's mouth should be a 'peony mouth'. To say that a face is 'like a peony petal' is still to insist on the logical distinction between face and flower, between the human and the non-human, and to create a picture that draws on the visual distinction between them. But to say that a mouth is a 'peony mouth' makes it difficult to discriminate, either logically or pictorially, between mouth and peony, between the human and the non-human. They compose in the visual picture not two images but one image, and that image more image of flower than of mouth.

Hardy's pictures and portraits are most remarkable of all when their surrealism derives neither from the thing itself nor from the simile or metaphor it generates but from both. The effect on such occasions is that of images logically divorced from each other but imaginatively joined in a highly-charged and almost unconscious association. That the sun should shine into Eustacia's mouth is in itself astonishing, but that it should shine into her mouth 'as into a tulip, and [lend] it a similar scarlet fire' is to add the astonishing to the astonishing, and to produce in sun and mouth and tulip and fire one dynamic composition of logically dissociated images. Again, that Tess's yawn should reveal to Angel Clare 'the red interior of her mouth' or that 'the miniature candle-flame [should appear] inverted in her eye-pupils' is in itself sufficiently grotesque, but that 'the red interior of her mouth' should show itself *'as if it had been a snake's'* or that 'the candle-flame inverted in her eye-pupils' should shine *'like a diamond'* is again to add one grotesque image to another and again to create, in red interior and mouth and snake, in candle-flame and eye-pupils and diamond, one inspired series of otherwise disconnected images. It would be rash to claim that Hardy saw human creatures in the same astounding ways that Cézanne and Picasso and Chagall would come to see them. He was a novelist after all and had to 'think' in sentences as well as 'see' in pictures. But it is a measure of the originality of his imagination that he should suggest comparison with them on any terms. Like them he would behold the human character not as the eye but as the imagination beheld it. Like them he would dehumanize the human character not in order to make it less human, but only in order to make it more vividly and more remarkably so.

For Henry James, Thomas Hardy was 'the good little Thomas Hardy'. But not for Lawrence. As the poet and novelist who would help to change this century's sense of life and character, Lawrence was able to recognize, as James was not, the originality of Hardy's provincial genius, the brilliant eccentricity of his art and imagination. The Hardy who witnessed strange stars and constellations, the crash of icebergs and the slide of snowhills, things altered to bronze in the sun or to gold in the moon, creatures with fire on their lips or with forests round their brows or with diamonds for eyes: such a Hardy was surely something more than 'the good little Thomas Hardy'. For all his faults and failures, this Hardy had entered states of life and being stranger by far and more mysterious than anything James and his friends knew existed. Reality was not exhausted after all by the human; it was conterminous with a natural cosmos that remained uncomprehended and incomprehensible. Nor was the human exhausted by the social; it was a part of the same non-human mystery by which it was surrounded, by the same natural cosmos out of which it came and into which it disappeared. It would be too much to say that without Hardy Lawrence would never have discovered a world fit for the imagination to expatiate in. But it would not be too much to say that no other novelist before Lawrence was even ready to admit the possibility of such a world's existence.

X

Walter F. Wright:

A NOVEL IS AN IMPRESSION, NOT AN ARGUMENT

In his 1892 preface to *Tess of the d'Urbervilles* Hardy makes a statement that may seem a truism, but which needs to be reiterated in the approach to literature, including Hardy's own novels and also his poems. He writes, 'Let me repeat that a novel is an impression, not an argument.' If we understand *argument* to mean any reasoned demonstration, not just an attempt to win a case, the assertion has at least two implications. First of all, it reminds the reader that, unlike a historical document or an objective biography, a novel has no validity as a statement of actual fact. At the risk of making Hardy's spirit writhe by the comparison, one might say that a novel is as 'fictitious' as any television commercial in which persons radiate joy upon choosing the virtuous product and presumably, like Bassanio and Portia, will live happily ever after. What the narrative work provides must be, by its very nature, a simulation; hence it can *prove* nothing. It can only give the author's impression.

The second implication of Hardy's pronouncement has to do with literature as an art form. Even an essay which by use of logic tries to persuade may, and indeed should, be aesthetically pleasing; a classic example is Swift's 'Modest Proposal'. If a novel or poem is not pleasing aesthetically, it may serve some topical propagandistic function to arouse readers to immediate action, but it will not carry out its true function of addressing the imagination and harmoniously appealing to those emotions which are inseparable from imaginative insight.

To return to the first implication, there is nothing a novelist can do to force us to believe what he tells us, no matter how hard he may argue. After all, what he is really reporting is not that an actual person did or said something, but that in his opinion the character he has invented might reasonably do so. We can disagree. If we wish, we can join those who refused to let Romeo and Juliet die in the tomb and instead permitted them to begin a long life together. Of course, we can maliciously continue the alternative version by adding a sixth act to take place decades later, in which Romeo, now very much out of the current of exciting events and living in sentimental reverie, tries to convince his little great-grandchildren that their great-grandfather was really quite a devil-may-care madcap when he went serenading. One can picture him as that friend of Falstaff, one Master Shallow, no longer quite sure whether it was a girl named Juliet or one named Rosalind who whispered of roses by moonlight.

And one may recall that a jurist friend told Hardy that no jury would have convicted Tess. So, if we wish, we can bestow upon her the fate which Hardy seems to designate for her sister, a lifetime with the somewhat chastened, but still rather dull Angel Clare. If we say that a different ending for the play or for the novel would be at least as probable as the actual ending, we must then ask what else is required of a work of literature. Would those alternative endings be significant? What impression would they support? And in contemplating that question we find that we are involved in something far more complex than logical probability and the following of a carefully reasoned argument. We are groping for insight into the very reason for our continuing to exist as imaginative and feeling beings.

On the other hand, if we merely indulge in undirected imaginative adventures, we have no assurance that the consequences will be other than a wandering in a wilderness or an indulgence in maudlin sentimentality. As for fiction, it would be devoid of theme. So one does find a need for demonstration, for logic, for abstract speculation. Some years ago one of our distinguished poets became annoyed because too many readers would not read a poem as poem, but insisted upon its containing a clearly definable meaning that could be paraphrased philosophically. The key line in his own didactic rebuke was, as you may remember, 'A poem should not mean, but be.' Oddly enough, it would seem that, paradoxically, he must have wanted his readers to know not only what his line *was*, but what it meant.

We must recognize the fact that throughout his reflective life Hardy was both poet-novelist and speculator in philosophy. Not being a professional philosopher, I am not sure as to the differentiation between the disciplined metaphysician and the amateur, but I suppose we could enrol Hardy's name among the names of those who begin with a staggering sense of bewilderment and try by deduction and analogy to achieve some kind of pattern by means of which to sort out and appreciate mental experiences. In short, his philosophic contemplation was inspired by the human predicament—an emotional, and hence literary, concern.

For examination of the relation of his philosophy to his works of art we may begin with the most nearly abstract statements and continue toward the ultimate picture of life in which whatever meaning there may be is, to borrow Hardy's own term for the life principle, 'immanent' rather than asserted. Actually, we cannot find the extreme of total abstraction, for Hardy could not think without using metaphors, which are not merely analogical but at least to some degree emotionally connotative. But following his own example, we can be concerned with his attempts at the philosophic definition of existence.

It is not by mere 'hap' that we begin with the poem, dated 1866, which is so entitled. Chance confronted Hardy, of course, as it does the rest of us, with events that seemed to make no sense and had nothing to do with one's wisdom or deserving. Hence the metaphor of 'dicing Time' and the different one with essentially the same implication, 'purblind Doomsters'. In the poem Hardy offers one alternative to chance, which, however, he at once rejects. This is that a 'vengeful god' has destined man to suffer for the god's own amusement. One may assume that Hardy did not have to open up his copy of *King Lear* to recall Gloucester's lines—'As flies to wanton boys, are we to the gods;/They kill us for their sport.' In other poems Hardy sometimes mentions and casually rejects the concept of a benevolent god. Actually these do not constitute three equal alternatives, because only a trust in benevolence would be totally pleasant. The concept of a vengeful god does have certain attractions, as it implies design, even though malevolent, and it gives dignity to man, as he fights against a 'Powerfuller than I', though such consolation does not assuage the suffering.

The concept of 'dicing Time' or 'Crass Casualty', however, if accepted fully, makes of life a mere contemptible travesty. The doomsters have not done mankind the courtesy of loading the dice either for or against him, as they are either indifferent or powerless. Actually, Hardy could never completely accept this intolerable third alternative, however pointedly he might state it. Most commonly he found himself entertaining the sensation perhaps not of a vengeful god, but yet of one who was impelled by conscious caprice. So it is that in *The Return of the Native* he can remark that if Eustacia had been a goddess on Olympus we should have had the same capricious meting out of joy and pain as now:

> There would have been the same inequality of lot, the same heaping up of favours here, of contumely there, the same generosity before justice, the same perpetual dilemmas, the same captious alternation of caressess and blows that we endure now.

The feeling comes out repeatedly in pronouncement in the poems and in often gratuitous authorial comments in the novels. For example, after pointing up the cruelty of circumstance that has compelled the 'half-dozen little captives under hatches' to sail in the ship piloted by their parents, the hapless John Durbeyfield and his childlike wife, Hardy cries out against such injustice:

> Some people would like to know whence the poet [Wordsworth] whose philosophy is in these days deemed as profound and trustworthy as his song is sweet and pure, gets his authority for speaking of 'Nature's holy plan'.

And in *Jude the Obscure*, Sue Bridehead, addressing Jude, provides Hardy's own sentiment after the death of the children:

> We said—do you remember?—that we would make a virtue of joy. I said it was Nature's intention, Nature's law and *raison d'être* that we should be joyful in what instincts she afforded us—instincts which civilization had taken upon itself to thwart. What dreadful things I said. And now Fate has given us this stab in the back for being such fools as to take Nature at her word!

Here not only is Fate an abstraction, but civilization is virtually one, too.

Elsewhere, for example again in *Tess*, Hardy blames society or convention as an oppression which the individual heroic spirit must endure. He even suggests that, having ceased to be a virgin, Tess, 'walking among the sleeping birds in the hedges, watching the skipping rabbits on a moonlit warren', was mistaken in seeing herself 'as a figure of Guilt intruding into the haunts of Innocence'. In reality, 'feeling herself in antagonism, she was quite in accord. She had been made to break an accepted social law, but no law known to the environment in which she fancied herself such an anomaly.' Somehow this illogically makes Nature good and society, with its conventions, bad, though both should be subservient to the purblind Doomsters or vengeful god. More typical is the sentiment expressed later in *Tess:* 'So the two forces were at work here as everywhere, the inherent will to enjoy and the circumstantial will against enjoyment.'

There is in this sentence something beyond mere argument—a limited dramatic concreteness in that the circumstantial will seems to be some kind of anthropomorphic emotional creature. Indeed, Hardy appears to have regarded Christianity as just as anthropomorphic as any other religion in its attempts to conceive of a divine power. In the Hardy library in the Dorset County Museum is a notebook of miscellaneous extracts from Hardy's reading. One of the quotations, identified as from Chesterton in 1906, reads, 'Paganism is Agnosticism which is sufficiently agnostic to admit the probability of spirits.' Hardy commented, 'For Paganism read Christianity.' Before *Christianity* he inserted *modern,* and then he restated the phrase to read 'Present-day Christianity'.

In his own attempt to achieve a philosophy that would not have multiple spirits, as you know, he adapted from Schopenhauer and others to come up with an Immanent Will. We need not explore the implications fully here, as one can read *The Dynasts*, in which the Will is the prime mover of all created things. Within our own framework what the concept of the Will amounts to is the postulation of one single force which expresses itself imperfectly through all things and all events and is unconscious. It is hoped that it will become conscious and work less imperfectly in future aeons. Thus, to put the concept in its post-Darwinian context, the survival of the fittest will come to have a favourable bias. And if human effort is to count for anything, then the collective effort of mankind, somehow at times freed from the Will itself, will assist in the Will's enlightenment. If all this sounds like mere words on paper, it is something more, for despite the apparent contradiction that makes the omnipotent learn from its helpless creation, the theory expresses what Hardy felt. He was acutely conscious of hap, and yet the very exercise of his own mind gave him some reason to feel that human effort must count in the universal scheme of things.

None of what we have scanned is highly original. The Greeks talked about the whimsicality of the gods and also about inexorable Necessity. As we began by noticing, it is not utterly abstract, as an argument would logically be. In context it seems even less so, and the power of such a statement as the reference to the circumstantial will against enjoyment consists in the fact that, analagous to the last line or couplet in a Shakespearean sonnet or the final chords in a piece of music, it brings an action to its close. For Hardy this means that it completes a vividly concrete representation of a specific human tribulation.

We can now move toward examples which, though using the methods of allegory and symbolism, are still more concrete and, without support from their context, carry something of Hardy's sense of life as he not only conceived it to be, but felt it in his very marrow. We turn, in short, to personification of qualities in the universe and in the human mind. Viewed as religion, this is simple polytheism. Considered as psychology, it amounts to sorting out the human faculties. We all, of course, use *reason, imagination, feeling, will,* and dozens of other terms as if they were precisely distinguishable, though we know that they are not. There is some evidence that Hardy himself was almost pedantic in trying to make discriminations. In his notebooks is a chart taken from Fourier which naïvely and arbitrarily attempts to classify human faculties. On the back are elaborate diagrams, dated 1863, apparently representing Hardy's own adapted classification, including such groupings as 'Human Passion, Mind, Character', 'Friendship, Love, Familism, Ambition', 'Impossible Monster of Instinct, Impossible Monster of the Will, Impossible Monster of the Passions', and 'Intellect, Passions, Will'. That Hardy should have felt the usefulness of such classifications shows his concern for analysis. Even when wandering in the realms of the imagination, he still wanted to be able to define and reduce to order what had come to him in a moment of revelation.

Sometimes personification helped him to express a human mind's sensation of the universe or of the nature of mortality. 'Purblind Doomsters', as we noticed, has a degree of concreteness and emotional fulness. More vivid is the image in a 'memorandum' of October 30, 1870:

> Mother's notion, and also mine: That a figure stands in our van with arm uplifted, to knock us back from any pleasant prospect we indulge in as probable.

In the poems there are many examples in which personified spirits not only present an intellectual concept, but convey intense emotion. Thus, in 'The Subalterns', the leaden sky, the chill north wind, Sickness, and Death all ask man's forgiveness because they themselves are subject to what the Greeks would have called, and Hardy elsewhere calls, Necessity. In the fifth and final stanza comes a resolution such as might round out a tragic novel:

> We smiled upon each other then,
> And life to me had less
> Of that fell look it wore ere when
> They owned their passiveness.

We do not know when 'The Subalterns' was written, but 'The Darkling Thrush' is dated December, 1900, to recognize the end of the year and century. In this poem Nature is not personified, but 'An aged thrush, frail, gaunt, and small, / In blast-beruffled plume' represents one voice of the natural world. The poet can only listen in wonder as in the bleak late afternoon of winter the thrush pours forth 'a full-hearted evensong / Of joy illimited'. The poem concludes with a mingling of melancholy and hope:

> So little cause for carollings
> Of such ecstatic sound
> Was written on terrestrial things
> Afar or nigh around,
> That I could think there trembled through
> His happy good-night air
> Some blessed Hope, whereof he knew
> And I was unaware.

Here Nature provides both what to human understanding is bleak and what, however inconceivable rationally under such seemingly painful conditions, is a carol of joy. Hardy is thus trying, through the conflicting manifestations of Nature in the gloom of the atmosphere and in the thrush's song, to suggest the mystery of our being at once a part of the natural world just as much as the thrush is and yet of our being incapable of comprehending its paradoxes and mystery. We are both native and alien. More important for our journey here, far more than in 'Hap' we are emotionally involved.

For the thrush, substitute Tess or Jude when for a moment they catch a glimpse of bliss in the midst of desolation, and we have a still greater mystery. To be sure, one could construct a statement of a philosophic substructure for the poem, but it would not be definitive. Indeed, one might find oneself playing with semantics and using question-begging definitions that would take one out of the reality of the poem to some kind of emotional vacuum. Most certainly, such an exercise would be after the fact, for Hardy has travelled no such path. He has simply abandoned systematic philosophy to accept, as one of his favourite poets, Keats, had done, the truth of the imagination.

To drop back several years to *The Return of the Native,* in the scene of the evening bonfire on the fifth of November, Hardy first paints a vividly graphic picture of the heath folk. Then, after some historical speculation about mankind's habit of building fires as the nights rapidly lengthen, comes an allusion to Prometheus as the bearer of fire from the gods to man:

> Moreover to light a fire is the instinctive and resistant act of man when, at the winter ingress, the curfew is sounded throughout Nature. It indicates a spontaneous, Promethean rebelliousness against the fiat that this recurrent season shall bring foul times, cold darkness, misery and death. Black chaos comes, and the fettered gods of the earth say, Let there be light.

The statement might be called generically concrete. 'Black chaos' sums up a possible infinity of specific evidence. And the 'fettered gods' include the thinker Clym Yeobright, the defiant queen of night Eustacia, who is the 'raw material of a divinity', and the pathetically grotesque Christian Cantle, all of whom share with Prometheus the torments inflicted by Zeus, the 'President of the Immortals'. The very use of the allusion admits that the concept is not original, and yet the passage does not merely echo Aeschylus's play; it takes human longing and frustration—which for Hardy is primarily a futility in man's search for understanding—and gives them a special immediacy in a nineteenth-century milieu.

As for the personification of the capacities of the human mind, the most extensive example is, of course, in *The Dynasts,* written in Hardy's early sixties. In the preface he loosely catalogues the spirits who from the 'Overworld' comment on the tragedy of the ten years of warfare, 1805-1815. To quote his own words:

> The phantasmal Intelligences are divided into groups, of which one only,

that of the Pities, approximates to 'the Universal Sympathy of human nature—the spectator idealized' of the Greek Chorus; it is impressionable and inconsistent in its views, which sway hither and thither as wrought on by events. Another group [primarily the Spirit of the Years] approximates to the passionless Insight of the Ages. The remainder are eclectically chosen auxiliaries whose signification may be readily discerned.

Of this remainder the Spirit Ironic is the principal spokesman.

We must keep in mind that as a philosophical argument—a justification of some celestial power's ways to man—the epic drama is dominated by the concept of one force, the Immanent Will, which is unconscious and yet works in patterns to create the 'web', the 'network' that enmeshes human souls in noble sentiments and base ones, in tragic sublimity and maniacal absurdity.

Hardy, of course, had ample precedent, in Milton and Shelley among other notable poets, for personifying attributes or perspectives of the mind. But what concerns us here is that he did so in a poem which was an attempt at a monistic philosophic interpretation of the creation and evolution of the universe of spirit. By allowing the Spirit of the Years, the Spirit Ironic, and the Pities to look in separate ways at an action, he was polytheistically abandoning monism in order to get at the reality of existence as he actually sensed it. To oversimplify, Years accepts Necessity; the human predicament has always been as we now know it, and there is no reason to expect it to change. In effect this is the best of all possible worlds and also the worst, because the ultimate longings of the human spirit and the capacity for sorrow are inseparable from human consciousness itself.

But it is also a preposterously absurd world. One may add parenthetically that one of our current absurdities is the readiness with which we have treated the so-called theatre of the absurd as an original phenomenon. It is the Spirit Ironic, supported by the cynical Spirit Sinister, that points out the absurdity of war itself and the ridiculousness of Napoleon's and other dynasts' ambitions. Indeed, Ironic's lesson is that of Ecclesiastes—'Vanity, vanity, all is vanity.'

Nevertheless, the generals, statesmen, and cannon-fodder alike, though victims of the Immanent Will, which impels them toward folly, remind us often of fettered gods and so are worthy of compassion. Hence there is a place for the Pities, even when desperately thirsty soldiers from both armies at Talavera rush to the rill that divides them, while drinking shake hands with their counterparts, and then inanely return to their ranks to start shooting each other again. As a personification the Pities here state the 'argument', but more important is the scene they describe—the rich embodiment of Hardy's impression.

'Save his own soul he hath no star.' Hardy quoted these words from Swinburne as an epigraph to the second part of *Jude.*

Whatever Swinburne meant—and he did sometimes overstate things—Hardy was certainly jolting his own search for a philosophy to its foundations. If one is at sea with no star from which to secure a reading, how can one find the way? About 250 pages later Jude, having returned to Christminster after long wandering in a spiritual wilderness, addresses the 'idle crowd' on Remembrance Day, which he rechristens 'Humiliation Day for me'. After defending himself against the taunts, stated or surmised, he continues:

> I am in a chaos of principles—groping in the dark—acting by instinct and not after example. Eight or nine years ago when I came here first, I had a neat stock of fixed opinions, but they dropped away one by one; and the further I get the less sure I am.

Now in the management of the external affairs of his life Hardy had examples and principles. But as a novelist he must, more and more, have come to recognize that 'fixed opinions' meant triteness, commonplace platitudes, superficiality. When he went beyond them he tried to find some kind of certainty, ultimately one single star, by which to take a reading and steer a philosophic course. And yet, finally, at his best as poet and novelist, while having ample landmarks for plotting the action and, indeed, not hesitating to use conventional melodramatic formulae in the mechanics of his craftsmanship, in his finest scenes and lyric passages Hardy had to depend on the equivalent of Jude's instinct, namely on his poetic impression of things.

I do not recall whether there is evidence that Hardy had read the famous passage on 'negative capability' in Keats's letter of 28 December 1817—'that is, when a man is capable of being in uncertainties, mysteries, doubts, without any irritable reaching after fact and reason'. Certainly as a poet and novelist Hardy had to accept just such a view as Keats's. For thinking man it was as irrevocable as Necessity itself. What does it mean in the given case? Essentially that we come to accept as truth that which the imagination has sensed.

The matter was fraught, to be sure, with danger, and evidence of Hardy's recognition of the problem appears in his annotation of a passage in Newman's *An Essay in Aid of a Grammar of Assent.* It will be noted that Newman asks his reader to use logic so far as he can, but then to venture beyond it in what can only be an imaginative leap of faith:

> so by a like dictate we are not justified, in the case of concrete reasoning and especially of religious inquiry, in waiting till such logical demonstration is ours, but on the contrary are bound in conscience to seek truth and to look for certainty by modes of proof, which, when reduced to the shape of formal propositions, fail to satisfy the severe requisitions of science.

Hardy was drawn toward Newman much as toward Wordsworth

and the mystic poet Henry Vaughan. Yet, having marked this passage, he added an exclamation mark, his typical expression of scepticism.

His own approach was dissimilar in that, instead of dealing with formal propositions, at his best Hardy dealt with specific human experience, and his resolution of his fictitious events was too complex to be described as formal proof. To illustrate this we may begin with the last paragraph of *The Return of the Native.* To be sure, Hardy was apologetic about the final section of the novel, which he gave the anticlimactic title 'Aftercourses', but had he left out an irrelevant happy ending for Thomasin and Venn, he still should not have omitted the concluding scene, which ends with something of a choral comment on the action that has gone before. It happens also to provide an oblique justification for the very writing of fiction itself.

The scene begins, as you will recall, with Clym preaching on Rainbarrow to a small gathering who 'listened to the words of the man in their midst, who was preaching, while they abstractedly pulled heather, stripped ferns, or tossed pebbles down the slope'. The scene and the novel conclude with the author taking the part of *Hamlet's* Horatio or *Lear's* Albany:

> He left alone creeds and systems of philosophy, finding enough and more than enough to occupy his tongue in the opinions and actions common to all good men. Some believed him, and some believed not; some said that his words were commonplace, others complained of his want of theological doctrine; while others again remarked that it was well enough for a man to take to preaching who could not see to do anything else. But everywhere he was kindly received, for the story of his life had become generally known.

What this says is that no system of philosophy will finally reach what the story has been about. The reference to the fact that some did and some did not believe does not mean that truth is a matter of opinion. It means, rather, that philosophic 'modes of proof' finally come up short. Argument will not suffice. But of one thing there can be no doubt. The tragic life of Clym, significantly referred to as 'the man in their midst', has not been a futile demonstration. What one has left at the end is a greater awareness of the human lot, a recognition of its dignity that amounts virtually to a sense of wonder, and finally compassion.

Let us return to the matter of man's relation to the universe, the subject of 'The Subalterns' and 'The Darkling Thrush'. In the first pages of *The Return of the Native* the very heath takes on a life of its own, as if it were sentient. More than twenty years later in Hardy's career the coneys and even the moles and snails share in the sense of destruction at Waterloo. It is not only, however, that Hardy felt compelled to identify all creation as part of a web. He also found the human sensation of Nature akin to the human response to humanity. Consequently as there was beauty in the midst of tragedy, so it was to be found in the natural world at its bleakest. A fine example is in the description in *Tess* of 'Cross-in-Hand':

> Of all spots on this bleached and desolate upland this was the most forlorn. It was so far removed from the charm which is sought in landscape by artists and view-seekers as to reach a new kind of beauty, a negative beauty of tragical blankness.

Sometimes it is not a blankness, but a sinister bitterness that seems to identify the mood of Nature with man's own. Thus in 'Neutral Tones', dated 1867, in which the theme is that 'love deceives', Hardy writes of the winter day when

> . . . the sun was white, as though chidden of God,
> And a few leaves lay on the starving sod;

and in the final two lines he identifies the beloved's face with the bleakness of the scene:

> Your face, and the God-curst sun, and a tree,
> And a pond edged with grayish leaves.

In *Tess*, as has been commonly recognized, the emotional pattern of the heroine's life is somewhat matched by the landscape and season, even to the entertaining of the validity of sun worship.

But although Nature is much more than a mere backdrop for human drama, Hardy's primary concern was always the latter, and, except in *The Dynasts* and those parts of *The Mayor of Casterbridge* dealing with Henchard and Farfrae, almost always a drama involving a man and a womn. Certainly Sue Bridehead is speaking for Hardy as well as for herself when she prefers to take the Song of Solomon not as religious poems but as love songs. Many a short lyric by Hardy above lovers is almost a novel in miniature.

One of the most poignant and beautiful is 'Beyond the Last Lamp', in which the narrator recalls vividly a scene witnessed thirty years before. On a rainy night near Tooting Common he came upon a man and woman who 'seemed lovers' walking sorrowfully back and forth. They were still there when he returned 'some hours beyond the droop of day'. He remembers the place, the weather, the darkness, but, above all, the lonely pair:

> And yet
> To me, when nights are weird and wet,
> Without those comrades there at tryst
> Creeping slowly, creeping sadly,
> That one lane does not exist.
> There they seem brooding on their pain,
> And will while such a lane remain.

As you may recall, he used the motif of the poem with a special twist in having a passer-by see Angel and Tess. In the poem the lovers are 'linked'. In the novel Angel has already destroyed the bond.

Since a poet and novelist is responsible both for the general architectonics and the fitting of each separate stone in his edifice, we may note briefly Hardy's skill or good fortune in hitting upon the apt poetic phrasing—an emotionally connotative, hence impressionistic language. We may recall the natural simplicity of Clym's words as he looks at his dead wife and for the first time allows himself to recognize what he had tried to believe was not very important when he married her. Clym tells Charley, 'You shall see her.' And then, turning to Venn, he adds, 'You would like to see her too—would you not, Diggory? She looks very beautiful now.'

In a scene in the Harper version of *Tess*, dialect contributes to the poetry. Having been rejected by Angel, Tess, whose language has generally been rather standard literary English, begins as usual, but suddenly lapses into her childhood speech, for she is in reality like a helpless little girl once more:

> I agree to the conditions, Angel, because you know best what my punishment ought to be; only—only—don't 'ee make it more than I can bear!

And in *The Woodlanders* Marty's final prose lyric at the grave of Giles is enhanced by both dialect and the use of *was* where *were* would be grammatical:

> If ever I forget your name let me forget home and heaven! . . . But no, no, my love, I never can forget 'ee; for you was a good man, and did good things!

One of the most tragic of all passages and at the same time one of the most expressive of the dignity of humanity is Henchard's soliloquy as he leaves Casterbridge for the last time. He has lived unwisely and accepts the consequences by identifying himself with the biblical prototype of all outcasts:

> 'I—Cain—go alone as I deserve—an outcast and a vagabond. But my punishment is *not* greater than I can bear!'

At the end of *Jude the Obscure* Hardy again draws from the Bible, the early part of the Book of Job, to give poetic universality to his obscure hero's fate. In *Tess*, with no mention of the Will, he permits Tess five days of peace which, if translated philosophically would mean five days of freedom from the Will. Though he may discuss philosophic matters, sometimes heavy-handedly, within the novels, significantly, the resolution, as in *Jude* and *Tess*, is poetic, in the harmonious subsiding of vast human passion. Man cannot escape his fetters through reason. The imaginative recognition and the unconstrained compassion that accompany tragedy are the only fitting dénouement. By identifying the individual case with the eternal human predicament Hardy establishes pattern and order where otherwise 'Crass Casualty' would prevail.

Man errs with equal likelihood from conscious, rational planning, as with Clym, and from unconscious impulse, as in Jude's attraction to Arabella. Hence the order is not a mere matter of the dominance of reason. For Hardy it comes through the encompassing of a vast range of awareness and the contemplation of that range with emotional, that is, poetic sensibility.

We must remember that Hardy was an architect, with a feeling both for the total design and for each separate ornament and window pane. Paradoxically, by confining space a cathedral intensifies one's sense of the vastness of the space it encloses. So, too, do Hardy's novels. The cathedral likewise suggests inexhaustible variety, as do the novels and the great epic drama, with its scores of individualized scenes. And the effects of dawn, early twilight, and darkness, of rain and mist, of warmth and chill are common to both the cathedral and Hardy's literary art. There is in each an impressive massiveness under the heavens, not defiant, but sturdy, with a grey sombreness and yet a tranquil mellowness as of time-weathered stone.

Generations, even centuries, contribute to the ageing of both famous cathedrals and obscure country churches far from the madding crowd. For Hardy's characters the time which brings change to their faces is compressed, but with the illusion of far-stretching years. For Clym the actual time is a few months of wondering about his mission, followed by a brief tragic marriage and a sudden, unanticipated self-discovery. For Tess there is swift alternation of hope, dejection, stoic endurance, a moment of madness, and the five days of peace. For Henchard—whose odyssey would seem to have aged him as much as repeated tempests age a forest of hemlock and pine, there are actually about two decades of battling, often blindly, with the Figure in the Van before he succumbs to Aeschylean acceptance of defeat. And for Jude there are a few short years of wandering physically and spiritually, with occasional cries of anguish which echo Job and also remind us of that eternal cry, 'My God, why hast thou forsaken me?'

We must remember that none of these, not even Clym or Jude, are philosophers. Yet their lives do accord with a comprehensible pattern. In his famous passage in 'Levana and Our Ladies of Sorrow' De Quincey writes of the sisters who are responsible for the education of the human spirit. Our Lady of Tears acquaints man with those sadnesses inevitable from the very nature of mortality. Our Lady of Sighs accompanies those—such as Henchard and Tess and Jude—who, for whatever reason, feel themselves alien among their fellowmen. And finally, Our Lady of Darkness, *Mater Tenebrarum,* may strike one with despair. Without sentimentalizing, De Quincey is still able to accept despair itself, because it, too, is a form of revelation; it 'educates' or, as De Quincey points out from the Latin meaning of *Levana,* it 'raise[s] aloft'. Hardy's Spirit of the Years would at least understand.

And then we can turn to the final lines of Milton's *Samson Agonistes.* The action is ended. The pillars have fallen, and the tragic hero is dead. Milton concludes:

> His servants he with new acquist
> Of true experience from this great event
> With peace and consolation hath dismist,
> And calm of mind all passion spent.

For Milton Samson's anguish is indeed intense. Whence then comes the calmness? Not from the reasoning of a Job's comforter, nor from the wishful thinking of a sentimentalist. It is the final impression we have achieved of an erring, but significant human spirit—a fettered god of the earth, whose tragic kinsman is Michael Henchard.

In *The Return of the Native* the very heath is described as 'like man, slighted and enduring'. Of Hardy's protagonists, all of whom are slighted by Fate, what matters is what endures. And what endures is a mingling of what Burke called the sublime and that which he termed the beautiful. It is as stern as the Spirit of the Years in *The Dynasts,* who will allow no glossing over of the folly and the suffering. But in the epic drama, while admitting the severe pronouncements of Years, the Spirit of the Pities reminds us that in the midst of the absurd and the painful there is a bitter-sweet beauty. And significantly, in the drama whose subject matter is the ultimate of the absurd and also of magnanimity and nobility, it is the Pities, who, as the preface warns us, are 'impressionable and inconsistent', that have the final word:

> But—a stirring thrills the air
> Like to sounds of joyance there
>   That the rages
>   Of the ages
> Shall be cancelled, and deliverance offered from the darts that were,
> Consciousness the Will informing, till It fashion all things fair!

The reference to the Will makes these lines complete the philosophic scheme of the drama. But they have the ring, the tone, of a poetic rhapsody. Translated into other language, they express the hope that the fettered gods may, as in Shelley's version of the legend of Prometheus, become unbound. What the total drama and the novels, too, leave with us in Hardy's *impression* of the human predicament and of the strength and resiliency of the human spirit, which can endure.

XI

Frank R. Giordano:

HARDY'S MOMENTS OF REVISION

The criticism of Thomas Hardy's poetry can be described, by and large, as a series of responses to the questions, 'What kinds of poems did Hardy write?' and 'What are the biographical bases of his poetry?' Both types of responses, the classifications and the biographical explorations, have emerged naturally and inevitably: Hardy's tendency, taken from Wordsworth and Arnold, to classify poems according to form and purpose encouraging the one; and his declaration that there is more about his personal life in a hundred lines of his verse than in all his novels, fostering the other. And both approaches, even when narrowly and exclusively pursued, have been of benefit in laying the groundwork for what should be our present and most important task, the understanding and assessment of Hardy's poetic art; for we can most fully appreciate the meanings and feelings in Hardy's poems when we are attentive to his sources and techniques in recording his impressions of his personal experiences.

In keeping with established customs for discussing Hardy's poetry, I wish also to identify, classify, and consider the genesis of a group of Hardy's poems, which I shall call 'moments of revision'. Though I shall limit my discussion to works that appear in *Wessex Poems,* this class in fact constitutes a large portion of Hardy's total corpus, and is especially evident in the early volumes. The importance of these works is that they help us to understand how Hardy's critical temperament often achieved expression in poetic forms; and they enable us more precisely to account for the impact of Hardy's reading upon his own works. I consider his reading, particularly in the great English poets of the nineteenth century, to be among the most important, though rarely considered, of the biographical facts about Hardy. Evidence of the poetic nurture he derived from his absorption in the poetry of his Romantic and Victorian ancestors is abundantly available in the *Wessex Poems.*

The class of poem called 'moments of revision' is to be contrasted with the more familiar category, Hardy's 'moments of vision', a type of poem to be found all through his volume of that name. In his recent book-length study, Paul Zietlow defines a 'moment of vision' as a brief work in an unpretentious and delicate style, which records an immediate response to a concrete situation, a tentative personal impression emerging from a momentary experience. Hardy's method in these poems, which deal with the 'homeliest

/Of heartstirrings', tends to be objective description of simple facts, things clearly seen, appealing to the human desire for meaning in a context of apparent meaninglessness and indifference. Such moments are often rooted in events and feelings Hardy actually experienced directly.[1] By contrast, the 'moment of revision' is a poem that originates as a response to, or a comment upon, an earlier work or works of literature. It is a poem that is 'influenced' in the best sense of that denigrated term. Ezra Pound once advised the would-be poet: 'Be influenced by as many great artists as you can, but have the decency either to acknowledge the debt outright or to try to conceal it.'[2] Hardy's practice seems to have anticipated Pound's advice, for his language in a 'moment of revision' is often deliberately artificial and allusive, even when the sources of the art or allusion are concealed. In these poems Hardy reconsiders the ideas and feelings expressed, or the problems raised and solutions posited in works of earlier authors, either revising or completing the experiences and refuting or criticizing their answers. Many of his poems, then, are to be regarded as refutations or qualifications, in short, revisions of the literary statements of earlier poets. For the most part I shall consider 'moments of revision' that respond to poems by Hardy's ancestors in the nineteenth century, especially the major poets Wordsworth, Shelley, Tennyson, Browning, and Arnold. T. S. Eliot has truly remarked that 'No poet, no artist of any art, has his complete meaning alone. His significance, his appreciation is the appreciation of his relation to the dead poets and artists. You cannot value him alone; you must set him, for contrast and comparison, among the dead.'[3] This paper will attempt such an examination of some of Hardy's relations to his poetic ancestors.

In developing my discussion of individual works and their relations to earlier poems, I rely on Harold Bloom's brilliant analyses of the modes of poetic misprision in his recent *The Anxiety of Influence*. Bloom describes with convincing and penetrating precision the dynamics of poetic influence; how, very often, poems are deliberate misinterpretations and corrective revisions of earlier poems; and how, in their disciplined perverseness, 'strong' poets necessarily misread their ancestors in order to clear imaginative space for themselves.[4] Bloom defines six modes of poetic misprision, at least three of which are characteristic of many of Hardy's 'moments of revision'. As these terms will recur later, let me define them now. First there is *clinamen*, a corrective swerve away from the meaning of a precursor's poem, which implies that the earlier poem went accurately up to a point. *Tessera* is an antithetical completion of the meaning of a precursor's poem, retaining its terms but valuing them differently, as though the precursor had failed to go far enough. *Kenosis* is a movement towards discontinuity with the precursor, the later poet humbling himself in relation to the stance taken by his precursor, undoing in himself the precursor's strength, with the ironic result that the precursor's strength is rendered suspect, even perhaps undone also.[5]

These three modes of poetic misprision, *clinamen, tessera, kenosis,* help to illuminate how poetic influence operates within Hardy's 'moments of revision'. Some of his poems are totally intent on revising a precursor's work; in other poems, only a few lines, a single stanza perhaps, are devoted to reinterpretation. In each case, our awareness of Hardy's revisionary relationships to precursor poets can provide a much more satisfying idea of Hardy's immersion in the main streams and traditions of English poetry, a more exact sense of the phenomenon of poetic influence, and a clearer and truer view of literary history.

The first two pieces in *Wessex Poems* prefigure the chief preoccupation of this volume's 'moments of revision'. 'The Temporary the All' and 'Amabel' raise a central problem for most of the Romantic poets, that of finding a satisfactory reconciliation between the human needs to imagine and pursue the ideal and to manage the real. Both poems revise or correct the typical solution proffered by the great Romantics. Where Wordsworth and Shelley affirm that the ideal is the only reality, and that the world of sense is only an illusion that must be penetrated in order to achieve a vision of the ultimate reality, Hardy usually finds that the gap between the real and the ideal is essentially unbridgeable. His title in 'The Temporary the All' insists upon the sole reality of the actual. The result of the idealist's quest for his true friend, his 'Wonder of women', his 'visioned hermitage', and his high aim to 'outshow' Truth and Light are suggested in the poem's opening and closing phrases: 'Change and chancefulness . . . Never transcended'. For Hardy, honesty and good sense require that one often assume a deeply anti-Romantic stance: one must face up to the disparity between real and ideal, even though the price one pays for a realistic vision is profound emotional pain.

In poems where the speaker longs for the ideal in spite of his knowledge that the real must always fall short of it, the tone may range from melancholy to bitterness. Hardy's typical poetic strategy in a 'moment of revision' is to allude to a particular poem, its diction, stanzaic pattern or rhythm, in order to recall for the reader the actual context he is revising. We shall consider numerous such instances shortly. At other times he simply revises ideas or feelings usually associated with a particular poet, and suggests his source through form and theme, but without actually alluding to the exact language of a particular work. 'Amabel' is such an instance, a symbolic poem dramatizing a Byronic narrator's bitter reflections about Time's tyranny. The idealized woman of the poem, a Shelleyan 'Well-beloved' or 'beautiful loved one', is revealed as all too humanly vulnerable to change, age, and custom. The obvious implication of 'Amabel' is to satirize and repudiate the Shelleyan concept, and to suggest the futility of demanding ideality from any woman.

The sonnet 'In Vision I Roamed' is in form a typical Romantic excursion lyric, an imaginary quest that ends in a transforming vision. The poem is characterized by Shelleyan and Keatsian diction with an unorthodox sestet, reminiscent of Keats's dissatisfaction with an experimentation upon the rigorous sonnet form. However, the usual Romantic theme of the inordinate inaccessibility of the idealized lover is revised by the narrator's scientific point of view. Extensive earthly distances are transformed into nearness when compared to the celestial distances of the speaker's imaginary 'traverse through ghast heights of sky/To the last chambers of the monstrous Dome,/Where stars the brightest here are lost to the eye'. The poem, illustrating the revisionary mode Bloom calls *tessera,* is informed by the usual thematic conditions of famous Romantic quest lyrics; but these conditions lead to a significantly different feeling when considered from the perspective of a scientifically knowledgeable narrator. Because of the speaker's corrective, antithetical perspective, attained through his knowledge of Victorian science, his lover's absence evokes 'pleasant thankfulness' rather than the Romantic's protracted painful longing.

'Her Initials' is a Wordsworthian memory poem that employs what Carlos Baker has aptly described as the 'double-exposure' technique of 'Tintern Abbey'.[6] The purpose of this technique, which involves the presentation of a speaker who has returned to a particular setting or situation after the passage of some time and who reveals the changes he has experienced since his first experience, is to dramatize the growth or spiritual development of that speaker. In 'Her Initials' Hardy employs the plain diction of *Lyrical Ballads* and Wordsworth's imagery of light to portray the speaker, who once associated two letters of his lover's name with some lines he was reading, undoubtedly in the poetry of Shelley. But when the speaker returns to the initialled page after some years, there is a breakdown in the unifying power of his imagination, a diminution of the original complex emotion. Thus the original experience is lost: for though 'the same / Immortal light illumes the lay / . . . from the letters of her name / The radiance has waned away!' From Wordsworth's ideas about the creative powers of the imagination and the preservative functions of the memory, and their relative roles in the production of poetry, Hardy seems to swerve. For him, as for Matthew Arnold, another great reviser of Wordsworth, the loss of youthful feeling is without recompense; it is sheer loss. His misinterpretation, or rather re-interpretation of those ideas in 'Her Initials' is an instance of *clinamen* or creative revisionism, the rendering of a mode of experience made possible by a reaction to an experience in an early poet's work. 'Her Initials' reveals that for Hardy poetry may result because of the *failure* to recollect in tranquillity the emotion that one spontaneously felt at an earlier time.

'Her Dilemma' begins with five lines of the kind of descriptive setting we find in Tennyson's 'Mariana'. In both works the theme of sexual frustration is developed with an abundance of images of sterility. But 'Her Dilemma' seems centrally inspired by Browning, from its parenthetical epigraph to its fascination with a moral dilemma that illustrates a moment in the development of a human soul. The paradoxical morality of Browning's 'The Statue and the Bust', that even a crime will do as the test to prove the soul's worth, seems vindicated in 'Her Dilemma' by the woman's lie to her dying lover: 'And hence she lied, her heart persuaded throughly / 'Twas worth her soul to be a moment kind.' The bold generosity of her act, however sinful it appeared, is only a Browningesque 'apparent failure'; actually, her lie is the means by which Hardy's woman antithetically completes Browning's poem, where both lovers lost life's set prize by their failure to commit a crime to gain it.

The sonnet 'Revulsion', which seems to have been written under the influence of Shakespeare's sonnet sequence, is a clever but not very moving refutation of Tennyson's adage in lyric 85 of *In Memoriam,* that ''Tis better to have loved and lost / Than never to have loved at all.' To Hardy's revisionist speaker, 'Out of the night there looms a sense 'twere better / To fail obtaining whom one fails to miss.' That is, ''Twere better *not* to have loved and lost!'

'Valenciennes' is a full-scale reworking of Robert Southey's subject, theme, and technique in 'The Battle of Blenheim'. Both poems use modifications of the traditional ballad stanza as their metrical base. In both works a conventional *naïf* reminisces about a famous victory of the English and their commander over their arch-enemy, the French. The narrators' emphasis upon the carnage of battle, and their obliviousness to the major questions of the purposes and the justice of the struggles, account for the effective though understated satire on war in both poems. Where Hardy antithetically extends Southey's tone and treatment is in his dramatic and passionate directness of presentation. Southey's disengaged irony is developed through an edifying debate between Old Kaspar and his grandchildren, as well as through Kaspar's expression of romantic and nostalgic sentiments. Hardy, on the other hand, employs direct narration by a participant in and victim of war's horrors. The corporal's realistic dialect, precise imagery and emotional ambivalence render his account a more immediate and psychologically authentic experience than that of Kaspar.

In 'The Burghers' Hardy submits again to the influence of Browning. The poem employs the earlier poet's characteristic method of distancing his subject by vaguely suggesting in the epigraph the time of the poem's events. The use of *terza rima,* the poem's conflict between the demands of the spirit and of the law, and its appeal to God alone as final judge of morally dubious choices, reveal the poem's indebtedness to 'The Statue and the Bust'. Here again, as in 'Her Dilemma', Hardy's protagonist vindicates Browning's morality; for when his soul is tested by a moral dilemma, whether or not to liberate his wife to flee with her lover, he responds promptly to the demands of charity, even when it involves sanctioning what the law would deem adultery. In its subject, moreover, 'The Burghers' also recalls the root situation of *The Ring and the Book,* where an apparently injured husband seeks revenge upon his errant wife and her lover. But unlike Browning's demonic Count Guido, the husband in 'The Burghers' is graced with the moral capacity for spiritual development; and, at the moment of his testing, he responds to his revelation of his wife's pure love and the marriage laws' inhuman tyranny by befriending the lovers and providing their daily bread in the spirit of charity. The husband is transformed from a potential Guido into a divine Father figure. His ambiguous last words reinforce the poem's moral values and suggest further the husband's divine-like prescience. In the end, 'The Burghers' seems an experiment in which Hardy dramatizes Browning's morality from 'The Statue and the Bust' by antithetically completing the conflict in *The Ring and the Book.* This complicated instance of *tessera,* however, is clearly stamped with Hardy's own moral courage, sympathy, and aversion to the dehumanizing consequences of too rigid laws.

'A Sign-Seeker' is a clear illustration of the revisionary ratio Bloom calls *kenosis.* Hardy's speaker throughout the poem assumes the stance of Tennyson's in *In Memoriam,* that of combing the universe for signs of an afterlife. That Tennyson's poem is Hardy's source seems without dispute. The stanzaic form and the continuous flow of verbal echoes and thematic strands make the link clear. But for all this repetition there is the major discontinuity between the two speakers. While Tennyson in lyric 95 of *In Memoriam* receives his sign of Hallam's continuous existence after his departure from the flesh, Hardy's seeker, in lines that allude to that very same lyric, admits the futility of his search:

> —There are who, rapt to heights of trance-like trust,
>   These tokens claim to feel and see,
>   Read radiant hints of times to be—
> Of heart to heart returning after dust to dust.
>
> Such scope is granted not to lives like mine . . .

Although like Tennyson he consults Scriptures and contemporary signs, and visits the scenes and homes and tombs of friends now dead, he lacks the ability to commune with the dead. This discontinuity with the Tennyson of lyric 95, which isolates Hardy's speaker by insisting on his humbler endowment than that of his precursor, is central to *kenosis*. Yet by undoing what his precursor did, Hardy achieves a breakthrough, a dialectical re-creation that represents an authentic liberation from the precursor and is marked with Hardy's own characteristic note. Moreover, the poem concludes by raising doubts about the validity of Tennyson's experience. Hardy's speaker's stance *appears* to be that of his precursor, but the meaning of that original stance is undone or, as Bloom puts it, emptied of its priority. Finally, the precursor himself is humbled (the source of *kenosis* is St Paul's account of Christ's humbling himself from God to man) by the later poet's apparent self-humbling.

The language of 'Her Immortality' recalls the common diction and stanzaic form of, among others, Wordsworth's traditional ballads, especially the Lucy poems. The speaker also seems a Wordsworthian in his associationist instincts and spiritualized imagination. But where Lucy's immortality is located 'in earth's diurnal course / With rocks, and stones, and trees', Hardy swerves away from Wordsworth's precedent by placing his speaker's dead love's immortality elsewhere.

> A Shade but in its mindful ones
>   Has immortality;
> By living, me you keep alive,
>   By dying you slay me.

For Hardy, then, immortality is a temporary state, lasting only as long as a dead one is remembered by living lovers. This 'moment of revision', this *clinamen*, epitomizes the extent of Hardy's intellectual separation from Wordsworth by implying the alienation between man and Nature and insisting upon the essentiality of shared loving-kindness.

'A Meeting with Despair' is an allegorical journey set on a lightless track of waste land. Hardy's quester is seeking solace even as he travels the gloomy, 'deadly dun' moor, a landscape that symbolizes his life. In its situation, setting, and technique, the poem recalls Browning's splendid grotesquerie in 'Childe Roland to the Dark Tower Came'. However, Hardy's delight in sporting with the terrible is unmixed with any quasi-religious redemptiveness; and he thus completes Browning's ambiguous work by permitting despair to dishearten the determinedly hopeful quester.

In 'Unknowing' Hardy imagines a relationship that seems to fulfil Shelley's hope for the matching of soul-mates: 'When, soul in soul reflected / We breathed an aethered air'. However, the purchase of such an illusion requires the neglect of all other friends and real concerns. Hardy's antithetical extension of Shelley's dream exposes the foolish selfishness of idealising human potentiality for love and the painful disillusionment and loneliness that 'knowing' brings.

'To Outer Nature' is a direct rejection of the Wordsworthian concept of Nature. The speaker's relationship to Wordsworth is established in the first two stanzas, where he recalls his early experiences in language that echoes 'Tintern Abbey'. The third stanza relates him to the Wordsworth of the 'Intimations' ode and reveals his loss of the visionary gleam. But here the continuity ends, and the remainder of the poem recounts the consequences of the speaker's passage from innocence. Significantly, he finds no 'abundant recompense' for his loss of the sense of Nature's radiance, its sweetness and meetness; he is a humbled, 'glow-forsaken' Wordsworth, without joy or perpetual benediction; and he lacks the sublime egotism of the original for reasserting his poetic power.

'In a Wood' rejects Wordsworth's characteristic feelings and beliefs about the joyous unity and the healing powers of Nature. Once again it is the mature Wordsworth of 'Tintern Abbey' who is evoked by the speaker's diction:

> Heart-halt and spirit lame,
>   City-opprest,
> Unto this wood I came
>   As to a nest;
> Dreaming that sylvan peace
> Offered the harrowed ease—
> Nature a soft release
>   From men's unrest.

But Hardy's Nature is actually found to be as contentious as men, her creatures causing one another suffering and death. The speaker recoils from his illusions when he is confronted with a Darwinian reality ('Since, then, no grace I find / Taught me of trees') and returns to the city, where at least 'now and then, are found / Life-loyalties'.

'Middle-Age Enthusiasms', dedicated to Hardy's sister Mary, invites comparison with Wordsworth's 'To My Sister'. Hardy's stanzaic form offers an analogue for the revisionary nature of this poem: his six-line stanza incorporates in its first four lines the rhyme scheme, tone, and themes of Wordsworth's four-line stanza in 'To My Sister', establishing a sense of continuity between Hardy's middle-aged lovers and Wordsworth's youthful ones. But Hardy's stanza also includes a subversive couplet, which reveals that, for all their temporarily recaptured joy and willing suspension of disbelief, the later strollers are unable to sustain their pleasant, romantic illusions. Implicitly a deeply insidious poem, 'Middle-Age Enthusiasms' imaginatively projects Wordsworth's youthful pair into maturity, whereupon it refutes Wordsworth's central ideas about nature, immortality, and the creative power of the imagination. All the temporary feelings of joy and harmony with nature, finally, amount to little more than 'Words! . . . Passed the mortal door / Our thoughts will reach this nook no more.'

'Nature's Questioning' should be related to 'A Sign-Seeker' and *In Memoriam,* which it resembles in its stanzaic pattern and spiritual questing. Blake's technique in 'The Tyger', where he asks a series of unanswered questions, which questions nevertheless imply balefully ambivalent qualities in Nature's creator, is employed here. The first two lines in the penultimate stanza contain allusions to Tennyson's final hope in *In Memoriam,* while the third and fourth lines are reminiscent of Arnold's 'The Last Word'. But again, as in 'A Sign-Seeker', the speaker is only a humble searcher, a questioner, not an answerer; again, the sincerity of his tentative posture creates in the reader an uneasiness about the forced optimism of both of Hardy's precursors.

'In a Eweleaze near Weatherbury' employs the double-exposure technique that Wordsworth perfected in 'Tintern Abbey'. But where Wordsworth uses the technique to dramatize the spiritual growth of his speaker, Hardy employs it for the ironic purpose of exposing his speaker's failure to grow. In fact, after the passage of time and her term as a teacher, Hardy's speaker desires to regress to her earlier self-regarding self-indulgence, shunning 'divinest duty' to resume the worship of Beauty. The spiritual inadequacy of her quest, however, is revealed through her allegiance to what she herself recognizes to be a perishable form of beauty. In this poem, through the revisionary mode of *tessera,* Hardy extends the potential of Wordsworth's reminiscential technique to achieve dramatic irony of the sort we usually associate with Browning.

The final poem I wish to consider is 'Heiress and Architect', perhaps the most complexly revisionary of all the poems in this volume. The richly allusive language of this poem, with its numerous echoes of Keats, Tennyson, and Milton, requires that we read it as a moral allegory and locate it in relation to the important

Renaissance and Romantic traditions that examine the moral implications of the soul's instinct to withdraw in godlike isolation into a splendid edifice or earthly paradise. To each request of Hardy's heiress, whether the request takes its spirit from Keats's narrator in the 'Ode to Psyche', Tennyson's high-born maidens in 'The Palace of Art' or 'The Lady of Shalott', or Milton's Eve, the architect returns a firm refusal. In an extensive revision, Hardy reinterprets the heiress's essentially Romantic aspirations as sinful selfishness; moreover, in condemning the heiress he enlists Milton's high moral authority by characterizing the architect through allusions to God the Father and the Son.

I began by asking questions about the kinds of poems Hardy wrote and their sources. The theoretical assumption behind those questions is that they will lead us to a clearer understanding of Hardy as a poet, since it is through poetic forms he expresses himself. I would like to conclude by asking, 'What do we learn about Hardy as a poet through our examination of his "moments of revision"?' Or, to put it another way, 'What is the relationship of the type of poem called a "moment of revision" to Hardy's artistic temperament and instincts?'

In the first place, the pervasiveness and the artistic significance of Hardy's 'moments of revision' reinforce our sense that Hardy is, above all, a poet of moments, a recorder of impressions and seemings, rendered in dramatic terms, rather than a poet who attempts to synthesize experience into a logically coherent and comprehensive vision. He is a tentative quester, a questioner, not an answerer or systematizer. In short, he is the kind of poet he described himself to be, time after time, in preface after preface, during all those years when critic and common reader alike, reflecting their own needs for intellectual certainty, tried to organize and fathom his 'philosophy' and pin a tag on it. In *Wessex Poems*, some of his most important and most characteristic poems are 'moments of revision' in which he undertakes what he surely considered the necessary critical examination and discrediting of inherited orthodoxies of his time, especially when those orthodoxies had been sanctioned by his century's sages and poets.

This critical temperament, so awesome a force in the author of *Tess of the d'Urbervilles* and *Jude the Obscure*, is the *genius loci* of the 'moments of revision'. Hardy's mature mental habits, developed so significantly by his reading of his contentious contemporaries, reveals his spiritual kinship to those Carlyle called 'Sceptical or Inquisitory Metaphysicians'. Inheritor of a questioning time-spirit, Hardy grew into his intellectual maturity during an era 'when the mind having widened its sphere of vision, the existing theorem of the Universe no longer answers the phenomena, no longer yields contentment; but must be torn in pieces, and certainly anew sought for in the endless realms of denial'. This Pyrrhonic endeavour, for Carlyle 'a pure, unmixed, though from time to time a necessary evil', was Hardy's life-long mission as an artist.[7] Ideas in theology, cosmogony, morality came regularly under his scrutiny; as did ideas, situations, and modes of feeling expressed in earlier poetry. When Hardy's usual instinct to record dramatic moments achieves expression in union with his characteristic critical temper, the poetic issue may be called a 'moment of revision'.

These moments, finally, reveal Hardy's dialectical relationships to his major precursor poets of the nineteenth century. Scholarship has long recognized Hardy's indebtedness to the great Romantics and Victorians, though very little in the way of precise explanations of the nature of the influences has been attempted. With the help of Bloom's insights, I have tried to describe some of the ways in which Hardy correctively revises his precursors. A full discussion of Hardy's indebtedness must also include those poems where he simply imitates or repeats his predecessors. It has not been my intention in any way to denigrate Hardy for his reliance upon the work of earlier poets. T. S. Eliot says truly that 'we shall often find that not only the best, but the most individual parts of [a poet's] work may be those in which the dead poets, his ancestors, assert their immortality most vigorously'.[8] In fact, Hardy's frequent struggles with and occasional conquests of his poetic fathers made possible the achievement of his own distinctive voice and redeemed him from the fate of being merely a latecomer and imitator. In these struggles he resembles Robert Browning's poet-narrator in *Pauline,* describing the progress of the poet as he works towards the establishment of his own poetic identity: 'I rather sought / To rival what I wondered at than form / Creations of my own.'

All good poets steal, T. S. Eliot also tells us; this is inevitable and necessary. Shelley implicitly demands as much when he says:

> one great poet is a masterpiece of nature which another not only sought to study but must study. He might as wisely and as easily determine that his mind should no longer be the mirror of all that is lovely in the visible universe, as exclude from his contemplation the beautiful which exists in the writing of a great contemporary . . . Every man's mind is . . . modified by all the objects of nature and art; by every word and every suggestion which he ever admitted to act upon his consciousness . . . [9]

The important matter, we should realize, is not whether or not a poet steals, but how well he uses his booty. Hardy records a reflection in his *Literary Notebooks* about artistic thievery with which, from the evidence of his works, he seems to have agreed: '*A true artist's method of appropriation*—He amalgamates the style of several masters—this is not the process of the copier.'[10]

From those same *Literary Notebooks* we have abundant evidence of how regularly Hardy's art was nourished by his appropriation of several masters' styles. The present reading of Hardy is founded on the conviction that very often the most important of the biographical influences upon the poetry is Hardy's reading of earlier poems, as this reading accounts for the subject and the treatment in an individual work, even when the work seems directly opposed to its source. For 'To do just the opposite is also a form of imitation, and the definition of imitation ought by rights to include both.'[11]

Far more 'objective' an artist than he has generally been recognized, Hardy is, like his revered Shelley, one of the most 'literary' poets of his time. I cannot help believing that his remarks, in his selection from the poems of William Barnes, are equally appropriate for defining the kind of poet he himself is: 'Primarily spontaneous, he was academic closely after.'[12] Though an event or a feeling Hardy actually experienced may be the ultimate source of a poem, before such raw materials are fashioned into poetry, they are subjected to comparison with, and rendered in language and formal structures employed by, previous poets who experienced similar events and feelings. Hardy's creative instinct is constantly to discover pre-existing analogues to his own experience, very often in works of literary art, with which he can associate or from which he can dissociate this experience. His representation of life, then, is deeply influenced by his absorption in art; so much so that it is accurate to say that in his 'moments of revision' Hardy's art imitates art rather than life. This tendency to render life's meaning in terms of pre-existing works of art is fundamental to the achievement of the universal stature of Hardy's characters, situations, and feelings. For today's critics of Hardy's poetry, an illuminating approach to the meaning of the works can be made by investigating their relationships to the parent poems from which they take their origins.

XII

Harold Orel:

AFTER "THE DYNASTS": HARDY'S RELATIONSHIP TO CHRISTIANITY

A man's relationship to his God, however private he may wish it to remain, invites scrutiny if it becomes the subject-matter of his art. The autobiographical substratum of much of Hardy's verse —what Hardy called the 'personal particulars' of his life—is inescapable, partly because Hardy claimed for himself the privilege of recording in verse views that he did not choose to express in novels, and partly because Hardy believed that his controversial views would excite fewer of the 'literary contortionists' who had attacked the appearance of each new novel. 'If Galileo had said in verse that the world moved, the Inquisition might have let him alone', he wrote dryly on October 17, 1896, at about the time he was renouncing the craft of novel-writing.[1] His concern with the formal Christianity he did not intellectually believe in became even more marked in his creative efforts after that date; poems seeking to define the grounds of a true Christian's faith in an increasingly non-Christian world may be found in every volume of verse that he published.

I believe in the sincerity and truth of the remark, dictated by an ailing Hardy to his second wife, that 'there is more autobiography in a hundred lines of Mr. Hardy's poetry than in all the novels'.[2] In my analysis, due credit will be given to the art, whether 'dramatic or impersonative even where not explicitly so' (Preface to *Poems of the Past and the Present)*, but an assumption to keep in mind throughout is that Hardy, shaken in his faith by theological arguments, reading, and independent thinking by the time he reached his early twenties, did not 'repent' on his deathbed.[3] A second cautionary note is that Hardy did not change his views dramatically or suddenly. The verse of his final years, when dealing with aspects of Christianity, may best be characterized as self-convinced, humanely sceptical, and occasionally tinged by genuine regret; these terms may equally well be applied to many earlier efforts.

Yet, before we move to the examination of specific poems, we should recall the intense interest with which Hardy watched and encouraged the efforts of the Church of England in the 1920s to revise its liturgy, to minimize the supernatural element, and to gather 'many millions of waiting agnostics into its fold'.[4] He knew of no other 'purely English establishment' that had comparable 'dignity and footing, with such strength of old association, such scope for transmutability, such architectural spell', that could 'keep the shreds of morality together'. Hardy noted that he himself had never been called 'churchy', though he thought the term more appropriate than many that had been applied, and added:

> . . . not in an intellectual sense, but in so far as instincts and emotions ruled. As a child, to be a parson had been his dream; moreover, he had had several clerical relatives who held livings; while his grandfather, father, uncle, brother, wife, cousin, and two sisters had been musicians in various churches over a period covering altogether more than a hundred years. He himself had frequently read the church lessons, and had at one time as a young man begun reading for Cambridge with a view to taking Orders.

The final moment in a series of moments of disenchantment came when *The Book of Common Prayer* appeared in new form, with what Hardy called its 'preternatural assumptions' still retained.

Arriving in London at the age of twenty-one (he had been a child of approximately eight the first time he saw the metropolis), Hardy carried two necessary letters of introduction, the *Bible* and *The Book of Common Prayer;* both books had been given to him by his parents. These he marked with pencilled references to events—those taking place between 1859 and 1897 in the *Bible,* and those of 1919 in the *Prayer Book.*[5] But what a young man might need in the way of spiritual solace inevitably changed as he grew older. A conviction that miracles lessened rather than enhanced scriptural authority became firm. 'Panthera', the poem which postulated the existence of a Roman soldier as the father of Jesus (a legend borrowed from Haeckel and Strauss), was part of a determined effort by Hardy to remove the myth from the *rationally* acceptable life-story of Christ. He made this effort in common with other distinguished Victorians like Matthew Arnold, in order to save the Christian religion from decline. One of the most telling poems of *Winter Words,* 'An Evening in Galilee', is cast in the form of a monologue by Mary, who wonders whether her son is mad; she makes no reference to any of his miracles that he is supposed to have wrought; she does not believe as he does ('He professes as his firm faiths things far too grotesque to be true . . . '), but he is a preacher, an expounder, a reader of unfamiliar philosophies, rather than a transformer into loaves and fishes, a healer who raises men from the dead, or a walker upon the water. Mary anticipates the 'tragedy-brink' of her son's life, the likelihood of his 'arrest, and death', but she does not know how to warn Joseph. Moreover, reacting with understandable bitterness to Jesus's denial of her relationship to him ('Who is my mother?), she poses—for him—the far more troublesome question, 'Who is my father?' The answer to that is known by Joseph, herself, 'and—one other', who will never see her again; what happened between herself and that 'other' is attributed to a chance encounter, she 'dreaming no ill' at the time it happened; in all likelihood Hardy alludes, however indirectly, to the Panthera legend. Mary is thus characterized as an artless, baffled, unhappy mother, incapable of perceiving the full meaning of either her son's preachings or his associations with 'the lowest folk' (fishermen, Mary Magdalene); most important, she is wholly human, and she thinks of Jesus as explicable, for all his erratic behaviour, without recourse to the imagery of supernatural agencies.

Hardy's sceptical attitude toward the suspension of natural laws is consistent. 'In the Servants' Quarters', a modernized rendering of the triple denial of Peter's relationship to Jesus, ends with the crowing of the morning cock. The poet follows the Gospels with sympathetic and imaginative fidelity, but the serviceable, homely realism of the exchanges between the servants, the constables, and Peter, does not state, or even imply, that Peter is convinced of the divinity of Jesus, who is referred to not as the Redeemer but as a 'criminal', a man being brought to judgement for blasphemies. 'A Drizzling Easter Morning' begins with the rhetorical question, 'And he is risen?' before it continues to point out, with more than a touch of melancholia, that 'dead men wait as long ago', and—if consulted—may not wish to rise again; they certainly do not rise again so far as the poet can tell. 'I stand amid them in the rain', he writes, and the old pattern of work ('the weary wain' and 'toilers with their aches') continues forever; those who live look forward to 'endless rest'. The point of the poem is that for them, no less than for those who are already in the grave, it makes no difference whether Jesus is risen. Jesus is said to have lived 'an innocent life' in 'The Clasped Skeletons', a poem written to commemorate the excavation of 'an Ancient British barrow near the writer's house', and Procula, Pilate's wife, does not weep for the son of God but for a man unjustly condemned. Indeed, in the series of rounds that constitutes 'Drinking Song', the history of civilization seems to turn out to be a number of speculations as to the nature of man—by Thales, Copernicus, Hume, Darwin, Thomas Kelly Cheyne, and Einstein—none of which is definitive, yet all of which offer respectable versions of reality for a given age. These speculations—or great thoughts—include the notion that miracles are unnecessary, and the rationalist's argument that Mary was not a virgin when she bore Jesus. 'Such tale, indeed,' Cheyne is made to say in his capacity as a scholar of Biblical texts, 'helps not our creed', and is 'a tale long known to none'.

Hardy's emphasis on the *naturalness* of religion should not be construed as being in any sense an attack on the emotional core of Christianity, for he regarded religion as necessary: it 'must be retained unless the world is to perish', he wrote in the Apology to *Late Lyrics and Earlier.* What he wanted was Christianity to earn the right to renewed credibility among those who had fled, in dismay, from many of its supernatural assertions. These, in turn, defied 'complete rationality' and boggled the imagination. But he became increasingly uncertain that the formal Church institutions of his age, besieged by textual disintegrators, scientific reorganizers of the sum of the world's knowledge, and the men of the cloth disinclined to change, would ever benefit from 'the interfusing effect of poetry', from what Wordsworth, in his Preface to the Second Edition of *Lyrical Ballads*, defined as 'the breath and finer spirit of all knowledge; . . . the impassioned expression which is in the countenance of all Science'.

The dilemma of Christianity is even more complex than that, however. Hardy informs us that the faith of Jesus—as distinct from the life-story, now hopelessly shrouded with story-telling inventions and fabulous artifices—has been systematized and transmogrified into something quite different from what Jesus believed it to be. 'In St Paul's a While Ago', a soliloquy by Hardy that may have been composed as early as 1869 but was first printed in *Human Shows,* Paul is characterized as 'that strange Jew, Damascus-bound', with a 'vision-seeing mind / Charmless, blank in every kind'. The 'eager, stammering speech' of Paul would have been dismissed by Hardy's contemporaries, had they been able to hear it, as the message of 'an epilept enthusiast'. The problem of learning what Christ had to tell us is twice compounded: first, by Paul's intoxicated visions (the 'drifts of gray illumination' that Hardy sees spilling down 'from the lofty fenestration' of the English Cathedral are symbolically fitting, for the joy of Jesus is not to be found within 'chilly Paul's, / With its chasmal classic walls'), and second, by the trivial interests of the modern age, as exemplified by statues of 'cadaverous' and 'wan' visage and by visitors to the Cathedral; the latter are 'all unknowing or forgetting' of the real Paul, and are given secularized names:

> A brimming Hebe, rapt in her adorning,
> Brushes an Artemisia craped in mourning:
> Beatrice Benedick piques, coquetting . . .

In 'Winter Night in Woodland', Hardy contrasts the fox-hunters, bird-baiters, poachers, smugglers, and drunken stay-at-homes against the Mellstock-singers 'just afoot on their long yearly rounds', who have set out 'to rouse by worn carols each house in their bounds'. Robert Penny, the Dewys, Mail, Voss, and the rest represent an age that had vanished even before Hardy's birth; the Mellstock quire (as in *Under the Greenwood Tree)* symbolizes an earlier and more innocent time. Hardy's first three stanzas describe various illegal and even brutal and murderous acts that in no way have been checked by the spirit of Christ's teaching, or modified by the meaning of 'the rhythm of voices and strings' carried through the countryside after midnight by the quire. Christ has had no effect on the perpetrators of these misdeeds.

Thus, it is not clear that Christ's having lived and died has improved the lot of mankind beyond expanding the choices available to those who want to believe in a credible God. A poem that illustrates this view is 'Christmas in the Elgin Room', begun (presumably) while Hardy was conducting research in the British Museum for *The Dynasts*, and completed very close to the end of his life (the dates appended to the poem are 1905 and 1926). Hardy imagines, in a characteristic irony of juxtaposed attitudes, what the Greek gods represented in the Elgin marbles ('those whom Christmas overthrew') might say about the pealing of Christmas bells. The Nativity which the occasion celebrates—according to those gods—was 'said to have been a day of cheer, / And source of grace / To the human race . . . '. But the fate of the Elgin marbles—to have been sold 'for Borean people's gold' and brought to London—was grim. Not only is England the land of the 'Borean people'; not only do the Greek gods recognize the fact that the British Museum houses them in an unworthy and demeaning 'gaunt room / Which sunlight shuns'; remembering where they had been, 'on Athenai's Hill', they sigh for the better times they have known: 'Before this Christ was known, and we had men's good will'. Hardy juxtaposes the pagan past and the Christian present, but not for cheaply ironic effect as, easily enough perhaps, he might have done. He is not, for example, suggesting that the 'deities fair' whom Pheidias sculpted represented a truer concept of religion than that which has replaced them. They have had their day; 'old Helios', 'the Ilissus River-god', Demeter, Poseidon, Persephone, and all the others are remembered today only because an Englishman —Lord Elgin—brought them from their ignominious repose (as broken limbs and 'shards beneath some Acropolitan clod') to a land where restoration had at least indicated a measure of their value to those who cared for their memories as the powerful gods they once had been. Hardy's note is more subtle and, correspondingly, more disturbing. The yesteryear when the Greek gods were 'radiant' will never come again; that he knows, and concedes. But the Christianity of the modern world, for all the sound of bells —variously described as shaking the light, clanging, and singing—is not presented as a cheerful condition of life either. Hardy could have suggested as much by allowing the gods to speculate on whether the significance of the Nativity had been truly understood; if men were acting on the basis of the meaning of the allegory that Christ's life provided. Even when we grant the limitations of perspective (the Greek gods, those 'of Zeus' high breed', cannot know for certain what is happening in the outer world), the poem provides no evidence that the new faith is 'radiant', based on mutual confidence between the people and the gods they worship, or serene. The gods are in exile, and a gloomy exile it has proved to be; they cannot be sure that the sun of Christ is any warmer than the 'cold' Aurore that enters their museum windows. Their ignorance may well be Hardy's uncertainty: how warming is the Christian faith to men of the twentieth century?

'Christmas: 1924', a quatrain, notes the ambiguity of the 'advances' of civilization. These have brought to us, and to Hardy only three years before his death, the perfection of a new weapon of mass-destruction, 'poison-gas'. But it is difficult to tell if Hardy laments here the tattering of the dreams of the League of Nations more or less than he laments the futility of the message preached by 'a million priests', the invocation of 'Peace upon earth!' which apparently means little or nothing to the modern world.

There is, however, no shading of ambiguity in the poem 'Unkept Good Fridays' which Hardy dated 'Good Friday, 1927'. It is a surprisingly powerful statement for a poem written so close to the end; the passion of the poem still has the power to move us more than a half-century later. Hardy believed that Christ's goodness (his human virtues) had led to envy, betrayal, and death; but this kind of sacrifice had not been unique in the annals of man. 'There are many more Good Fridays / Than this, if we but knew / The names . . . '. The sacrificial victims, the 'nameless Christs', will remain forever uncounted because their agonies have been unpenned. Such is the drift of four of the five stanzas, which essentially repeat the commonality of the fate of other martyrs; they were slain for their 'goodwill' by the rulers and the mobs who tortured, smote, and trampled them under into unmarked graves, on unscored dates.

If Hardy had concluded with the fourth stanza, the poem might have remained a conventionalized and unsurprising statement of Christian doctrine: the good man is fated to be scorned, to live through 'days of bonds and burning'; there are many Christs, and their Good Fridays will never be commemorated. But the fifth stanza goes much further, and argues that the failure to remember who they were really doesn't matter: 'The world was not even worthy / To taunt their hopes and aims . . . .' We have not been worthy of them or of Jesus. We have already dishonoured the memory of the Christ we knew. Why, then, should we assume that we could or would honour the memory of any of the nameless Christs—'these Christs of unwrit names'—if in fact we were to be informed of the nobility of their individual moments on Calvary? The final message of Hardy's poem is best characterized as bleak. Christ was, and remains today, too good for us. We rejected him, and all who followed in his footsteps, and we are where we are today because our Christianity is hollow. 'Unkept Good Fridays' can thus be read as a final comment on 'Christmas in the Elgin Room'. The old gods are exiled, imprisoned in the British Museum, devitalized; but the god of Christianity, the true and living Christ, may never have been believed in, and even worse, it is not in human nature—as the New Dark Age moves in, engulfing us—to understand and appreciate the meaning of Good Friday.

Now all of this goes beyond many of the critical commentaries on Hardy's concept of Immanent Will, which place so much emphasis on the mocking detachment of the Spirits, particularly in *The Dynasts*, where the meaning of the Will is most fully expounded and interpreted. It will be recalled that several of the Spirits are denominated as pitying, as sinister, as ironic; with one or two minor exceptions they do not participate in the action of the fated decade between 1805 and 1815; they remain far above the action; and the Immanent Will never speaks for itself anyhow. It has been easy for many critics to assume that Hardy identifies with his Spirits, and has adopted a pose of superiority to the agonies of mankind, the 'shapes that bleed, mere mannikins', each of which 'has parcel in the total Will'. At any rate, the temptation has not been consistently resisted.

But it may be questioned whether, in his final decade, Hardy's perception of a failed faith was impersonally rendered in such poems as we have been considering, or whether Hardy, like the Ezekiel whose Book he had been reading on at least one Good Friday, responded to the barbarities of his age with increasing concern and a sense of deepening personal involvement. Those familiar with the magnificent speech of the Chorus of the Years at Waterloo, remember how the poet imagined the war as seen from the height and perspective of the small animals and birds on that bloody battlefield; but equally poignant was the speech that followed, uttered by the Chorus of the Pities (Part 3. VI. viii):

> So the season's intent, ere its fruit unfold,
> Is frustrate, and mangled, and made succumb,
> Like a youth of promise struck stark and cold!

Hardy's unhappiness over the broken promises of the Christian religion is closely related to his conviction that the Church of England in the 1920s could not respond to felt needs, to his perception of the vastness of the gulf between institutionalized worship and the intellectual like himself who wanted to return to a simpler faith, and to his concern that the human race as a whole had already denied the possibility of its redemption; like Peter in 'In the Servants' Quarters', we had known the Christ and refused to acknowledge him. As Peter said:

> 'No! I'll be damned in hell if I know anything about the man!
> No single thing about him more than everybody knows!
> Must not I even warm my hands but I am charged with blasphemies?'

It is true Hardy denied that he spoke directly in his poems. He expressed frequently his willingness to believe that critics read 'meanings into a book that its author never dreamt of writing there'. In his final tart comment on 'licensed tasters', contained in his Preface to *Winter Words,* he wrote that their odd verdicts arose not from wilful misrepresentation but from a failure to read what he had written. It would be strange indeed if Hardy did not occasionally—in poems on a topic so close to his heart as the Christian faith and the difficulties that he stumbled over as he sought to partake of its blessings—sound an unmistakable personal note. In two poems particularly he described his private feelings at what should be the most joyous season of the year: 'Christmastide' and 'A Nightmare, and the Next Thing'. In 'Christmastide' Hardy contrasts his own mood as he strides 'despondently' through the rain with the mood of a poor man headed toward the Casuals' Gate of the Union House, where he will be fed and housed for the night; the tramp, too, is sodden, but he has not lost his cheer, and the poem ends abruptly. After the tramp has shouted a salutation, 'A merry Christmas, friend!' Hardy does not tell us whether the greeting has improved the spirits of the poet. In 'A Nightmare, and the Next Thing', again, the contrast is deliberately set: on the one hand, the poet depressed by the 'fogged and blurred' empty street of a 'nightmare Christmas Day' and, on the other, 'three clammy casuals' headed toward the Union House, laughing, alive, and unaware of any reason why they should share the poet's melancholia. No one else, in fact, sees the 'gray nightmare / Astride the day, or anywhere'. Is 'the next thing' of the title Death itself, as J. O. Bailey surmises?[6] If so, the depressed mood of the poem must be tied closely to old age, debilitation, fragile health. Yet only the presence of the poem in Hardy's last volume suggests lateness of composition (it is undated, as indeed are many of the poems we would like to know more about). Without speculating on the relationship of 'A Nightmare, and the Next Thing' to Hardy's conviction, in his late eighties, that he had outstayed his welcome, we may still observe that both poems present Christmas as a personally gloomy experience. Hardy does not deny that others may feel invigorated by the season; but the poet, speaking as the 'I' of each poem, is plunged deeply into a mood that Christ's birth seems powerless to lighten.

Hardy's final poems are sadder and more measured in pace. They turn backward to earlier and happier times; it is only natural that thoughts of Christmas in the post-war world should suffer by comparison with thoughts of Christmas enjoyed while a child. In 'Yuletide in a Younger World', for example, Hardy recalls, from his own boyhood, 'doings of delight', speculations on phantoms crossing a 'bridge or stile', the craft of divination to 'read men's dreams . . . / Even as wheels spin round', and a sense of closeness to 'the fartime tones of fire-filled prophets / Long on earth unseen . . . '. But, he admits these have long since gone: 'Now we are blinker-bound.' There is a finality to this recognition. Not only have the happy events and innocent beliefs of childhood receded into a remote past for the poet, but the possibility of ever reclaiming them is now seen as hopeless. Nor is his recollection of those moments of pleasure afforded the innocent eye spoiled by the wisdom of his eighty-sixth birthday ('He Never Expected Much'). Life, from the very beginning, warned him that he would experience 'just neutral-tinted haps and such', that the World would not all be fair. Most ageing poets would understand Hardy's mood of steely-edged nostalgia, and do.

Preparation for a final reckoning informs many of the poems in Hardy's last volumes of verse, and those with religious content seem peculiarly final in their point of view. I find particularly poignant 'Sine Prole', a poem Hardy wrote in deliberate imitation of a medieval Latin sequence by Adam of S. Victor, for here Hardy faced the certainty that he would have no descendants, children or grandchildren, because his family tree had run out:—'To the moment where I stand / Has my line wound: I the last one . . . '; and even if Hardy's view of post-war Europe was to harden a generalized conviction that no child could or would grow to manhood cheered by the prospects of an eternally barbarous mankind, the thought of dying childless was inevitably personal.

Human Shows is rich in these penultimate musings, which suggest that the nature of the Immanent Will had long since been settled to the poet's satisfaction, and that other questions now crowded front and centre. In 'The Graveyard of Dead Creeds', for example, Hardy treated all the religions of the past as 'old wastes of thought' which had outlived their usefulness, 'Catholicons' or cure-alls that no longer might solace 'created man, through his long groan'. Hardy did not consider it necessary to identify the 'heir' who would bring 'new promise' to the world, who would, in the words of the spectres of the 'dead creeds', 'make tolerable to sentient seers / The melancholy marching of the years'. The nature of that heir had been defined elsewhere: in his Apology to *Late Lyrics and Earlier;* in the hints about the self-conscious awakening of the Will in the After Scene of *The Dynasts,* as well as in a number of the Spirits' comments earlier; and in an extended passage written during January 1907, and later incorporated into the *Life,* where he spoke of the need for a non-magical, non-superstitious religion that thinking men might respect. Perhaps Hardy underestimated the difficulties that such a religion might pose for the great mass of his fellow-countrymen, and he surely did not want to be considered an original—and hence controversial—speculator on theological doctrine. But there are more than passing traces of regret in his comments on the value of ceremony and liturgy, even while, at the same time, he admitted to being unhappy with the twentieth-century stress on the morality and altruism of Jesus ('an entirely different meaning from that which it bore when I was a boy'). The meaning of Christianity had been altered, refracted, by the Higher Criticism, which he regarded as the unpleasant opposing extreme of the mysticism against which it had reacted; but how was 'Sinceritas'—'the Would-be-Religious'—to define the middle ground?

Hardy took keen interest in the possibility that a comparative study of religions might answer the questions that interpreters of Christianity avoided in their insistence on dogma or on their disintegrative analysis of texts. Toward the end of his life he quoted in his *Notebooks* a sentence used by the *Oxford Dictionary* to illustrate the meaning of sentience, quoted from FitzEdward Hall's *Hindu Philosophical System* (1862): 'The Sankhyas use them [the works of God] to prove that the whole world, every constituent part of which is for an end, has for its author that which possesses no sentience—nature.' He read widely in 'other moral religions within whose sphere the name of Christ has never been heard', and which taught the same doctrine 'of nobler feelings towards humanity and emotional goodness and greatness'.[7] He made notes on psychic phenomena, worried over the possible relevance of Einstein's doctrine of relativity, read with some scepticism Worsley's *Concepts of Monism,* and gave full credit to the significance of Comte's 'Positive Religion'. The usability of various philosophical works—by Mill, Stephen, Spencer probably more than by others—has been defined in a long chapter, 'Impressions of Reality', in Walter Wright's *The Shaping of the Dynasts: A Study in Thomas Hardy* (1967), and the whole matter of Hardy's eclecticism in both philosophical and religious readings is best summarized by Wright's sentence, 'We must keep in mind that Hardy wavered between alternatives in his search for a cosmic view' (p. 53). Hardy retained reservations about *all* men's systems; institutionalized religion, as he saw it, was a human construct, and could not help but be vulnerable to examination and questioning, as any human construct must be.

There is no way to measure the solace that Hardy derived from the limited and severely rationalized Christianity of the late nineteenth century. The poems offer dramatized versions of what are certainly conflicting—not necessarily 'developing'—points of view. Hardy believed that a writer was obliged only to write as well as he could what he knew and felt; the term 'pessimism' he regarded as an irrelevant criterion, one that might have been more appropriately applied to Gray's 'Ode on a Distant Prospect of Eton College' than to his own poetry. 'Oh, Gray is an unbearable poet', he burst out while talking to Vere Collins (October 29, 1921); ' . . . I suppose "pessimism" is an easy word to say and remember. It's only a passing fashion.'[8] Yet his poems dealing with religion, those that articulate in some way the religious impulse, become increasingly melancholy in the final volumes, and are inseparably bound up with his sense of the unlikelihood that men could benefit from Christ's example. Writing to Sydney Cockerell on 28 August 1914, he mused, glumly, 'As for myself, the recognition that we are all living in a more brutal age than that, say, of Elizabeth, or of the chivalry which could cry: "Gentlemen of the Guard, fire first!" (far more brutal, indeed: no chivalry now!) does not inspire one to write hopeful poetry, or even conjectural prose, but simply makes one sit in an apathy, and watch the clock spinning backwards, with a mild wonder if, when it gets back to the Dark Ages, and the sack of Rome, it will ever move forward again to a new Renascence, and a new literature.' He added hastily, 'But people would call this pessimistic, so I will stop . . . .'[9]

As a consequence, a critic's emphasis may fall on the hopelessness contained in the speeches of the wind ('A Night of Questionings'), which proclaim the unchanging evil of man's nature; human beings breathe 'dark-drawn breaths' and 'knave their neighbours' deaths', revert 'to type', and will never grow purer. Or it may identify, as more genuinely expressive of Hardy's longer-term belief, the hopefulness contained in such late poems as 'There Seemed a Strangeness' and 'Xenophanes, the Monist of Colophon', which look forward to the ultimate awakening of the Will, and the revelation of God's intentions:

'Men have not heard, men have not seen
Since the beginning of the world
   What earth and heaven mean;
But now their curtains shall be furled,

'And they shall see what is, ere long,
Not through a glass, but face to face;
And Right shall disestablish Wrong . . .'

But, over-all, Hardy's views are more mordant than sanguine. The possibility that the Will may never awaken from its complacent sleep is marked by quoted speeches in 'There Seemed a Strangeness'; (Hardy never says directly and personally that a 'Great Adjustment' will take place: he has a vision in which 'vermilion light' floods 'the land's lean face'; he hears 'a Voice'; these things seem to be and cannot be said actually to be), by the rumblings in letters and comments preserved by visitors to Max Gate, by a number of poems in which inclement weather becomes symbolic of defeated hopes for the triumph of loving-kindness.

It is not unreasonable, then, to end with a consideration of 'Evening Shadows', a poem in *Winter Words* that had appeared first in *The Daily Telegraph on* 7 May 1928. It was one of Hardy's final meditations on the religious impulse. Hardy muses on the relationship between pre-Christian burial mounds—in this case, Conquer Barrow, not far from his home—and the 'earthen cyst' in which some day he will lie buried himself. It was a convenient opportunity to platitudinize: to suggest, for example, that he will ultimately be forgotten. After all, the identity of the Britons who are covered by the barrow had long since been obliterated. Or he might have pointed out that Christianity has not more claim to permanence than the dead creed of the pagan dead. Such, indeed, is part of the poem's message; but only part. Hardy is not sure what will happen after his own death, whether the chimneys of Max Gate will continue to smoke and cast their shadows 'upon the greensward'. More important than his speculation that Conquer Barrow may still 'spread around' its shade many years hence—he does not know for a fact that it will—is his belief that now, in the last decade of his life, the Christian faith is as unregarded, as unbelieved in, as when Conquer Barrow itself was created:

> And nothing says such shade will spread around
> Even as to-day when men will no more heed
> The Gospel news than when the mound was made.

In brief, Hardy's final attitude seems to be that in his own lifetime Christianity had lost its powers to convert the would-be believer, and to cheer or comfort 'Sinceritas'—Thomas Hardy himself, grown poignantly old.

XIII

Tom Paulin:

TIME AND SENSE EXPERIENCE: HARDY AND T. S. ELIOT

In that highly sonorous poem 'A Broken Appointment', which he designed like a piece of clockwork, Hardy describes himself as a 'time-torn man'. No one would disagree with him. Again and again the poems insist upon the cruelties and tyrannies of time and, because Hardy was an agnostic, they seldom if ever suggest the beneficent view of time which we find, for example, in *The Winter's Tale* and *The Tempest*. Hardy's attitude to time is the attitude we meet in Shakespeare's sonnets: Time devours, Time tyrannizes, Time destroys. As Auden says:

> Time and fevers burn away
> Individual beauty from
> Thoughtful children, and the grave
> Proves the child ephemeral.

Without flinching, this is what Hardy states in 'Going and Staying'. The short last line of each stanza emphasizes its points in a curiously static, resonant fashion, like the final deep boom of a bell. The last line, 'Alike dissolving', sounds fixed and final, though what it actually says is that everything—the good and the bad, the sinister and sublime—are all melting and dissolving together like leaves on a compost heap. As the old woman says in 'Autumn in King's Hintock Park':

> Just as my shape you see
>   Raking up leaves,
> I saw, when fresh and free,
>   Those memory weaves
> Into grey ghosts by me,
>   Raking up leaves.

Again, the brief last line, which is used as a refrain in the poem, expresses the passing of time with weary resonance. The woman is one with the leaves she sweeps. Life reduces itself to a grey mass. As Hardy says in one of his last poems, 'Drinking Song':

And now comes Einstein with a notion—
 Not yet quite clear
 To many here—
That there's no time, no space, no motion,
 Nor rathe nor late,
 Nor square nor straight,
But just a sort of bending-ocean

There are no absolutes, no certainties, only a dissolving mass of relative perspectives.

'In the Mind's Eye' sets, with insidious irony, a very suspect form of permanence against this cosmic blur:

Now, as then, I see her
 Moving at the pane;
Ah; 'tis but her phantom
 Borne within my brain!—

Foremost in my vision
 Everywhere goes she;
Change dissolves the landscapes,
 She abides with me.

Shape so sweet and shy, Dear,
 Who can say thee nay?
Never once do I, Dear,
 Wish thy ghost away.

Here he says that the only fixity in a dissolving world is his ideal fantasy of the girl. The last two lines have a sinister ring because the irony is self-directed: he is in love with an ideal ghost and yet subject to time like the two doomed, platonic lovers in that poem of Browning's which Hardy so much admired, 'The Statue and the Bust'.

For Hardy memory is a graveyard, and graveyards are a kind of racial memory. Their permanence is all there is, but it stops far short of the real permanence he sought. And in 'In Front of the Landscape', where he plays long, deliberately contorted lines against short, static, four-syllable lines, the verse-movement is like the rise, the hold, then the toppling of waves; his mind, filled with his memories of the dead, is the exact counterpart of the graveyard where these dead people now lie:

Instruments of strings with the tenderest passion
 Vibrant, beside
Lamps long extinguished, robes, cheeks, eyes with the earth's crust
 Now corporate.

The concept of mind here is ruthlessly physical because it makes it merely a bundle of dissolving sense impressions. Hobbes described memory as 'decaying sense', and said that memory and imagination are really indentical: the poet does not create out of nothing; his work is always the product of his memory and experience. And this essentially reductive concept of the imagination is one which Hardy appears to endorse tacitly in this poem, though as I shall show later his attitude to imagination and memory is more complex than this.

One can read Hardy and feel that he always thought of time as a ghostly machine with revolving arms that sweeps everything into its maw like a great threshing-machine. This is the way he symbolizes time in 'Going and Staying', while in 'The Five Students' he appears to be suggesting, or anticipating, a film projector as an alternative, and equally pessimistic, symbol of the movement of time:

The sparrow dips in his wheel-rut bath,
The sun grows passionate-eyed,
And boils the dew to smoke by the paddock-path;
As strenuously we stride,—
Five of us; dark He, fair He, dark She, fair She, I,
All beating by.

The air is shaken, the high-road hot,
Shadowless swoons the day,
The greens are sobered and cattle at rest; but not
We on our urgent way,—
Four of us; fair She, dark She, fair He, I, are there,
But one—elsewhere.

The seasons change with undeviating rapidity; one by one the students drop away until only he is left stalking past a wintry graveyard.

The first four lines of each stanza have a firm iambic beat with the addition of an anapaest that increases their speed like a smooth gear-change. This swift rhythmic machinery makes the images of the seasons flash past so that the five students seem to be literally 'beating by' like the jerky, pathetic, semaphoring figures in a silent film. Their movement is intent, rapt and serious, but also comic and futile because the rapidity of their walking is a figure both for the confidence of their ambition and the speed of time which will rob them of their ambitions. The real destination they are hurrying towards is death, though they are not aware of it.

This might serve as a brief account of Hardy' view of time, for, granted that he sees time as a destructive element that wears people and things down, any demonstration of this must become a virtually endless series of examples. If memory was the one way open to Hardy of preserving existence, it, too, was subject to time and left him back in time with no way of escaping from it. As he says in 'His Immortality':

> I saw a dead man's finer part
> Shining within each faithful heart
> Of those bereft. Then said I: 'This must be
> His immortality.'

But, as the dead man's contemporaries also die, his immortality falls back into time:

> Lastly I ask—now old and chill—
> If aught of him remain unperished still;
> And find, in me alone, a feeble spark,
> Dying amid the dark.

And the only possible attitude to this dissolving universe where people wither and die away, and where memories also crumble, is a mood of stoicism, a wistful, plaintive stoicism which is beautifully caught in 'Waiting Both'. Trapped in change, both Hardy and the star wait for their final change. There is no heaven, no life ever after, no permanence. They are wearily resigned to this godless universe.

Inevitably, then, the alternative to this view of time must be religious, but as Hardy was an agnostic he could not adopt it. He would have agreed with all but the last line of this stanza from T. S. Eliot's 'The Dry Salvages':

> There is no end of it, the voiceless wailing,
> No end to the withering of withered flowers,
> To the movement of pain that is painless and motionless,
> To the drift of the sea and the drifting wreckage,
> To the bone's prayer to Death its God. Only the hardly, barely
> prayable
> Prayer of the one Annunciation.

For Hardy, that prayer of the 'one Annunciation' was not 'barely prayable': it was impossible, however much he hoped it might not be. And when Eliot insinuates in his softly magisterial tones that:

> There is, it seems to us,
> At best, only a limited value
> In the knowledge derived from experience.
> The knowledge imposes a pattern, and falsifies,

Hardy again would agree, though for him the knowledge derived from experience—empirical knowledge—is all there is. He followed Hobbes, Locke, and Hume in believing that all our knowledge is the product of our sense experience, that our minds are the sum of our sense impressions, and that we know only by reflecting passively. The weary passivity of the attitude in 'Waiting Both' is one result of Hardy's acceptance of the empiricist's view that the mind possesses no active, transcendental powers.

This places him with those two sensual empiricists, Donne and Webster, in Eliot's 'Whispers of Immortality':

> Donne, I suppose, was such another
> Who found no substitute for sense,
> To seize and clutch and penetrate;
> Expert beyond experience.

Hardy, like Donne, could find no substitute for sense experience, and it is Eliot's effort in *Four Quartets* to discover that transcendental substitute which would take him beyond time and experience. Because of his commitment to this search and because of its accompanying detestation of sense experience—not just sex, but all human experience—Eliot is a much more negative poet than Hardy. In 'East Coker', for example, he describes a country dance from an essentially Manichean viewpoint:

> The association of man and woman
> In daunsinge, signifying matrimonie—
> A dignified and commodious sacrament.
> Two and two, necessarye coniunction,
> Holding eche other by the hand or the arm
> Which betokeneth concorde.

The Elizabethan language distances this dance historically so that it appears only as a fanciful costume-piece which is utterly unlike a painting by Breughel or any of Hardy's descriptions of country dances in the novels and poems. For if Hardy almost always points to death and despair lying just beyond the joyous affirmation of the dance, he can allow the dancers their moment of happiness. Not so Eliot. His dancers keep the rhythm of the seasons in their dancing:

> The time of the seasons and the constellations
> The time of milking and the time of harvest
> The time of coupling of man and woman
> And that of beasts.

Almost unconsciously he has begun to convert a harmonious affirmation into a negative rejection:

> Feet rising and falling.
> Eating and drinking. Dung and death.

Time and sense experience interfere with the dance's triumph over time and draw it down into futility. There is no victory over time in this life.

In a way one could argue that this underlying sense of futility is there in 'Transformations' and 'Voices from Things Growing in a Churchyard', which elaborate a natural concept of immortality:

—The Lady Gertrude, proud, high-bred,
  Sir or Madam,
Am I—this laurel that shades your head;
Into its veins I have stilly sped,
And made them of me; and my leaves now shine,
As did my satins superfine,
  All day cheerily,
  All night eerily!

—I, who as innocent withwind climb,
  Sir or Madam,
Am one Eve Greensleeves, in olden time
Kissed by men from many a clime,
Beneath sun, stars, in blaze, in breeze,
As now by glowworms and by bees,
  All day cheerily,
  All night eerily!

One can easily object that this is just an imaginative development of the banal utilitarianism implicit in the phrase 'pushing up daisies'. And this is Eliot's objection when he says at the end of 'The Dry Salvages' that we are

content at the last
If our temporal reversion nourish
(Not too far from the yew-tree)
The life of significant soil.

Our 'temporal reversion' is to become one with the soil of a graveyard and the growth of a yew tree. As Hardy says:

Portion of this yew
Is a man my grandsire knew,
Bosomed here at its foot.

And if one disregards, for the moment, Eliot's point that a reversion into the natural time-cycle is just as significant and non-significant as soil, one can see that Hardy is able to use this familiar, obvious, and uninspiring idea of immortality to profound effect in 'Voices from Things Growing in a Churchyard'. Lady Gertrude's proud, essentially snobbish and sterile character comes through in the comparison of her shining laurel leaves to her 'satins superfine'. The evergreen leaves with their dark green gloss and the stagnant darkness beneath them develop, with superb economy, a sense of her deeply unhappy, frustrated and superficial character.

On the other hand, Eve Greensleeves, who ironically succeeds this lady of the manor and who was 'the handsome mother of two or three illegitimate children', has now been changed into an 'innocent withwind', a climbing plant that is also called 'virgin's bower'. The irony is not cheap: rather it suggests her essential innocence and generosity. She has been kissed by many men

'Beneath sun, stars, in blaze, in breeze, / As now by glowworms and by bees'; and this beautifully suggests a feeling of dazzling light fresh breezes and life-giving warmth, which also become the expression of her free sexuality and her innocent trust. As ever she is eternally virgin and promiscuous. And here each of her names has subtle reverberations which also help to give a profound sense of female character.

This ability of Hardy's to employ a natural, temporal concept of immortality to great imaginative effect—to make the soil significant—is also present in a marvellously mellow poem, 'Regret Not Me', which is a sort of rustic 'Sailing to Byzantium'. The richly melodious, gradually expanding triplets build a wonderful feeling of ripeness; life and happiness are gaily praised, but there are no regrets, no dismissal of triumphant, harmoniously timed dancing as the mechanical, bestial routine of 'dung and death'. The poem is rich, witty, and warmly peaceful; both serenely static and humming with a vibrant energy. The balance between flux and permanence is perfect.

This concept of immortality as laurels, dancing leaves and sunny trees is obviously humanist and secular. Immortality is naturalized and given a physical, not a spiritual, basis. But for the Christian, for a poet like Eliot, this is in no way satisfying. And for Hardy, too, it was not enough, though this does not mean that he had religious beliefs, only that he was dissatisfied with the knowledge derived from experience, with time-bound, time-torn knowledge.

There is a passage in 'East Coker' which in some ways resembles certain moments in Hardy's poetry where he offers an alternative feeling of eternity, of time still and unmoving, though it has to be said that Hardy presents it very firmly in terms of sense experience. Near the beginning of the poem Eliot says:

> In my beginning is my end. Now the light falls
> Across the open field, leaving the deep lane
> Shuttered with branches, dark in the afternoon,
> Where you lean against a bank while a van passes,
> And the deep lane insists on the direction
> Into the village, in the electric heat
> Hypnotised. In a warm haze the sultry light
> Is absorbed, not refracted, by grey stone.

It is then, in this sultry silence, that he has the vision of the dancers I quoted earlier. So, too, in Hardy's 'The Revisitation', which describes a middle-aged soldier making a midnight visit to a place where he used to court a girl called Agnette, there is the same use of warmth absorbed by stone to symbolize the past in the present. The soldier tells how the ancient Sarsen stone:

> On whose breast we had sat and told the zephyrs many a tender vow,
> Held the heat of yester sun.

The old stone contains the heat of the previous day—the past in the present—and it is just as he touches it, as some ghostly peewits rise against the sky, that Agnette reappears to him after an absence of twenty years. Though she is not a ghost (the irony lies in the fact that she is a faded, middle-aged woman), the poem works through its description of a close warmth held in the present—a retained warmth which, as in 'East Coker', releases the vision. This also happens in that great poem, 'Friends Beyond', where Hardy says:

> 'Gone', I call them, gone for good, that group of local hearts and heads;
>   Yet at mothy curfew-tide,
> And at midnight when the noon-heat breathes it back from walls and leads,
>
> They've a way of whispering to me—fellow-wight who yet abide—
>   In the muted, measured note
> Of a ripple under archways, or a lone cave's stillicide.

The warm walls of the midnight graveyard breathe back a stored warmth, and the dead return to life; the past infuses the present. The poem has a beautifully soft, subtle, cheeping tone. Hardy based its metre and rhythm on Browning's haunting 'A Toccata of Galuppi's', and both poems share a ghostly, creaking sound. As Browning says:

> Yes, you, like a ghostly cricket, creaking where a house was burned—
> 'Dust and ashes, dead and done with, Venice spent what Venice earned!
> 'The soul, doubtless, is immortal—where a soul can be discerned.

Again, in 'The Musical Box', Hardy describes a moment of warm stasis when time stood still—though only for a moment:

> I had slowed along
> After the torrid hours were done,
> Though still the posts and walls and road
> Flung back their sense of the hot-faced sun,
> And had walked by Stourside Mill, where broad
> Stream-lilies throng.

For Hardy, this is a moment of transfiguration, and when he describes such moments in his poetry he never allows them to shed their human qualities. Instead of a numinous moment in a rose-garden, we see the past transfiguring the worn-out present in a way that, in 'A Church Romance', is both touching and witty. Here his parents' moment of recognition and committed love has a transcendental quality, and that quality is firmly tied to the lovingly-detailed names of the hymns his father was playing.

Still, we can object that such intense encapsulations are not really permanent. The poem's distinction between the grinding, disappointing ordinariness of temporal experience—'when Age had scared Romance'—and the transcending image of the ardent violin player claiming the proud woman, is a false one because that image is also subject to time like the images in 'Memory and I':

> 'O Memory, where is now my youth,
> Who used to say that life was truth?'
>
> 'I saw him in a crumbled cot
> Beneath a tottering tree;
> That he as phantom lingers there
> Is only known to me.'

Each of the images in this poem is like a blurred and perishing black and white transparency. The mnemonic image is decaying like the 'spectral mannikin' in 'His Immortality'. As the brain decays, so do the images which compose the memory: their permanence is only temporary. In other words this is another escape route which has closed. But for Eliot, and I think at times for Hardy, there was a way out, a way which is taken through what Eliot, in 'Burnt Norton', calls:

> The inner freedom from the practical desire,
> The release from action and suffering, release from the inner
> And outer compulsion, yet surrounded
> By a grace of sense, a white light still and moving.

This is an escape, Eliot says, from a world which moves

> In appetency, on its metalled ways
> Of time past and time future.

Desire is movement; that movement is practical and utilitarian (the movement of cars, railway trains, bodies, Hardy's five hurrying students), but, just in moments, it is possible to break out of this practical motion and know a moment of transcending grace and freedom: 'a grace of sense, a white light still and moving'.

The banal, journalistic setting of Hardy's 'At the Railway Station, Upway' might seem the most unpromising condition for such a moment of freedom, but it is nevertheless what that poem is about:

> 'There is not much that I can do,
> For I've no money that's quite my own!'
> Spoke up the pitying child—
> A little boy with a violin
> At the station before the train came in,—
> 'But I can play my fiddle to you,
> And a nice one 'tis, and good in tone!'

The man in the handcuffs smiled;
The constable looked, and he smiled, too,
As the fiddle began to twang;
And the man in the handcuffs suddenly sang
With grimful glee:
'This life so free
Is the thing for me!'
And the constable smiled, and said no word,
As if unconscious of what he heard;
And so they went on till the train came in—
The convict, and boy with the violin.

This transcending feeling of liberation is the real subject of this poem. And the same is true of 'Midnight on the Great Western' and 'The Darkling Thrush' where the thrush's song, like the violin playing in 'A Church Romance', is a moment of pure joy, an existential affirmation like the last lines of Browning's 'Childe Roland to the Dark Tower Came':

Dauntless the slug-horn to my lips I set,
And blew. *'Childe Roland to the Dark Tower came.'*

For Eliot, such moments are visionary; they are part both of the personal and racial memory, and so they transcend the monotonously practical rhythms of time:

Time past and time future
Allow but a little consciousness.
To be conscious is not to be in time
But only in time can the moment in the rose-garden,
The moment in the arbour where the rain beat,
The moment in the draughty church at smokefall
Be remembered; involved with past and future.
Only through time time is conquered.

Though they are remembered in time these images are also beyond time. Their existence is a victory over its tyranny.

This is the substance of the lecture which the Absolute delivers in Hardy's 'The Absolute Explains', where we learn that 'Time is toothless' because everything is 'shaped to be / Eternally'. In this absolute dimension Hardy sees the permanence of everything:

There fadeless, fixed, were dust-dead flowers
Remaining still in blow;
Elsewhere, wild love-makings in bowers;
Hard by, that irised bow
Of years ago.

There were my ever memorable
Glad days of pilgrimage,
Coiled like a precious parchment fell,
Illumined page by page,
Unhurt by age.

If there seems, as Eliot says, 'no end to the withering of withered flowers', here is their real and absolute existence. Their apparently time-bound images have drifted up into a transcendental medium where they are kept free from time, perfected and permanent. However, the difficulty with this poem is that it does not convince: it states but it does not prove what it says.

'At Castle Boterel', one of Hardy's very greatest poems, holds an overwhelming conviction that within or beyond temporal experience there is a permanent reality which is not subject to the cruelties of time. The third to sixth stanzas show Hardy's characteristic view of time as the monotonously practical rhythm of wear and tear: the hill has been climbed, 'foot-swift, foot-sore, / By thousands more'. The rocks are primeval and the countless human lives wash over them and disappear. But the poem does not just say this, because against the erosion of time Hardy sets a moment of intense happiness, that 'time of such quality' which, like Eliot's 'moment in the arbour where the rain beat, / The moment in the draughty church at smokefall', is a liberation from normal time. It is his transcendental substitute for temporal sense experience. The still simplicity of 'It filled but a minute' arrests the poem for a moment before we pass back into the ordinary rhythms of 'foot-swift, foot-sore'. The sound and rhythm of this poem are very difficult to define, but they carry so much of its sense both of victory and loss. The long vowels of 'dry March weather' beautifully create a feeling of smooth stasis. They draw the phrase out to give a complete permanence, and they help to ensure that this is not simply a poem of time remembered and time lost.

The same is true, I think, of 'During Wind and Rain', though there is much in it which suggests that time is totally cruel and destructive. The last two lines of each stanza have a lacerating cruelty (as in the fourth):

> Ah, no; the years, the years;
> Down their carved names the rain-drop ploughs.

This is time's 'unflinching rigour', hard, cold and grinding as the symbol of the glacier in 'Drinking Song' implies. The bunched stresses of that last line set one's teeth on edge, like the screeching of chalk or brakes tightening. And this is an immediately recognisable view of time, a medium that is as practical as a corrosive acid or a chisel. But this is only part of what the poem means because the images in the first five lines of each stanza are in fact very similar to what Eliot is saying in the closing lines of 'Burnt Norton':

> Sudden in a shaft of sunlight
> Even while the dust moves
> There rises the hidden laughter
> Of children in the foliage
> Quick, now, here, now, always.

While Hardy's refrains are saying what Eliot follows these lines with:

> Ridiculous the waste sad time
> Stretching before and after.

Though Hardy shows that the waste time of clocks and the elements is terrifying rather than ridiculous.

This wasting, unhappy time is a knowledge derived from sense experience, while the time in the rest of Hardy's stanzas is outside this practical realm—it is a transcendental way of knowing. And between these opposite epistemologies there is a row of dots, a disconnection like the torn leaf on a calendar. There is no point in saying 'only connect', because nothing can bridge the two. There is no way of joining this visionary image:

> They sing their dearest songs—
> He, she, all of them—yea,
> Treble and tenor and bass,
> And one to play;
> With the candles mooning each face . . .

with this practical and realistic refrain:

> Ah! no; the years O!
> How the sick leaves reel down in throngs!

The visionary image is filled with ecstatic happiness and glowing light: the candles are 'mooning' each face. The detail is perfect and it would be wrong to object that the light, like the light of the moon, is reflected and therefore dead. Rather, the light is both absorbed and returned by their faces, like the day's heat breathed back at midnight in the poems I discussed earlier. This light is radiant and alive.

We have to respond to both the actualized idealism of the visions in each stanza and the uncompromising bitterness of the refrains, but we are wrong if we use those refrains as a touchstone for the rest of the poem. The elders and juniors, a completely happy family, are busily clearing the 'creeping moss', and if we know that their task is in a sense useless because the moss will win in the end, it would be ridiculous, to use Eliot's word, to say that they are wasting their time: their gardening is an affirmation of that 'inner freedom', just as the handcuffed convict's singing is also an assertion of a freedom which is superior to the utilitarian practicality of handcuffs, policemen, and railway trains. If we simply listen to the refrains and call this freedom an illusion, we are siding too absolutely with the pessimistic foresight of the architect in 'Heiress and Architect':

Then said she faintly: 'O, contrive some way—
Some narrow winding turret, quite my own,
To reach a loft where I may grieve alone!
It is a slight thing; hence do not, I pray,
  This last dear fancy slay!'

  'Such winding ways
  Fit not your days',
Said he, the man of measuring eye;
'I must even fashion as the rule declares,
To wit: Give space (since life ends unawares)
To hale a coffined corpse adown the stairs;
  For you will die.'

The utilitarian architect is right, but he is also hopelessly wrong.

This paradox is also there in 'During Wind and Rain', where triumph over time and defeat by time co-exist within each stanza. Hardy does not assert, as Eliot does, that

all shall be well and
All manner of things shall be well.

But neither does he offer us a series of remote, rather empty, visionary moments: the rose garden, the lotos, the hidden children, the draughty church at smokefall. Hardy's visions have a richly human detail absent from Eliot's: a Victorian musical evening, the family gardening, a summer breakfast-party, a vigorously optimistic removal to a new house. This detail must obviously exist in time but, simultaneously, it has an idealistic radiance, a glow, which raises it above time and makes it permanent.

XIV

Keith Wilson:

THE PERSONAL VOICE IN THE POETRY OF THOMAS HARDY

The poetry of Thomas Hardy has over the last few years emerged from the critical neglect which for so long made of it a kind of fortuitous appendix to the main business of the novels. Donald Davie and Philip Larkin have both, in their different ways, encouraged a view of the poetry as a beginning rather than an end, as the seed from which developed a crop of twentieth-century British poetry rather than as a late flowering of exhausted Victorian dilemmas. However, despite this reappraisal, virtually no attention has been paid to the theoretical assumptions about the role of the artist that lie behind Hardy's work. Eliot's notorious attack on Hardy's 'personality'[1] could scarcely have avoided being more virulent had he been aware of the views that Hardy endorsed. The *Literary Notebooks* into which Hardy transcribed extracts from his readings of other writers, and the autobiography that he dictated to his wife, are filled with material that, while not adding up to a fully formulated manifesto, points to a body of consistent presuppositions that clarify the strengths and limitations of Hardy's own practice. Also clarified is Hardy's role as a poet who, by becoming the spokesman for what could be called the personal voice in poetry, can be seen as the obvious counter to Eliot's championship of impersonality.

Into the second of his *Literary Notebooks* Hardy transcribed a quotation which he ascribed to Andrew Lang: 'We can only utter the message of our temperament.' This is a condensed statement of a tenet that is basic to Hardy's beliefs about the inevitable subjectivity of the artist's response. While he was capable of being consistently annoyed by simplistic charges of pessimism (and nagged into involved arithmetical disproofs)[2] Hardy made no bones about his constitutional idiosyncrasies. The 'message of his temperament' seems to have made itself clear from an early age. There are strange suggestive episodes mentioned in the *Life* which are explicable only as embryonic manifestations of a constitutional bias:

> One event of this date or a little later stood out . . . more distinctly than any. He was lying on his back in the sun, thinking how useless he was, and covered his face with his straw hat. The sun's rays streamed through the interstices of the straw, the lining having disappeared. Reflecting on his experiences of the world so far as he had got, he came to the conclusion that he did not wish to grow up.[3]

His eye was for the evocative—and what was evoked seems an autumnal melancholia:

> In those days the staircase at Bockhampton . . . had its walls coloured Venetian red . . . and was so situated that the evening sun shone into it, adding to its colour a great intensity for a quarter of an hour or more. Tommy used to wait for this chromatic effect, and, sitting alone there, would recite to himself 'And now another day is gone' from Dr. Watts's Hymns, with great fervency, though perhaps not for any religious reasons, but from a sense that the scene suited the lines.[4]

Like Dickens' Paul Dombey, Hardy must have been a provokingly 'old-fashioned' child, and the following entry from the second *Literary Notebook* was perhaps transcribed because it struck a personal note in Hardy's memory:

> From Pierre Loti's (M. Jules Viaud) address on his reception into the French Academy:
> ' . . . As a child he was a little sensitive creature, vaguely suffering from everything, uneasy at the unknown of life— . . . tendency to suffer from everything, even from happiness.'

The phenomenon is of course familiar from the novels, most apparently in the egregious Father Time of *Jude*. The nature of the sensitivity that Hardy displayed as a child seems in retrospect a clear pointer.

The application of these inevitably vague temperamental proclivities to Hardy's writing becomes clearer in the light of his theorising. He writes in the 'General Preface to the Novels and Poems':

> Differing natures find their tongue in the presence of differing spectacles. Some natures become vocal at tragedy, some are made vocal by comedy, and it seems to me that to whichever of these aspects of life a writer's instinct for expression the more readily responds, to that he should allow it to respond.

The point is explored more fully in a clipping—that Hardy transferred to his second *Literary Notebook:* his agreement with the writer was sufficiently strong for him to underline the extract almost *in toto:*

> It is the same with beliefs as with art. Two artists may paint the same scene and may produce utterly different pictures of it: yet each picture may be as beautiful, and each may give as truthful a representation of reality, as the other. This does not mean that a painter can play with reality as he chooses, or that picture-making is an arbitrary game. Reality is one sure fact and the artist's mind is another, and between these two facts there is a certain relation which it is the artist's business to express. If he tries to give us the relation between reality and the mind of some other artist his picture expresses nothing, and has no real beauty or significance.

The kind of comments that Hardy abstracts show remarkable

consistency in their emphasis on the primacy of the subjective emotional response:

> *Poetry*—'Primarily poetry is a purely subjective thing—the expression of emotion for the sake of the relief or heightening of the emotion which the expression gives. The fact that the expression of the emotion becomes at the same time the means of transmitting it to the consciousness of others is almost accidental . . .
>
> What is essential in poetry is, firstly, that it should be charged with emotion, and secondly, that the moods of this emotion should have aesthetic or ethical value . . . '.

It is not far from this to a conception of the artist as a speaker of truths, as a seer:

> *Imaginative Literature.* 'The first and noblest aim of imaginative literature is not either to tickle or to stab the sensibilities, but to render a coherent view of life's apparent incoherence, to give shape to the amorphous, to discover beauty which was hidden, to reveal essential truth. The great artist may force you to laugh or to wipe away a tear, but he accomplishes these minor feats by the way. What he mainly does is to see for you. If in presenting a scene, he does not disclose aspects of it which you would not have observed for yourself, then he falls short of success. In a physical and a psychical sense his power is visual, the power of an eye seeing things always fresh, virginally, as though on the very morn of creation itself.'

The poet's role as seer is again emphasised in extracts Hardy took from J. A. Symonds' *Essays Speculative and Suggestive.*

> The poet is less a judge than a seer and reporter. If he judges, it is as a light, falling upon an object, showing its inequalities, discovering its loveliness, may be said to judge.

But in putting on the robes of a seer the poet neither can, nor should, surrender his subjectivity:

> The artist cannot avoid modifying his imitation of the chosen object by the infusion of his own subjective quality; but he is at liberty to reduce this subjective element to a minimum, or, on the other hand, to regard it as his chief concern.

As a corollary to these assumptions, the critic's job is seen as in part to decide whether the artist's responses are perceptive or merely unhelpfully quirky (Hardy prefaced the section of which these extracts form a part with 'Excellent rules for the critic'):

> Since then all art expresses what the artist has perceived, thought and felt, concerning external nature, mankind and himself, the critic asks: How far in this case is perception just, accurate, penetrative, subtle . . . how far is the representation adequate to fact? Does the artist show himself to be a man of normal or abnormal temperament?

What these various extracts seem to add up to is a conception of the poet or artist as a passionate and subjective spokesman who discovers, or highlights, truths which extend beyond personal significance to universals, universals which give voice 'to what is indestructible in human life and character'. Such assumptions are conveniently summed up in an entry with the assuring title, 'Law in Poetry':

> Professor Courthorpe lectures to the effect that all fine poems combine the individual, or peculiar, with the Universal, or common: 'In all these [great verses] the total effect produced was simple, natural, universal: and yet the individual character was strongly marked . . . Such a reconciliation of opposing qualities was the universal condition of all fine art!

The intensity of personality is a *sine qua non* of 'fine art', and especially vital in lyric poetry:

> In lyrical poetry, more than in any other form of art, it is only the distinctively individual that can outlive its period of review. It is the *personal* cry, in a note that is somewhat, if not entirely, new, for which we ask: this alone is the badge and title-deed of the true poetic lyrist . . . Take the distinctive personality—the mind, attitude and the ego—from Heine, Béranger, Burns, Moore and the most prominent of our Elizabethan lyrists, and what is there left?

It is scarcely surprising to find a correspondence between this *mélange* of other writers' comments and what we have of Hardy's own speculations. 'The Poet takes note of nothing that he cannot feel emotively', he writes,[5] and *what* he feels emotively is governed by the constitutional bias that causes 'differing natures' to 'find their tongues in the presence of differing spectacles'. Hardy expounds on the necessity of the seer's temperamental subjectivity, and incidentally justifies his own practice, in a comment in his *Life:*

> June 3. [1882] . . . As, in looking at a carpet, by following one colour a certain pattern is suggested, by following another colour, another; so in life the seer should watch that pattern among general things which his idiosyncrasy moves him to observe, and describe that alone. This is, quite accurately, a going to Nature; yet the result is no mere photograph, but purely the product of the writer's own mind.[6]

Just as responses to life are inevitably, and desirably, the result of the particular idiosyncrasy, so any view of an objective phenomenon is decided by the state of mind of the viewer. Indeed, the phenomenon is given significance *only* by that view: Hardy writes 'the beauty of association is entirely superior to the beauty of aspect, and a beloved relative's old battered tankard to the finest Greek vase'.[7] And if a viewer's state of mind changes, so too does the objective world: 'The poetry of a scene varies with the minds of the perceivers. Indeed, it does not lie in the scene at all.'[8] By such lights any engagement with a supposed 'reality' has to be subjective. The poet's subjectivity, however, is of a special order in that its distinctiveness allows him to give voice to a truth which might otherwise go unnoticed. We have already seen Hardy noting that the artist discloses aspects of a scene 'which you would not have observed for yourself': he echoes the sentiment in his *Life*:

> So then, if Nature's defects must be looked in the face and transcribed, whence arises the *art* in poetry and novel-writing? which must certainly show art, or it becomes merely mechanical reporting. I think the art lies in making these defects the basis of a hitherto unperceived beauty, by irradiating them with 'the light that never was' on their surface, but is seen to be latent in them by the spiritual eye.[9]

The poet's 'spiritual eye', judging from the comments that we have seen Hardy endorsing, would seem to be the consciousness that marks out the human race tuned to a vibrantly responsive pitch. This responsiveness bestows upon him the office of seer, which involves engaging with the objective world more subtly than the average man is capable of doing. Later Hardy relates this perceptual role directly to the individuality of the artist, awakening echoes of the comments he transcribed into the *Notebooks:*

> Art is a changing of the actual proportions and order of things, so as to bring out more forcibly than might otherwise be done that feature in them which appeals most strongly to the idiosyncrasy of the artist . . . Art is a disproportioning . . . of realities . . . [10]

These speculations, forming as they do such a central part of Hardy's literary notes and journals, indicate clearly the basic impetus behind Hardy's own poetic practice. Equally clearly, the process by which the engagement between the individual mind and the objective reality is shaped into a poem is vital. Yet time and again Hardy displays a willingness to assume that the process of perception and the process of shaping that perception into poetry are utterly discrete. The most widely promulgated judgement, and hence the most notorious one, comes in Hardy's *Life:*

> Poetry. There is a latent music in the sincere utterance of deep emotion, however expressed, which fills the place of the actual word-music in rhythmic phraseology on thinner emotive subjects, or on subjects with next to none at all. And supposing a total poetic effect to be represented by a unit, its component fractions may be either, say:
>
> Emotion three-quarters, plus Expression one-quarter, or
> Emotion one-quarter, plus Expression three-quarters.[11]

This reduction to a formula appears naïvely mechanical. Yet it is typical of Hardy's striving for absolute definitions of what makes a poem. This tendency is reflected in his frequent readiness to create a metrical mould into which to pour a poem, or in his capacity for writing ideas out in prose and then searching for the best metrical vehicle to enclose them. It is paradoxical that Hardy's insistence on the personal voice should coexist with the rigorous impersonality of predetermined and often awkwardly imposed metrical forms. The engagement of the intensely subjective, temperament-dictated response with the dispassionate shaping mind often seems the distinctive mark of Hardy's poetic probing.

The paradox is made more complex when one considers the seminal importance of the cover-all term 'consciousness' in Hardy's work. In Hardy's use of the term the areas of 'thought' and 'feeling', of rational organisation and of instinctive response, are inextricably linked. The association can best be seen in the 'philosophical' poems that speculate on the evolution of the human consciousness from primal nescience. In writing of 'the birth of consciousness' in the poem 'Before Life and After', Hardy refers to the emergence of 'the disease of feeling'. The manuscript of *Time's Laughing-stocks* reveals, however, that the line which now reads 'But the disease of feeling germed' read originally 'But the disease of thought engermed'. At the level of what Hardy seems to mean by consciousness, the power both to experience emotions and ponder on their significance, thought and feeling are complementary and seemingly used interchangeably. The bridge between the two activities is sometimes made by the use of words which have come to cover both thought and feeling. The manuscript of *Late Lyrics and Earlier* shows that the lines in the final stanza of 'The Children and Sir Nameless' which now read 'They thought an effigy so large in frame / Best fitted for the floor' originally read 'They felt . . . '. The change hardens the reaction into a more purely intellectual one. In 'Under the Waterfall' line forty-one originally read 'From the past awakens the feel of that time' but was changed to the more open 'a sense of that time'. The word 'sense' widens the associations to combine the activities of both brain and nerve-endings. In the realm of what Hardy means by consciousness, 'the disease of feeling' and 'the disease of thought' are dissolved into the all-inclusive disease which is the human ability, or liability, of responding in various ways to an unconscious and unresponding world. The individual poet, in articulating the responses of his consciousness, is speaking the message of his temperament. The words which Hardy invariably uses to describe these responses are significant: 'moods', 'seemings', 'intuitions', 'unadjusted impressions', 'moments of vision'. All imply types of responsiveness in which thought and feeling are inextricable, in which the poet is simultaneously experiencing and exploring the significance of the experience. Hardy's best poetry, rooted as from first principles his writing is in the personal response, occurs when his consciousness—his thought modified by feeling, his feeling modified by thought—is in fullest engagement with his material.

To understand the centrality of the individual consciousness for Hardy, one has only to turn to the recurring assumptions that he articulates imaginatively throughout his writing life, in both prose and poetry. The truth that the subjective view is of supreme value because ultimately it is the only view is one that dawned early on him. In one of his earliest poems, the second of the 'She, to Him' sequence, written in 1866, he pictures a woman imagining herself summed up through the eyes of a disenchanted lover as a 'Poor jade':

> And thus reflecting, you will never see
> That your thin thought, in two small words conveyed,
> Was no such fleeting phantom-thought to me,
> But the Whole Life wherein my part was played;
> And you amid its fitful masquerade
> A thought—as I in your life seem to be.

Three years later Hardy covers identical ground, in almost identical words, in his first novel *Desperate Remedies*, as Cytherea kicks against the social duty that compels her to live with a husband she does not love; she reaches the conclusion 'Nobody can enter into another's nature truly, that's what is so grievous.' And in *Tess*, Angel Clare is concerned that he should not treat Tess's regard lightly:

> Tess was no insignificant creature to toy with and dismiss; but a woman living her precious life—a life which, to herself who endured or enjoyed it, possessed as great a dimension as the life of the mightiest to himself. Upon her sensations the whole world depended to Tess; through her existence all her fellow creatures existed, to her. The universe itself only came into being for Tess on the particular day in the particular year in which she was born.
>
> This consciousness upon which he had intruded was the single opportunity of existence ever vouchsafed to Tess by an unsympathetic First Cause—her all; her every and only chance.[12]

This emphasis on the subjective reality that is seen by every individual consciousness stays with Hardy throughout his career as poet, and dictates the central position that personal experience has in his major work, work in which the man who experiences and the poet who transmutes that experience into expression are in complete, and indivisible, alliance.

Against this context I want to consider initially two opposing manifestations of the personal voice in Hardy's poetry. The one seems to be productive and leads directly to Hardy's major work, the 'Poems of 1912-13'; the other produces a kind of automatic writing in which the personal voice is nothing more than the imposition of a particular preordained attitude upon a manipulated set of circumstances. The poem 'Her Secret' from *Satires of Circum-*

stance has, in a limited sense, the distinctive Hardy tone:

That love's dull smart distressed my heart
He shrewdly learnt to see,
But that I was in love with a dead man
Never suspected he.

He searched for the trace of a pictured face,
He watched each missive come,
And a sheet that seemed like a love-line
Wrought his look lurid and numb.

He dogged my feet to the city street,
He followed me to the sea,
But not to the nigh, still churchyard
Did he dream of following me!

Here is a poem in which one immediately senses the idiosyncratic Hardyan preoccupations. The poem offers a cameo situation in which various standard motifs of Hardy's combine—the despair, deceit, and suspicion of love, the grief that derives from the fact of mortality, the ironic truth that escapes the jealous husband. But though these personal trademarks are clear, they are deceiving —a kind of personal symbol from which any genuine personality is drained. The situation is developed purely to carry the ironic load and to express a predetermined view of life's vagaries, albeit a view in accordance with Hardy's temperamental proclivities. Such poems are what might be called 'closed-situation' ones. The situation is in no sense exploratory, opening up to provide a personal and speculative view as the act of interpretation takes place. On the contrary, the act of interpretation is a *fait accompli* before the situation which it is made to hang on has been constructed. The secondariness of the idea to the situation is reflected in the hollow language. Although there is overtly a very dramatic situation—a lover's triangle, in which one of the members is dead but retains the affection of his surviving mistress, a jealous husband, intercepted letters, clandestine visits to the churchyard—the language conveys nothing beyond the surface statement of that situation. It is tiredly conventional: 'love's dull smart' distressing the heart, 'watched each missive come' (the manuscript originally had 'the postman', which is rather less austere and avoids the awkward 'watched each'), 'wrought'—all thinly 'poetic'. The alliterative echoes are cacophonous—' . . . like a love-line / Wrought his look lurid and numb', although this is perhaps an improvement on the version in the first edition which read 'Made him look frozen and glum'. What one has therefore in this poem is a supposed personal dramatic situation, described in the first person, with no personality to support it because Hardy is concerned with the mere display of irony.

The factor that makes the ironic stance so obtrusive in poems such as this is the situation in which the poet places himself *vis-à-vis* the events of the poem, with which he is concerned entirely objectively. Such closed situations allow Hardy a kind of vicarious intellectual existence by providing him with situations conforming to the attitudes that the thinking part of his consciousness has troubled him with. One wonders whether the effect was partially therapeutic. By placing himself in this uncommitted situation Hardy could articulate the ironies of existence without himself being touched by them. The situation is closed: there is no way out for the protagonists. But Hardy himself is not one of them, and to be able to see over the ironic is to be able to gain some temporary power over, and temporary immunity from, it. One of Hardy's most notorious poems, 'In the Days of Crinoline' (incidentally one of those which he defended by the claim that it was based on an actual occurrence), reveals this stance clearly. Again the situation exists only to demonstrate an ironic point, and is evoked in the most general and arbitrary terms. At no time is the poet himself engaged with the subject, which explains the easy superficial invocation of an ironic view with very little embodied substance to it. To the extent that the poet has a position at all in this type of poem, it is similar to that occupied by the Spirit Ironic in *The Dynasts*. He stands outside the events and enjoys the special knowledge that a protagonist lacks. The form that the assumptions about human nature and the human situation take bears the mark of Hardy; but there is no emotional commitment to the observation. Hardy is taking note of something that he can 'feel emotively' in no genuine sense. What one remembers is a series of baldly stated images—vicar, wife, hat, bonnet, leaze, heath, wood, garden—with no integral connection to a precisely evoked situation.

If we turn to a poem in which there is primacy of situation, in which a situation leads into interpretation and is not preceded by it, the personal voice becomes more than an empty posture. 'Neutral Tones' from *Wessex Poems* is a deservedly familiar, and surprisingly early, poem. Again a personal voice is very apparent. But this time the personality comes not from the facile application of a trademark but from the active engagement of an individual consciousness with the external stimuli that help to shape it. If the events of 'Her Secret' or 'In the Days of Crinoline' are obtrusively shaped by Hardy, one senses that Hardy himself is in some degree being shaped by the events in 'Neutral Tones'. The most immediate factor is the subtlety with which the situation is placed by the use of sparse but integral images. The white sun, the 'few leaves . . . on the starving sod' and the ash tree are intimately linked by the evocativeness of their wintry decay with the experience of which they are a visible cipher. The experience and its surroundings are so integral that subsequent 'lessons that love deceives' conjure up not only the emotion but the ghostly physical surroundings in which it was experienced. The verbs pick up the mixture of disenchantment and aimlessness which is the dominant mood of the experience: the leaves lay, eyes 'rove / Over' and words 'played between', the grin 'swept'—words suggestive of the lassitude and motiveless movement which implies the fact of transitoriness. The meandering but basically regular rhythm matches this aimlessness.

Like 'Her Secret' and 'In the Days of Crinoline', 'Neutral Tones' is a 'situation' poem. It is concerned with a particular set of circumstances, narrated (like 'Her Secret') in the first person by one of the participants. But in 'Neutral Tones' the situation is open: to the extent that the speaker comes to a decision about his experience at all, it is one which has not been preordained but is gently and sadly moved towards as the subtleties of a particular personal interchange harden into a decisive shape. The eyes and smile are articulate, but what they articulate is a non-specific alienation whose cause is left shadowy in the irony and ambiguity of the lifeless smile. Perhaps the single most impressive aspect of the poem is the positiveness with which a tentative and colourless state—a state which is indeed 'neutral'—is caught, so that one feels the force of a first-hand experience filtered through a responsive consciousness that has found the exact words and technical form to convey the experience. The sense of a genuine personal experience is so strong that the poem's integrity implies something more universal about the half-light of a decaying love.

The treacherous—because vague—word 'sincerity' is often used to define the achievements of Hardy's best poetry.[13] The word does, however, suggest the kind of commitment that the active engagement of the poet's own consciousness produces. Its validity can be seen even from a relatively minor, but distinctively Hardy, poem such as 'The Self-Unseeing' from *Poems of the Past and the Present.* The mood of nostalgia here is one which inevitably involves the simultaneity of thought and emotion, the engagement of consciousness in both its intellectual and emotional senses. The mood is impossible without the possession of knowledge brought by hindsight, and knowledge of a sort that has something to say about the human situation. Hardy makes an emotional statement which is rendered possible only by the knowledge that his intellectual faculty has brought him—the knowledge of inevitable transitoriness, of lost opportunity, of failure fully to recognise happiness while still in possession of it. The precision of the setting validates the experience that is being described: the physical details are sparse but individual enough to prove their primacy to the situation. This conviction is a direct result of Hardy's personal involvement with the state which he is describing.

The pervasiveness of the personal voice has borne more blighted critical fruits than merely the antipathy of Eliot. It has encouraged a prodigious amount of biographical speculation. But as we have begun to suggest, the personal element is neither a blemish nor a device for writing a coded diary. Ultimately it is the acknowledgement in practice of the fact that 'reality is one sure fact and the artist's mind is another, and between these two facts there is a certain relation'. Whether the personal reaction has anything of a more universal significance to offer depends, paradoxically, on the extent to which its personality convinces. And equally paradoxically, biographical burrowing is not going to help us to decide. Take, for example, the brief and very personal poem 'The Little Old Table' from *Late Lyrics and Earlier*. The desk is important only for what lies beyond it for the speaker. Whatever else we find out about the event that inspired the poem, we shall not discover anything new about what the poem is doing. The reader will not respond in the same way as Hardy to events that have specific meaning only for him. We shall respond only to what is archetypal in Hardy's experience, even though that experience is a convincing archetype only because it is so convincingly personal. The poem invites this response because again the table and the experience that it objectifies are not discrete. The table inevitably activates in the speaker's mind an incomplete past scene that exists for him alone. But that personal picture has much wider implications. The poem, in its small way, is directly concerned with the lack of human communication—'she looked at me with a thought / That I did not understand'; it is concerned with the passage of time and with the inevitable disappearance of all human experience, however vital it once was to the experiencer; it is concerned with the very fragile hold that a past love has on existence, a hold that lasts only as long as the surviving partner; it is concerned with the inevitable ignorance of subsequent generations about their forefathers.

It is this meeting of event and genuine response that is the hallmark of Hardy's achievement in the 'Poems of 1912-13'. All the assumptions that we have seen Hardy making about the writing of poetry, and about the nature of the individual's engagement with the world that surrounds him, find productive ground in the situation that Hardy found himself in at the time of the writing of these poems. As with 'Neutral Tones', the fact of personal reaction to events is the basis of the series' success. The pattern can be summed up by a detailed consideration of the first poem of the group, 'The Going'. One of its most immediately distinctive features is the expression of what appears to be an instinctive musing in a highly stylised metrical form. The conversational tone liberates the metre, but is still enclosed within the regular patterning of the alternate stanzas. The result is a combination of seeming spontaneity and careful control, which accounts for the tone of restrained, almost stoically accepting emotion, that distinguishes these poems. Constantly one discovers in the group an eerie coupling of uncertain, colloquial speculation with a very certain and symmetrical poetic framework. A study of the manuscript and first edition indicates that some of what appear the most integral and instinctive touches are in fact the result of revision. In the first edition 'Or lip me the softest call' reads 'Or give me the softest call'. The change to 'lip', a favourite Hardy verb, places a stronger emphasis on the softness of the call and allows the possible associations of both intimacy and indifference; to 'lip' can mean either to kiss, or that the call is made as the merest gesture with no conviction behind it. A similar change from a neutral word to a more evocative one occurs with the alteration of the manuscript version from 'And think for an instant it's you I see' to 'And think for a breath . . . ', which captures the suggestion of fleeting shock. 'Darkening dankness' read 'creeping dankness' in the manuscript; the change emphasises the blight that has overtaken Hardy's life, and works in conjunction with a later change from 'the next spring weather' to 'this bright spring weather'.

The revisions suggest the responsiveness to the associations of particular words that Hardy had, indicating something of the way in which he strove to convey the particular texture of a subtle emotion accurately. This sense of particularity is hardened by the fact that the poem is concerned not only with a past occurrence and the events surrounding it—Emma's death and Hardy's reactions—but with a present moment in which the poem is written. The first line asks a question about a past event, but asks it of an imagined ghostly Emma whom the speaker is presently addressing; not only are the events of the past being considered from the present, but there is also a new dramatic context that exists only in the present. Each of the alternate stanzas begins with a present question about the past, and this produces the musing rather than assertive tone of the poem. They are questions to which, by their very nature, there can be no answer, articulating uncertainties that elsewhere—in the non-personal poetry—Hardy turns into obtrusive ironies: questions about lost opportunity, about important events occurring while the person they affect remains completely unaware, about the hollowness of a place associated with someone now dead. Nothing is demonstrated, and no easy intellectual conclusion reached. The pained puzzlement is a function of Hardy's positions within the poem. Indeed, the third stanza provides a key not only to this poem, not only to the 1912-13 group as a whole, but to all of Hardy's personal poetry. It is concerned entirely with what the individual, Hardy, sees. He imagines fleetingly that he sees Emma 'At the end of the alley of bending boughs' but is quickly pulled back to the 'yawning blankness / Of the perspective'. The yawning blankness is both the sight of the darkening alley and the special sense of loss that that sight forces upon him. This particular perspective is one that only Hardy can have. The alley of bending boughs is an objective phenomenon, but its importance is defined by the special subjective associations it has for Hardy.

One is in a position now to chart a general pattern in Hardy's poetry. That Hardy is some kind of ironist is axiomatic—the titles of such volumes at *Time's Laughingstocks, Satires of Circumstance, Human Shows, Far Phantasies, Songs and Trifles* are in themselves a superficial indication of the native bent. But equally axiomatic, as has been seen from his theorising, is his belief in the personal and emotional basis of poetry. The two are not easy bedfellows, since the one normally implies dispassion and the other involvement. And indeed, dispassion is precisely what one finds in much of Hardy's work. The dominant ironic mode of *The Dynasts* is expressed in the distinction between the reality experienced by the human protagonists, and the reality observable to the uncommitted commentators of the Overworld. The dominant ironic mode in such closed poems as the 'Satires of Circumstance' is expressed in the distinction between the reality experienced by an unsuspecting protagonist and the reality that a designing poet / ironist has in store for them. But the dominant ironic mode of the personal poems is expressed in the distinction between two types of reality, both of which have equal claims and neither of which is artificially weighted. The one reality is the world as it is to the uncommitted observer; the other is the world as it is experienced by the individual whose own consciousness is his 'every and only chance'. The latter is a world in which a desk, a violin, a house, a hill, open on to vistas that only one mind can fully penetrate to; the other is a world where the scope of such objects is limited to their purely physical natures. Out of the abrasiveness between the two—neither of which can become an ultimate reality —Hardy makes his most distinguished work.

NOTES

Abbreviations for references:

Life: F. E. Hardy, *The Life of Thomas Hardy,* London and New York 1962.

Orel: Harold Orel (ed.), *Thomas Hardy's Personal Writings,* Lawrence, Kansas, 1966 and London, 1967.

Purdy: R. L. Purdy, *Thomas Hardy, A Bibliographical Study,* Oxford, 1954 and 1968.

II
pp. 21-38

1. Purdy, p. 336.
2. See R. C. Schweik, 'The Early Development of *Hardy's Far from the Madding Crowd*', *Texas Studies in Literature and Language,* Autumn 1967, pp. 415-28.
3. R. C. Schweik suggests the extent to which the early portions of the novel underwent a radical revision in 'A First Draft Chapter of Hardy's *Far from the Madding Crowd*', *English Studies,* August 1972, pp. 344-49.
4. Hardy had originally identified the location of the Fanny-Troy meeting as at Melchester; then, in later printings of the novel, he amended this to achieve the anonymity of 'a certain town and military station, many miles north of Weatherbury'.
5. In some places, for example, Hardy describes Boldwood in language which suggests a kind of mechanical equilibrium: 'the perfect balance of enormous antagonistic forces—positives and negatives in fine adjustment' (XVIII); when he becomes interested in Bathsheba he feels 'the symmetry of his existence to be slowly getting distorted in the direction of an ideal passion' (XIV), and he speculates as to whether Bathsheba's movements 'were as geometrical, unchangeable, and as subject to laws as his own' (XVII). Elsewhere Hardy uses elemental and organic metaphors: Boldwood's feelings are either 'stagnant or rapid'; he is a 'hotbed of tropic intensity', and a man of 'wild capabilities' and potential 'high tides' whose feelings can be kindled to a 'great flame' (XVIII). In still other places the analogy is to a fortress whose walls have been breached: Bathsheba's triumph we are told is her 'consciousness of having broken into that dignified stronghold at last' (XVII),

and Boldwood's face subsequently shows that 'he was now living outside his defences for the first time, and with a fearful sense of exposure' (XVIII).

6. An index indication of the care with which Hardy composed these rural matters may be seen in the manuscript of the novel, which reveals the extraordinarily heavy revision he lavished on the description of the Great Barn in Chapter XXII. Hardy's artful conduct of the narration in this chapter is the subject of a close and appreciative analysis by J. Hillis Miller in *Thomas Hardy: Distance and Desire,* Cambridge, Mass., 1970, pp. 57-66.
7. This included a self-imposed deadline to finish the novel before his marriage in September 1874.
8. Hardy took the business of Coggan's tracking skills seriously enough to provide in the manuscript a series of carefully drawn patterns of horses' hooves illustrating the various gaits which Coggan interprets; these, however, were never printed.
9. *Life,* p. 100.
10. The phrase is taken from Michael Millgate's discussion of *Far from the Madding Crowd* in *Thomas Hardy: His Career as a Novelist,* London and New York, 1971, p. 82.

III
pp. 39-59

1. R. Altick, *The English Common Reader,* pp. 125-6.
2. Tennyson, 'Ode Sung at the Opening of the International Exhibition'.
3. G. Saintsbury. In *The Academy,* 1881.
4. Penelope Vigar, *The Novels of Thomas Hardy: Illusion and Reality,* 1974.
5. *Life,* pp. 98, 273, 298.
6. The evidence for Hardy's interest is found in his 'Trumpet-Major' Notebook; see *The Thomas Hardy Year Book,* 1973-4, p. 95.
7. See *The Thomas Hardy Year Book,* 1971, p. 28.
8. *Life,* p. 172.
9. Orel, pp. 108-9.
10. From 'Let Me Enjoy' in *Time's Laughingstocks.*
11. Orel, pp. 214, 216.

IV
pp. 60-73

1. The four scenes referred to will be found in Chapters XXIII, XXXIII, XXXII, and XX.
2. Chapter XI, on the question of following Stephen Smith, to be married by licence.
3. 'The actual innocence which made her think so fearfully of what, as the world goes, was not a great matter, magnified her apparent guilt . . . tale' (Chapter XXXI).
4. *Life,* p. 114.
5. *A Pair of Blue Eyes,* XXX and *Tess,* XXXVI.
6. The scenes occur in Chapters XXV, XXXI, and XXIX.
7. From Chapter XLVI.
8. *The Hand of Ethelberta,* VIII and *Tess,* X.
9. From Chapter XLIII.
10. Book I, Chapter IV.
11. Book III, Chapter II.
12. From 'In the Moonlight', the last poem in *Satires of Circumstance* (final arrangement).
13. In the Apology to *Late Lyrics and Earlier.*

V
pp. 74-85

1. *Life,* p. 313.
2. Orel, pp. 30-31.
3. *Life,* p. 239.
4. It should be remembered that (as R. L. Purdy pointed out) the story was written for the Exhibition Number of *Scribner's Magazine,* May 1893, which was specially prepared for the Chicago World's Fair.
5. In a letter to the editor of *The Times Literary Supplement* (Orel, p. 142).
6. See *The London Magazine,* Autumn 1958.

VI
pp. 86-105

1. J. Hillis Miller, 'Howe on Hardy's Art', *Novel,* Spring 1969, p. 276.
2. *Life,* pp. 87, 104. Subsequent references to this work are given in the text.
3. Orel, pp. 127, 107.
4. Most of Hardy's notebooks have been destroyed. Among the

few preserved are two volumes labelled 'Literary Notes I' and 'Literary Notes II' respectively. About half the entries in these volumes are now published as *The Literary Notes of Thomas Hardy,* Vol. I, Gothenburg, 1974. The second half is being prepared for publication. Subsequent references to the 'Literary Notes' will be made in the text and will, wherever possible, relate to this edition (by Lennart A. Björk) and to the entry numbers rather than to the page numbers. Where quotations are from notes not yet published, references are to the pagination of the manuscript volumes. The description of the Fourier material follows to some extent the annotation to the first entry in the *Literary Notes.*

5. Nicolai Ryazanovskii, *The Teaching of Charles Fourier,* Berkeley and Los Angeles, 1969, p. 239.
6. C. Fourier, *The Passions of the Human Soul,* I, 347. Subsequent references to this work will be made in the text.
7. Frank E. Manuel, *The Prophets of Paris,* Cambridge, Mass., 1962, p. 215.
8. Manuel, p. 221.
9. Charles Morgan, *The House of Macmillan,* London, 1943, pp. 89-90.
10. Michael Millgate, *Thomas Hardy: His Career as a Novelist,* pp. 21-24.

VII
pp. 106-124

1. *Life,* 207-8.
2. Purdy, p. 89.
3. *Life,* p. 269.
4. *Life,* p. 278.
5. General Preface to the Novels and Poems (Orel, p. 45).
6. *Life,* pp. 250-51.

VIII
pp. 125-139

1 See the poem 'Why Do I?' at the end of *Human Shows.*
2. *Life,* p. 330.
3. 'Yell'ham-Wood's Story' at the end of *Time's Laughingstocks.*
4. *Life,* p. 149.
5. *Paradise Lost,* IX. 780ff.
6. *Life,* p. 271.

IX
pp. 140-153

1. Joseph Conrad, *Notes on Life and Letters,* London, 1949, p. 17.
2. Harry Moore (ed.), *The Collected Letters of D. H. Lawrence* in two volumes, 1962: II.993, I.226, I.291, and I.77.
3. *Life,* pp. 291, 104.
4. William Archer, *Real Conversations,* London, 1904, p. 45.
5. *Life,* p. 185.
6. *Life,* p. 153.
7. Lawrence, *Phoenix II,* London, 1968, p. 227.
8. *Collected Letters:* I.281.
9. *Ibid.,* p. 566.
10. Lawrence, *Phoenix,* 1936, p. 579.

XI
pp. 168-179

1. Paul Zietlow, *Moments of Vision: The Poetry of Thomas Hardy,* Cambridge, Mass., 1974, p. 229.
2. Ezra Pound, 'A Few Don'ts', *Poetry,* March 1913, p. 202.
3. T. S. Eliot, 'Tradition and the Individual Talent', *Selected Essays,* 1932, p. 15.
4. Harold Bloom, *The Anxiety of Influence,* New York and Oxford, 1973, p. 5.
5. Bloom, pp. 14-15.
6. Carlos Baker, Introduction to William Wordsworth: *The Prelude, Selected Poems and Sonnets,* New York, 1954, p. xvii.
7. Thomas Carlyle, 'Characteristics'.
8. Eliot, p. 14.
9. Shelley, *A Defence of Poetry,* quoted in Bloom, pp. 102-3.
10. Lennart A. Björk (ed.), *The Literary Notes of Thomas Hardy,* Vol. I, 1974, p. 22.
11. Bloom. quoted Lichtenburg, p. 31.
12. Orel. pp. 79-80.

XII
pp. 180-191

1. *Life,* p. 285.
2. *Life,* p. 392.
3. At the final moments Hardy wished read to him 'The Listeners' by Walter de la Mare; 'Rabbi Ben Ezra' by Robert Browning;

and a single verse from FitzGerald's translation of the *Rubáiyát of Omar Khayyám.* Hardy, unlike the dying Keats, was not feverishly attempting to rediscover the validity of Christian perspectives. Keats, as readers will recall, requested that Severn bring him a number of religious works, including Jeremy Taylor's *Holy Living and Holy Dying,* but none of these reassured him.

4. Orel, p. 57.
5. Kenneth Phelps, 'Annotations by Thomas Hardy in his Bibles and Prayer-Book', Toucan Press, 1966, *passim.*
6. J. O. Bailey, *The Poetry of Thomas Hardy,* Chapel Hill, N.C., 1970, p. 592.
7. *Life,* pp. 332-33.
8. V. H. Collins, *Talks with Thomas Hardy at Max Gate, 1920-22,* London, 1928, p. 63.
9. Carl J. Weber (ed.), *Letters of Thomas Hardy,* Waterville, Me., 1954, p. 100.

XIV
pp. 205-217

1. T. S. Eliot, *After Strange Gods,* London, 1934, pp. 54-5.
2. There is a stubborn entry in Hardy's hand on the fly-leaf of his proof-copy of *Human Shows:*

   Total: 152 poems
   —of these there are, roughly,
   60 poems of tragedy, sorrow or grimness
   (65 of a reflective dispassionate kind
   92 (11 of the nature of comedy
   (16 love songs and pieces, mostly for music
   that is
   Tragedy or sadness 2/5 of the whole
   Reflection, love, or comedy 3/5
3. *Life,* pp. 15-16. This experience was later used in *Jude the Obscure,* I.ii, and in the poem 'Childhood Among the Ferns'.
4. *Life,* p. 15.
5. *Life,* p. 342.
6. *Life,* p. 153.
7. *Life,* pp. 120-21.
8. *Life,* p. 50.
9. *Life,* p. 114.
10. *Life,* p. 228.
11. *Life,* p. 311.
12. *Desperate Remedies,* XIII.4, and *Tess,* XXV.
13. The most fruitful exploration of this treacherous quality in relation to Hardy is F. R. Leavis's essay 'Reality and Sincerity', *Scrutiny,* XIX, 1952.

NOTES ON THE CONTRIBUTORS

Dr Lennart Björk, Professor of English at the University of Stockholm, is the editor of *The Literary Notebooks of Thomas Hardy*, Volume 1, 1974.

Melvyn Bragg is a well-known novelist and B.B.C. literary interviewer.

Frank Giordano is an Assistant Professor of English at the University of Houston, Texas, and the author of a number of articles on Hardy.

Dr. Desmond Hawkins is the author of the recently published *Hardy: Novelist and Poet*, and a successful adapter of Hardy's novels for B.B.C. serial dramatization.

H. A. T. Johnson is Head of the Department of Language and Literature, Mather College, Manchester, and author of *Thomas Hardy*, 1968. He organized the Manchester Thomas Hardy Festival in 1974.

Roy Morrell, formerly of the New University of Ulster, and author of *Thomas Hardy: The Will and the Way*, 1965, is a Visiting Professor of the International Christian University of Japan, 1975-6.

Harold Orel, Professor of English at the University of Kansas, is the author of *Thomas Hardy's Epic: A Study of 'The Dynasts'*, 1963, and editor of *Thomas Hardy's Personal Writings*, 1966. His most recent book is *The Final Years of Thomas Hardy, 1912-1928*.

John Paterson, Professor of English at the University of California, is the author of *The Making of 'The Return of the Native'*, 1960, and *The Novel as Faith*, 1973.

Tom Paulin, Lecturer in English at the University of Nottingham, is the author of *Thomas Hardy: The Poetry of Perception*, 1975.

F. B. Pinion, recently a Reader and Sub-Dean at the University of Sheffield, is the author of *A Hardy Companion* (revised 1974) and *A Commentary on the Poems of Thomas Hardy* (due 1976). He is the editor of *Two on a Tower*, and (with Evelyn Hardy) of *One Rare Fair Woman* (Hardy's letters to Florence Henniker), 1972.

Dr M. A. Quinn is a Lecturer in English at Trinity College, Dublin. Her doctoral thesis is on Hardy and Edward Thomas.

Robert C. Schweik, Professor of English at the State University of New York, is the author of many articles on Thomas Hardy, particularly on the text and composition of *Far from the Madding Crowd.*

Dr. K. G. Wilson is an Assistant Professor of English at Carleton University, Ottawa, and the author of a number of articles on Hardy.

Walter F. Wright, Marie Kotouc Professor of English at the University of Nebraska, is the author of *The Shaping of 'The Dynasts'*, 1967.

Index

Antell, John 115-16
Arnold, Matthew 114, 122, 127, 131, 133, 181

Bloom, Harold 169-70
Browning, Robert 172, 173, 178, 199, 201

Carlyle, Thomas 50, 177-8
Comte, Auguste 89, 119, 134, 135, 189
Conrad, Joseph 104, 140

De Quincey, Thomas 166-7

Eliot, T. S. 169, 178, 195-6, 197, 198, 200, 201, 202, 205
Ellis, Havelock 40

Fielding, Henry 47-9
Forster, E. M. 53
Fourier, Charles 86-7, 88-92, 98, 100, 101, 102, 103, 158-9

Good Words 39-40
Guerard, A. J. 41-3

HARDY, THOMAS:
anti-rationalism 87ff.
natural imagery 141ff.
social criticism 92ff.
works:
The Dynasts 158, 160-61, 167, 186
novels:
Desperate Remedies 10, 11, 17, 71-72, 73, 95-8
Far from the Madding Crowd 10-20, 21-38, 56, 64-5, 141, 144
The Hand of Ethelberta 65-9, 73
Jude the Obscure 98-104, 106-24, 127, 132-4, 139, 161-2
A Laodicean 69-71, 73
The Mayor of Casterbridge 16, 72, 78, 147, 148, 151
A Pair of Blue Eyes 11, 14, 15, 16, 18-19, 62-4, 73
The Poor Man and the Lady 10, 92, 93
The Return of the Native 12, 18, 49, 125-9, 142, 143, 147, 150-51, 160, 163
Tess of the d'Urbervilles 64, 65, 67-8, 134-9, 142, 143, 144, 146-7, 152, 157, 164
The Trumpet-Major 39-59, 60-62
Two on a Tower 69, 73, 141
Under the Greenwood Tree 13-14, 14-15, 26, 45
The Well-Beloved 11, 71, 73
The Woodlanders 12, 16, 129-32, 142, 145, 148
poems:
The Absolute Explains 201-2; Amabel 170-71; At Castle Boterel 202; At the Railway Station, Upway 200-201; Autumn in King's Hintock Park 192-3; Beyond the Last Lamp 164-5; A Broken Appointment 192; The Bullfinches 136; The Burghers 173; Christmas in the Elgin Room 184-5; Christmas: 1924 185; Christmastide 187; The Church-Builder 134; A Church Romance 199-200, 201; The Clasped Skeletons 182; The Darkling Thrush 159-60, 201; Discouragement 135, 138; Drinking Song 182, 193, 202; A Drizzling Easter Morning 182; During Wind and Rain 129, 202-4; An Evening in Galilee 181-2; Evening Shadows 191; The Five Students 194; Friends Beyond 199; The Going 215-17; Going and Staying 192, 194;

The Graveyard of Dead Creeds 188; Hap 156; He Never Expected Much 188; Heiress and Architect 176-7; Her Dilemma 172; Her Immortality 174; Her Initials 171; Her Secret 211-12; His Immortality 195, 200; In a Eweleaze near Weatherbury 176; In a Wood 175; In Front of the Landscape 193-4; In St. Paul's a While Ago 183; In the Days of Crinoline 213; In the Mind's Eye 193; In the Moonlight 71; In the Servants' Quarters 182, 187; In Vision I Roamed 171; The Lacking Sense 135-6; The Little Old Table 215; A Meeting with Despair 174-5; Memory and I 200; Middle-Age Enthusiasms 175-6; The Musical Box 199; Nature's Questioning 176; Neutral Tones 164, 213-14; A Night of Questionings 190; A Nightmare, and the Next Thing 187; Panthera 181; A Plaint to Man 134; Regret Not Me 198; The Revisitation 198-9; Revulsion 172; The Self-Unseeing 214; She, to Him 211; A Sign-Seeker 173-4, 176; Sine Prole 188; The Sleep-Worker 136; The Souls of the Slain 51-2; The Subalterns 159; The Temporary the All 170; There Seemed a Strangeness 190-91; To Outer Nature 175; Transformations 196; Unkept Good Fridays 135, 185-6; Unknowing 175; Valenciennes 172-3; Voices from Things Growing in a Churchyard 196-8; Waiting Both 195; Why Do I? 128; Winter Night in Woodland 183-4; The Workbox 85; Xenophanes, the Monist of Colophon 190; Yell'ham-Wood's Story 129; Yuletide in a Younger World 188.

short stories:

Absent-Mindedness in a Parish Choir 75; Alicia's Diary 76; Barbara of the House of Grebe 77; A Changed Man 80-81; A Committee-Man of 'The Terror' 76; The Distracted Preacher 75; The Doctor's Legend 85; Fellow-Townsmen 78; *A Few Crusted Characters* 76, 77, 79; The Fiddler of the Reels 79, 80; For Conscience' Sake 79; *A Group of Noble Dames* 76, 77; An Indiscretion in the Life of an Heiress 92; Interlopers at the Knap 75; A Mere Interlude 84-5; The Melancholy Hussar of the German Legion 75, 81; Netty Sargent's Copyhold 84; plots for unpublished stories 83; The Son's Veto 79, 80; The Superstitious Man's Story 75; The Three Strangers 85; Tony Kytes, the Arch-Deceiver 76-7; A Tradition of Eighteen Hundred and Four 74, 78, 82; The Waiting Supper 80, 85; What the Shepherd Saw 81-2; The Withered Arm 75, 85.

Harrison, Frederic 135, 138
Heine, Heinrich 127-8, 132
Howells, W. D. 75-6

Johnson, Samuel 59

Keats, John 160, 162, 171

Lawrence, D. H. 18, 119, 124, 140-41, 145, 146-7, 149, 152-3

Mill, J. S. 79, 101, 119, 128-9, 135, 189
Milton, John 133, 137, 167
Moule, Horace 107, 116, 117

Newman, John Henry 108, 162-3

Pater, Walter 127, 139
Pound, Ezra 169

Shelley, P. B. 170, 171, 178
Smollett, Tobias 47
Sparks, Tryphena 120
Stephen, Leslie 26, 32, 39, 107, 118, 189

Tennyson, Alfred (Lord) 172, 173-4, 176

Thomas, Edward 50

Wordsworth, William 140-41, 170, 171, 174, 175-6, 183

CONTRIBUTORS

Lennart A. Björk

Melvyn Bragg

Frank R. Giordano

Desmond Hawkins

H. A. T. Johnson

Roy Morrell

Harold Orel

John Paterson

Tom Paulin

F. B. Pinion

Maire A. Quinn

Robert C. Schweik

Keith Wilson

Walter F. Wright

UK £3.60 net
US $9.00 net